NORTH-EAST LOWLANDS OF SCOTLAND

by

JOHN R. ALLAN

Yeadon's

This edition published in 2009 by Yeadon's
an imprint of Birlinn Limited
West Newington House
10 Newington Road
Edinburgh
EH9 1QS

www.birlinn.co.uk

First published in 1952 by Robert Hale & Company, London
Copyright © the Estate of John R. Allan
Foreword © copyright Jack Webster 2009
Introduction © copyright Charlie Allan 2009

ISBN: 978 1 84158 830 8

British Library Cataloguing-in-Publication Data
A catalogue record for this book is available from the British Library

Facsimile origination by Brinnoven, Livingston
Printed and bound by the MPG Books Group

CONTENTS

YEADON'S OF ELGIN AND BANCHORY

In 1887 James Dawson Yeadon took over the premises at 62 High Street, Elgin. The business he began there introduced a wide range of services to the community. In addition to selling new books and stationery, Yeadon was an antiquarian bookseller of distinction, boasting Prime Minister Ramsay MacDonald among his regular customers. He also ran a bookbinding business, a lending library and a printing office, publishing books of local history and community interest. His 1914 book, *Elgin Past and Present*, by H.B. Macintosh, stands out as a remarkable achievement by a provincial bookseller. Scholarly and immaculately produced, it remains a significant contribution to the historical literature of Moray.

In May 2007, Edinburgh-based publisher Birlinn Limited purchased Yeadon's of Elgin, opening a second store, Yeadon's of Banchory, in December that year. After a period of many years, this publication of John R. Allan's classic *North-east Lowlands of Scotland* re-establishes Yeadon's as a publisher of books of local and national importance.

FOREWORD

You could search for a lifetime and not find a book about his native heath that comes even close to this masterpiece of John R. Allan. Seldom has a factual examination of a region turned into such a literary delight that you can hardly put it down. At the root of it, of course, is the author's magnificent use of the English language. It will have you pausing time and again to re-read that passage, to savour the sound and sense of it, as well as the wit and wisdom. It forces readers to re-assess their view of an area they may know so well but have understood so little. John R. Allan illuminates it all with his own brand of genius.

As a teenager I was lucky enough to have discovered his 1935 short classic, *Farmer's Boy*, a mixture of fact and fiction, much acclaimed by novelists like Howard Spring, and I had already met him in person, as the officer returning from war to his native Aberdeenshire with the courage to oppose that legendary orator and parliamentarian Robert Boothby in the 1945 General Election. Mercifully, his political defeat persuaded him towards the more noble pursuit of writing. As a youngster boldly seeking to found a magazine for my local village, I plucked up the courage one day to call at his home, Little Ardo, and ask if he would write an article for me. Ignoring the impertinence of youth, he greeted me with warmth and encouragement—and did indeed write that article. I sang all the way home.

It was two years after that 1949 meeting before John R. Allan first wrote the book now in your hands. There were later up-dates. But it was patently obvious, then as now, that here was the definitive view of life within that Grampian cocoon which looks towards the city of Aberdeen.

The author was himself a true son of the North-east soil, not favoured with an easy beginning but blessed with an appetite for the life around him and a gift of perception that took him through the University of Aberdeen and onward to a writing career of distinction.

He turned his mind to the city of Aberdeen, old and new, and charted its interdependence with that rural hinterland, once dour and grudging, which was finally tamed and transformed into some of the finest cattle country in the kingdom. That may have broken the back and the spirit of many a man but it forged a native character of strength and honesty and dependability that is celebrated in this book. It is, after all, the people who make the story.

Mindful of that first edition of more than half a century ago, it is fascinating to read of John R. Allan's writing contemporaries who were all alive at that mid-century point. We are reminded of Agnes Mure Mackenzie, Nan Shepherd, Catherine Gavin, Mabel Cowie (Lesley Storm), Rachel Annand Taylor, Neil Gunn, Eric Linklater, G.S. Fraser and Neil Paterson, all from his own area and most of them graduates of Aberdeen University.

Allan devotes more space to two of the North-east's greatest scribes who, by that time sadly, had met premature deaths. There was the incomparable Leslie Mitchell, better known as Lewis Grassic Gibbon, whose fictional trilogy, *A Scots Quair*, is the all-time North-east classic. He was gone before his thirty-fourth birthday. And there was Ian Macpherson, author of *Shepherd's Calendar, Pride in the Valley, Land of Our Fathers and Wild Harbour*. John R. Allan had the good fortune to befriend Macpherson in 1922 when both were studying English literature at Aberdeen University. He regarded him as 'the most wholly and intensely alive person I have ever known', the very spirit of the north. But he, too, was gone in his thirties, killed in a motor-cycling accident in 1944.

Thankfully, John R. Allan had a longer span, delighting us in this book with many a humorous cameo, such as the football match in the village park or the dire performance of the local dramatic society! Then he turns serious, with his personal philosophy on education, surely a blueprint of wisdom for the way our schools should be run.

I must hinder you no longer from the treat that lies ahead.

Jack Webster
November 2009

INTRODUCTION

John R. Allan was brought up on a small farm in the heart of the North-east Lowlands by his grandparents, who found him in the institution in which his mother had left him before she fled his secret birth to Canada. His grandparents gave the boy a comfortable and loving, but not lavish, upbringing on their farm outside Aberdeen, and taught him the history which was not about kings and conspiracies but about how things were, and how they came to be.

This beautifully written and amusing book is not a burst of song from an illiterate peasant, for his grandparents spent the last of their modest resources on his education. When his grandfather died his grandmother told him, 'If there's the money, and you've got the brains, you'll get to the college.' The old lady didn't quite live to see it, but the boy got an honours degree in English and set out to earn his living as a journalist on the *Glasgow Herald*. When he went to buy his train ticket he had the last of the family fortune in his pocket. It came to £30.

As he writes: 'To my shame I once despised Dungair [his grandparents' farm]. The University and its society of cheap wits seemed to offer a noble culture and an ampler humanity. I climbed the steep ascent towards a morning coat and an English accent, and managed to wear both with distinction. I cultivated philosophies, took part in movements, earned a good income, saved money and was a credit to society. But it was no good. We were lost in a world of words and pretensions. We had no reality. So I said goodbye to the morning coat and returned in all humility to the place from where I began.' Allan wrote that fully ten years before he did it, returning from service in Hitler's war not to the Bohemia from which he had been called-up, but to Aberdeenshire and his wife's family farm.

It is well that he did, for not long after his return John R. Allan turned his hand to defining the essence of his homeland, the North-east Lowlands of Scotland. I doubt if it could have been done half so well away from the heart of the area.

The book he produced should be prescribed reading for everyone who moves into the area—and there have been so many in the last forty years since oil was found in the North Sea—or anyone who wants to understand it from afar. It is the masterpiece of one who knew every stone of the lowland strip of Scotland that runs from

Montrose to Caithness, and who loved, hated and laughed at them all. If you want to understand why these Lowlands are so far from being Highland, and yet are almost as far, culturally, from the industrial Lowlands, then this is your encyclopaedia and your bible.

Allan is not anti-Highlands, but what he writes is a powerful antidote to the view that the essence of Scotland is in the Highlands. The iconic status of the Highland bagpipe, the Gaelic language, the Highland games, the Gaelic Mod, and tartan and Highland dress is seen as a sad case of a large and vibrant dog being wagged by a moribund wee tail. The tartan shortbread tin carries a picture of Highland cattle by a Highland loch, though the main ingredients are grown and the biscuits and the tins are made in the Lowlands. The author's own regiment, the Gordon Highlanders, was recruited, and had its headquarters in lowland Aberdeen: 'Nothing so annoys a true native of these lowlands than the suggestion that he is a Highlander. Even when it is meant as a compliment—and it always is—we know it as a deadly insult.' I wish my father had lived to see the bilingual road signs that now adorn the main artery that runs through the northern part of his North-east Lowlands.

This book was originally written as a guidebook in the national series called County Books. Being such, Allan treats the whole of each of the counties from Kincardine (now part of Aberdeenshire) to Caithness, though the upland parts of each belong to the Highlands. He sees the coastal strip as the western edge of the continental plain that spreads across Europe to the Steppes of Russia, when the Highlands were its western ramparts against the Atlantic. When Britain separated from Europe the North-east lowlands was cut adrift, and the 'Dutch fringe' was left clinging between the sea and the mountains.

The narrative takes us on a voyage from earliest times and from south to north. Allan is a great guide. The narrative is full of wisdom and anecdote. He tells us how whisky is made in terms that can be understood even by those from whom it should be kept a secret: 'It is a clear spirit of heroic strength and only heroes or distillerymen could drink it in that state . . . it should be matured in a cask for at least five or seven years to lose any harshness or bite; for it is not worthy to be drunk till it goes over the thrapple like milk and then glows up like a rising sun.' We learn about illegal stills and about the exciseman who eventually traced an alcoholic smell to a church where the beadle had cunningly adapted the central heating system to his own purposes. 'It is a nice thought that, while the congregation were listening to the Word, the spirit was circulating in the warm pipes beneath their feet.'

Often Allan's observation is kindly, like his account of the Highland gentleman in Inverness who lifted his hat to a lady, a little act of chivalry he said could not have happened in Aberdeen without an introduction. And the Highland level crossing where, because there were fewer road vehicles than trains, the gates were kept closed and were only opened if a car came along. The Black Isle is to him kindly, and he would not trade a hundred acres of it for a whole country of highlands.

Sometimes he is waspish, like towards tourists, 'the incredibly elegant American babes that look as if they were assembled out of brass fittings on a conveyer belt; their males who so ably carry on the English tradition of loud voices and bad manners abroad'. And his description of a day out to the Falls of Shin to admire 'a small stream falling down an inconsiderable height; the boarding house teas with wasps and jam; the long twilight evenings while the mists came down, and the gulls squeaked louder; the concert where a fat man in a kilt made speeches between songs and two bagpipers played duets like all hell let loose in a small space.'

But Allan is happiest and has the surest touch when he is describing the lowland farmland. The best way to see the mountains is from a distance and over a field of grain where 'the care of the land was a sort of religion, perhaps nearer to our hearts than anything the churches teach'. He is strong on the improving lairds who in the eighteenth century modernised their estates with the help of innovations like the turnip, which made it possible to fatten cattle and sheep in winter. And the lowland lairds managed to avoid the mistakes of lairds elsewhere. Their improvements 'left no common feeling of injustice such as the Enclosures in England and the Clearances in the Highlands. Both those movements drove people out of the countryside—making in England rich but silent fields and in the Highlands desolate empty glens. The improvements in the lowland north nourished the land and kept it full of people for more than a hundred years.'

There is pathos in Allan's telling of the struggles of the squatters as land hunger drove them further up the hills. And how the North-east survived the Depression on a diet of locally landed fish and locally grown chips. Whereas the English farming aristocracy retreated from the land, those in the North-east cut their cloth. Where, in England, so much sumptuous land was allowed to go back to the heath, in the North-east we hung on. The English peasantry had gone soft in a culture where 'seven daughters could be as bad as seven wet harvests and a day at the races worse than the year of the short corn'.

Then there's the capital. 'Take away Aberdeen and the North-east would be a poor dismembered thing.' Aberdeen sits so comfortably in its environment. Allan finds it astonishing to find such a big town so far north. Aberdeen is an industrial town that became a resort. 'The third town of the kingdom lived by cultivating its own backyard . . . The salmon came up the river to the fishermen's door; the whale was not so convenient in its habits. By 1819 they had brought home oil from 48 whales and 668 seals yielding 688 tons of oil and an intolerable stink around the oil works.'

There is much, much more. There are chapters on the ballads, the supernatural, pastimes, cattle shows and the 'lads o pairts' who left the land to have their lives opened up at the university which sits so prettily in its old town. John Allan didn't have to leave home with a barrel of salt herrings and a sack of oatmeal for, when they were torn from the land by his grandfather's death, he lived with his granny in a tiny fisherman's cottage within a mile of the college. So the university was not something that was far, high and almost out of reach. Going there was, for John Allan 'as if I had opened a door in my own house and walked straight out into celestial fields'.

Before writing this introduction I re-read the *North-east Lowlands* with a plan—I would mark all the memorable bits of insight, wit and wisdom. After thirty pages I had to abandon my plan for I had marks on every page. It is just the most wonderful book. The re-reading has left me with an even deeper appreciation of my father and a heightened desire to tell him how much I admire him. Sadly, what he taught me gives me no optimism that I will get the chance.

Charlie Allan
Little Ardo
November 2009

ACKNOWLEDGMENTS

As I was writing this book I realised, always the more, how greatly I was in debt to those who worked before me. To those who made the North-east, for instance: and to those who spent long time and labour in preserving its history. In this book I have tried to say what I think and feel about the first; now I must acknowledge my debts to the second:

To the First, Second and Third Spalding Clubs in Aberdeen, for their editions of burgh records and family papers.

To Professor Henry Hamilton of the University of Aberdeen for his *Monymusk Papers* (Scottish History Society) and *An Aberdeenshire Estate, 1735–1750* (The Third Spalding Club), which set out the beginnings of the agrarian revolution in the North-east.

To Dr W. Douglas Simpson, Librarian of the University of Aberdeen, for his monograph on Archibald Simpson, the architect.

To Miss Edith Olivier for her biography of Alexander Cruden the Corrector, published by Faber and Faber.

To the Royal Highland and Agricultural Society for its *Transactions*, in which so much of the history of the North-east has been reported as current events for more than a hundred years.

To Alexander Keith, for his history of the North of Scotland Bank, which contains so much about the growth of capital in the early nineteenth century—and which introduced me to Alexander Anderson.

To the Reverend J. M. McPherson, sometime Minister of Rickarton, for *Primitive Beliefs in the North-east of Scotland*, which has been a world of wonders to me.

I am very grateful for the facts that I have borrowed from those and from many others. If I have misused them, perhaps my creditors will understand. Error is an occupational hazard of the literary life. As soon as a man sets pen to paper he sets himself open to two sorts of error: one, his own, which is bad enough; and, two, the misunderstanding of those who read him, which is infinite. I hope mine has fallen just this side of infinity.

There must be those from whom I have borrowed and to whom I have made no acknowledgment, either here or in the text. If anyone finds a good observation, that he made long ago in a moment of intellectual passion, pass here as a piece of traditional wisdom, or even as a little thing of my own, he should console himself that it must have been a good one: he is like the mother who gives birth to a genius and finds very soon the genius belongs not to her but to all mankind.

In the chapter on ballads I have quoted extensively from memory, but memory has been reinforced—and often greatly helped out—by reference to Child's great collection and to John Auld's *Bothy Songs and Ballads of the North-east*.

I wish to acknowledge every debt; and so I divest myself of almost everything, except responsibility for the use I have made of my borrowings. For all that is set down in this book I am wholly responsible. Although the sins of the fathers may be visited on the children, the sins of the children are not to be cast back upon the fathers—not in this book.

I would like to give my very best thanks to the Librarians and to the staffs of the University Library and the Public Library in Aberdeen for so much help over so many years. They have always been so prompt to lend although I was so slow to return. There are many of us who remember them amongst our most helpful teachers—even though we did not always understand their insistence on quiet in their reading rooms.

Little Ardo, Methlick.
Whitsunday, 1952.

CHAPTER I

THE LIE OF THE LAND

I AM in some difficulty in trying to account to you for the district I have to describe: its shape, for instance, looks quite improbable. So I am forced back to the days when I was a small boy in a country school here. We spent a great deal of time on geography, which was proper, for I had seen no more than lay within a five-mile radius of my home, and within that small space I understood very little. My ignorance was amended very quickly. I could recite Omsk, Tomsk and Tobolsk, and find them on the map. I knew the rivers of Africa, the capes of Australia and the Mountains of the Moon. And there was Chile, a long and ragged strip, coloured yellow on the map, like a selvedge that the moths had been at. We spent a lot of time on Chile, which must have been famous for something at the time, and our teacher used many epithets in the hope of fixing the country in our minds. At last she found one of which she must have been rather proud, because she used it so often. Chile, she said, was the Britain of South America. It was a pretty stroke at describing the unknown in terms of the familiar, and it was successful. I still think of Chile as the marrow of Old Machar, a familiar country where farmers drive their gigs from pub to pub and the ploughman sings rude songs to the music of the melodeon. We never forget what we learn in those impressionable years: and so the tattered South American country comes to my hand at the time of need. I can hardly do better than describe these lowlands as the Chile of the north; the narrow selvedge the worm of time has eroded.

It is no more than the border of counties along the North Sea and the Moray Firth—Kincardine, Aberdeen, Banff, Moray, Nairn, Inverness, Ross and Cromarty, Sutherland and Caithness. To be exact it is much less than those, for the limits of those counties were drawn without any regard to geography. Each one consists of a coastal plain which soon gives place to hills that rise steeply into mountain country. The upper part of each of my counties belongs to the Highlands in the matters of soil and climate and all that follows from them, and my real concern is with the narrow belt of farmland between the hills and the sea. As, however, it is hardly practical to draw such an indefinite line I will take the counties as my limit, except for Inverness and Ross and Sutherland that are so preponderantly highland.

In this matter of highland and lowland it may seem that I am paying

I

too much attention to geography; or else that I am trying to make a distinction so fine as to be imperceptible. Please believe me, that is not so. Nothing more annoys a true native of these lowlands than the suggestion that he is a highlander. Even when it is intended as a compliment—and it always is—we know it as a deadly insult. Our racial background is different from that of the highlanders, our language is different, our habits of thought and our manners are different; and, most of all, our attitude to life and work is different. The highlanders are Celtic, and we are what soil and climate and time and the migrations of Continental tribes have made us. The people of Caithness have a very marked Scandinavian strain and are quite different from their neighbours in Sutherland and Ross. As for the people along the coasts from Moray to Kincardine—the gentleman who once described us as "the Dutch fringe" may have spoken well.

Even if the racial business is all nonsense, as most of it is, geography would make us different from the Celtic people of the Atlantic coast. They live by the Gulf Stream, in the mild airs and the copious warm rain. We live on the east in the dry winds and the cold currents off the vast sub-Arctic plains. Because of that, whoever our ancestors, the climate would have made us nearer to the Dutch and to the Danes than to the dwellers beyond the mountains who catch upon the breeze remote enchantments of the Mexique Bay. The seal-woman never sings upon the rocks of Buchan; the wind would chill her to the bone.

Then there is the difference of soil. This lowland fringe is arable country, whereas highlands by their very nature are always pastoral. It is not the height above sea level which decides those matters, but the presence of enough soil to make a tilth for a seedbed. Now some land in these lowlands may be rather dour stuff but it has been brought under the plough. Though not rich by nature it can be made fertile, and that brings an echo from across the sea. The story of how the north-east was brought under the plough has been repeated at a later time, in Jutland. The problems were the same, for the North Sea that divides the two countries is only an accident.

Perhaps we are indeed the Dutch fringe: and the lowland strip, so improbably hanging to the mountains, is the western limit of the great European plain. This is all so well known, or so often conjectured, that we are apt to forget it, but it is amusing to remember it in passing. There would have been a time when the continental mass included Scotland, and the Highlands were its ramparts against the Atlantic. Somewhere between the coasts of Caithness and Norway the Rhine found a way out to the sea. Then at one of the earth's cataclysmic tremors, the land subsided and the water flowed in to make the German Ocean, leaving a narrow strip high and dry at the foot of the western rampart.

There is just one more thing to notice before we leave the so speculative past. The mountains of Scotland are very hard. They stood throughout several ice ages, and at the end of every age they sent their glaciers down upon us. Geologists calculate that the glaciers of several periods came our way and in several directions—from the west, from the south-west and from Scandinavia. Sometimes the glaciers coincided on us—as, for instance, ice from the Perthshire highlands, moving roughly north-west, was met and deflected by greater ice moving across from Scandinavia. These matters are perhaps too remote, but their effect is still with us. The north-east corner was ploughed and harrowed by the streams of ice; and when the ice melted, it laid down whatever burden of soil it carried from its native place. Thus in the north-east corner we have not one sort of soil but many—earth and stones casually laid down by the glaciers—the rakings of Western Europe. The granite and the gabbro are our indigenous rocks, but we have stones from Scandinavia, and along the coast of Aberdeenshire there are pockets of the red clay from Strathmore. The Laigh of Moray is a light and chingly soil, probably an old sea bed with masses of beautiful red and yellow sandstone. The shores of the Beauly and Cromarty Firth have rich alluvial soil; Caithness the Old Red Sandstone. It may be very confusing but it does make for variety. And variety is an important part of our heritage.

As you come to the northern lowlands by road or train from Perth you pass through some of the best country in Scotland. That is the wide valley of Strathmore, with low rounded hills on the right and the Grampians on the left, blue in summer and glittering under snow in winter. The farms in Strathmore are of a good size; some of them are large by our ideas, being 600 or 700 acres under the plough. The farmhouses are solid, square and sometimes a little pretentious, like the people who live in them. There are castles—Cortachy, Kinnaird, Glamis and Brechin, guarded by old woods and enclosed in high walls, the outposts of the Middle Ages. And everywhere trees. Now trees are very significant features of a countryside. If they are Scots firs, their roots are clenched round the primeval boulders. If they are rowan and silver birch, there is more for the week-end artist than the husbandman. If they are beech and ash that stand diffidently on one leg like hens in a thunderstorm, there is no bounty at their roots. But from a good soil trees rise like a mighty fountain of life; and that is how they rise in Strathmore. The soil there is the Old Red Sandstone, red in colour, free from stones, easy to work, yet strong and retentive of moisture. It is a soil of great heart which responds to high farming as if that were its birthright. An old farmer from those parts, putting down an upstart from the north, said, "Just mind this —Strathmore has been well farmed for five hundred years; not, like Aberdeenshire, scraped up atween the stones in two-three generations."

You cannot go far through Strathmore without getting a sense of that age and amplitude. Life is good and easy on the Old Red Sandstone; and, considering the farmers there, it needs to be. You must have been raised on a hard soil in a cold climate to appreciate the true inwardness of Strathmore and its continuation, the Howe of the Mearns. It is so rich, so protected by the long range of the hills, so sheltered by noble trees. You can feel, as the old farmer implied, that people have enjoyed a good life there for a very long time. I have never passed Balbegno Castle at Fettercairn without being riven by the thrust of envy and the desire to possess a house so old and plain and beautiful in the decent native way. The ruins of Edzell Castle have not the melancholy of a house thrown down; they are so nicely ordered, so sheltered and so calm, you might think the genius of the house still lived in the empty walls. The countryside is old with good life; and with memories of an older, wilder past. At the Mill of Kincardine behind Fettercairn there was, by tradition, a royal castle where Fenella lived, one of those women, half witch, half queen, that move mysteriously in the gloaming between folklore and history. Earlier still, Grassic Gibbon says, the good people of the bronze age enjoyed a civilisation simple and harmonious, from which all that has happened since has been a process of corruption and decay. At times, about the end of a summer day, it is easy to believe there was a golden age once in that fortunate land.

Where the streams come down by the mountains there are a few glens that have a peculiar interest, for they are highland and yet they have a lowland accent. The best known of these is Clova which runs up along the South Esk to the heart of the Grampians. Three hundred years ago, and long before that, Clova was a passage from the north to which men came with cattle and whisky over the hill paths between the mountains, and from which marauding clans returned with the spoils, human and bestial, snatched from the lowland lairds.

The narrow glen of the North Esk, which runs up for twenty miles behind Fettercairn, is not only charming in its natural features of hill and water, but it is a piece of social history, agreeably displayed. Along most of its length the glen is narrow, one farm's breadth on each side of the river, or maybe two. These are proper glen farms, with a certain acreage of low arable land and then an extensive range of rough grazing up to the ridge of the hills. The arable land is still cultivated and gives a small return of cash crops, but its real value is in the winter food it provides for the sheep and cattle on the hills. For some miles from Edzell the road winds along the glen, now alongside the waters of the Esk as they slip and splash along the stones, sometimes swinging away but always to return. At Tarfside it reaches the village that is now the centre of the community—a dozen houses, a post office, a church and a hall. At this point the tributary Tarf comes down from the north, and the Glen in consequence is not only wider, but allows, along the banks of the Tarf, a glimpse across fields to a lonelier place where perhaps the hungry anthropophagi have their dreadful habitation. The road continues now close to the river, for the glen is narrower, but there are still cultivated fields, though more restricted by the rough grazing beyond them. A few miles from Tarfside there is another church, a decent small house among the few trees at the roadside; obviously the kirk of a quiet parish; too quiet, for the kirk is seldom used, the minister having moved down the glen to get at closer grips with the devil in the metropolitan bustle of Tarfside. But this was once the parish kirk and presumably the centre of the parish from the point of population. It is obvious that the centre of population has shifted: the people have been leaving the remoter glen. A little way further, where the Water of Mark joins the Esk, there is a douce plain house that was the minister's manse, with a walled garden and a steading behind. A patient eye may discern on the moor the ridges that once were dykes and the brighter green of what was once the minister's glebe. A little further through the trees, there is a sign of older things—Invermark is a ruined square tower by the roadside, four grim broken walls with the holes that were windows and the other hole that was the door ten feet up the wall. It belonged to no golden age; the memories in those walls are dark and dangerous. It is nearly the end of the journey; another few hundred yards and the glen opens out into a great pool of light ringed round by the dark hills: Loch Lee among the ruins. Where the road meets the loch there is the oldest church of the glen, humble and now roofless; and, still to be found by the side of the loch and on the lower slopes of the hills, the marks of primitive houses and crofts long, long since deserted. The people have gone, all gone, though there must have been many once upon a time; and there was some culture too, for the poet of Lochlee is buried in the kirkyard and his work is not forgotten. It is easy to guess why the people went: as soon as prosperity came to the lowlands it must have drawn the younger ones away. Some return—but only at the weekends in summer to enjoy the quiet of that empty place.

I once lived in the old manse of Lochlee at a time when petrol was very scarce and people in remote places had to depend, more than ever, on their own resources. It was an experience of the rare sort that makes up for a lot of tiresome living and which cannot ever be forgotten.

The house had the feeling of a place that has been well-lived in and loved. That cannot be defined, but anyone who has a feeling about houses will understand what I mean. I have gone into a house— even an empty one—and thought at once, this has been a well-loved place. Sometimes I wonder if it is not that something has reminded me of the old house in which I received so much kindness when I was a child. Or it may be just a matter of good proportion and simple beauty. I cannot believe that love can enter into stone and lime or that the souls of good men and women return to bless the places they loved. But—there was a something about that old house. Even on the wildest nights when the snowstorms raved and battered at the windows, the house sat immovable and quiet around us. There was no uneasiness in that place.

We were out of the world, yet we were not lonely. We had some neighbours who were very kind to us; and, though there were only half a dozen families, they were a real community. I would not say that people liked each other more than they do in villages or towns; but, when we were so few, we had to be tolerant for the sake of company. We made the most of each other.

There was something more which was difficult to define. Even when we saw no one for days we were not lonely. The road that came up to our gate continued through a wicket and, as a rough track, to a shepherd's house three miles away and thereafter as a hill path over the mountains and down into Deeside. Now and then on a summer evening we heard the latch of the wicket and voices on the road and saw young men and girls pass who had walked over the hills. They were the latest of a company that had been a long time on the road. The drovers had come this way with their cattle from the highlands; the bands of young men and women had gone this way to the harvest in the low country, carrying their boots round their necks to save the leather, and this way they returned, with their boots worn out but a harvest fee in their pockets. So many people had gone our way through so many years it is no wonder I heard, or imagined I heard, the beat of hooves on the grassy road or the echoes of young girls' voices dying upon the river.

There was a quiet spirit in the old house and in the big walled garden. There was—almost I might call it companionship. Of course that was partly in the abundant company of birds and animals—the blackbirds that whistled in the firwood, the grouse that called and whirred across the heather, the sheep that strayed round the kitchen door, and in midwinter the herd of deer that pawed the snow from the grass close by the garden wall, then, suddenly alarmed, listened for a second and, all together, leaped away in a flight of panic. There were so many natural presences, some inanimate—the Water of Mark, that murmured or rumbled beyond the garden gate according to the season; the wind that swept down strong and lightsome and flowed in a sort of muted music through the firs and larches; and the silence —the utter silence of the deep country where the mind is at peace and the hobgoblins slain: powers inanimate that touched the imagination and took life in it so that they became for us beings vast, unhuman, but never to us unfriendly.

6

Glenesk, Strathmore, the Howe of the Mearns—they are beautiful names and fine places. I have often been sad when I had to leave them. I am sad now.

As you come further north into the Howe of the Mearns the valley grows narrower and the Grampian Hills come near, sweeping round towards the sea. Beyond Fordoun the road climbs a little, the hills come right across the way, the red soil begins to lose its bloom; and once over the hill you have lost it. The Highland Fault is the cause of this change. Some unimaginable disturbance once cracked the face of the land. Thus on one side of the line there is the Old Red Sandstone, and on the other, hard rocks strewn with the burden of the glaciers. The Highland Fault meets the sea at Stonehaven, and when you cross it you say goodbye to ease and amplitude. By the stony fields and the diffident trees you may guess you have come to a soil very roughly ground through the mills of God. This is my country.

Stop for a little while in Stonehaven. Although it does not immediately catch the eye, the little town has atmosphere and character, in the part from the square to the harbour. It is quiet and grey and looks like a place that people built to live in—a northern fishing village that grew into a small, a very small, county town, on a bay sheltered by two great arms of stone. On the cliff top to the south there is Dunnottar Castle, a famous strong place which the Earl Marischal used to hold for the King. It is now a ruin and may be visited by those who like to moralise on fallen glory, at the cost of a small fee. On the other side of the town there is Ury House, a fine big mansion where a Glasgow ironmaster set up a county family long ago. Now the noble woods that surrounded it have been cut down, the gentlemen are gone, and the house has been bought by a local authority for some purpose of the common people. Time passes: Dunnottar roofless looks across to Ury bare; temporal powers outlast their day and so decline.

The northern part of the Mearns lies on the last rocks of the Grampians that end in a cliff wall between Stonehaven and Girdleness at Aberdeen. It is a cliff-top country; the trees lean inwards away from the tormenting of the south-east gales, and indeed the place has a worried look. Though there are good pockets of land, the rocks too often stand out of the soil and the whins wait at the dykesides to recapture the fields. A short distance inland the farms give way to the moor and the moor to the hills. There are fishing villages along the coast, small villages of bare, rectangular houses on the top of the cliffs; in keeping with the trade of the fisherman who tills an unfriendly element. Inland many of the small farms are no less bare and you may get the idea that the farmer tills an element no friendlier and often less productive. Of course it is always dangerous to make general statements: around Muchalls Castle and Elsick you will find that blessed state amenity, but in this part you may guess what the history of the north-east has been—a long effort to bring fertility out of a hard soil, to make a living in hard conditions for a reward that even in the best of times is hardly generous. Further away from the sea, large forests are being established. These might be extended. If ever a countryside needed to be buried deep in trees, it is here.

As you come over the last hill out of the Mearns, you are likely to be surprised, for Aberdeen lies on the slope anent you. Whatever you expect, Aberdeen is bound to be just a little more. It is a big town to be so far north. By the streets of new buildings you can see that it is growing quickly, yet it has none of the more obvious signs of industry. The granite sparkles when the sun comes out after the rain, making the town seem unreal—too clean and too cold to be a human habitation. But it is real enough and many people—one hundred and eighty thousand of them—find a living here, a sign that there is more in the north-east than meets the eye in the scrag end of the Mearns.

Aberdeenshire falls naturally into five divisions—Deeside, Donside and Strathbogie, Formartine and Buchan. I would say something about them in that order.

DEESIDE

The Dee is a charming little river; no other adjective is pretty or familiar enough to describe the setting of water and wood and hill. It is so picturesque: wherever you look, the elements compose themselves into a view. If there must be highland glens, let them be like this, where the brown heath is purple heather, the wood is shaggy in a graceful way and the mountain and the flood have no terror in them.

Where the river meets the sea, the motor boats come dancing in over the harbour bar, home from the inshore fishing; and the trawlers tread a more stately step from the North Sea banks. Once into the arms of the breakwater, they slip softly up the Dee, each with its convoy of seabirds that swoop and scream behind it. Old men lean over the side of the breakwater; a man in a jersey swings a line for flounders on the pier, watched by a large black cat; across the slipping stream the lighthouse stands up slender and white on the black rocks. The boats ride up the stream with a purr from their engines while a fisherman washes down the decks with a bucket deftly thrown in and drawn from the river. Another throws a last offering of harrigals to the birds; and the skipper, leaning out of the wheelhouse window, measures the distance to the harbour gates and home.

Upstream from the harbour the Dee becomes urban with a cemetery on one side and a prison on the other; and trees on both. Past the Old Bridge of Dee there are suburbs all the way to Culter; villas and bungalows of the people who have done well; while on the south side there are some bigger houses of the people who have done even better.

Thereafter along the South Deeside Road all is quiet and exquisitely arranged: a border of trees; the river beyond; Park House balanced and serene on a green lawn; Crathes Castle, baronial, forbidding and old, high on a crag in the woods; Banchory, Kincardine O'Neil, Aboyne, Ballater, Braemar—the road always winding, the river between dry selvedge of silvery stone; the obstinate firs, the elegant, drooping silver birches, glimpses of green fields and corn; and, suddenly rediscovered a hundred times, the deep-blue peaks of Cairngorms standing always nearer in the west.

Clear skies and bright colours—Deeside in autumn is just a little incredible. Nature should not be as pretty as a picture, as bravely coloured as a romance. Deeside has everything. Castles—yes, like a fanfare of trumpets: Crathes in the cleft of the woods; Aboyne, a stronghold of the Gordons; Birse, a perfect little thing from a fairy tale in the empty Forest; Braemar, fantastically turreted, where the standard was raised in 1715 for the Old Pretender's rebellion; Balmoral—ah, Balmoral, how the willing heart can be stirred by the old loyalties. So many other fine things—mansions and shooting lodges where parties go out in the morning to shoot birds, accompanied by women whose tweeds are nearly as loud as their voices. I can't go on—this heart is not willing, except to be stirred the wrong way round by romantic and social Deeside.

I do not understand blood sports very well; and in so far as I do understand I deplore them. Not that I can take up a high moral attitude in the matter. As a farmer I breed cattle that eventually go to the butcher. As one who likes a good diet of meat I will wring the neck of a duck. Indeed, all who like a steak or a cut off the breast should have to kill and disembowel occasionally in case they become over-refined. I have killed birds and beasts, but always with a sense of regret, or even guilt. When you take a trout from the water and that most exquisite agility dies between your hands, you have destroyed something you can never replace. There is no essential difference between taking the life of a bird or a fish and the life of a man or a woman; the difference is only in degree. In our defence we can quote only the necessity that knows no law greater than itself. It is part of the human predicament that there is so often a conflict among our instincts and impulses. I destroy the lovely caterpillars that strip the leaves from my young poplar trees because I am in great need of trees for shelter, but as I destroy them I feel a slight chill, an intimate desolation, at the ruin of those innocent and lovely creatures. I doubt if there is any escape from the predicament. We live only by the death of others. Of course the vegetarians have an answer; but how valid is it? Who knows what agonies the cabbage suffers as the reticulations of its heart are shredded down to recreate a classical economist? We must accept the fact that we are beasts of prey and live by murder.

We can, of course, try to keep our hands clean of blood. We can leave the killing to professional slaughterers who take a hundred lives a day and think nothing about it. We may argue that the killer is purely professional and there is no emotion in his work. I am unhappy about that argument. I feel it is bad that there should be no emotion about the taking of a life; it implies an atrophy, a callousness. It is necessary that a professional slaughterer should feel no emotion. If he carried with him a sense of guilt for all the lives he takes, he would be hunted into madness by the Furies. We may say that society delegates him the job and therefore society must take the blame. But should society delegate that which leads to atrophy of feeling? It is cowardly or dishonest to try to get out of it that way. Of course some one must do the killing. Perhaps it would be good if slaughterhouse service were like jury service—if ten citizens of each town received an order from the Sheriff to attend at the slaughterhouse next morning and kill the day's intake. Not to cut up the meat—that's nothing once the life has gone; but to deliver the bolt at the broad forehead and strike with the agony of death and see the fading of the bright eyes. What a sauce it would be at dinner that day; the high sharp sauce of realising that all our pleasures are taken precariously on the lip of the grave, that the hunters at any moment become the prey.

The slaughterer kills because it is his living. What can we make of the people who kill wholesale in the name of sport? When a gentleman goes to the moor with several friends and they shoot two hundred grouse and various other birds and creatures, they can hardly plead necessity. On the contrary, the fact that the killers are neither hungry, nor forced to kill for a living, is a mark of very high social position. To enjoy a successful day with the guns must require a great atrophy of feeling, an advanced state of decadence. As for the idea that there is something manly about shooting game, it is a little comic. What fortitude is required to hit a bird with shot scientifically prepared to be propelled out of an expensive gun? Fortitude—there was a lot more shown by that fine old sportswoman the farmer's wife when she cut off the tails of the three blind mice.

The great grouse shoots were one of those forms of vulgarity that sometimes become marks of social distinction. They were marks of conspicuous waste and very expensive at that. The grouse shooters were often rather pathetic people, going through a ritual imposed on them because they could afford it. They came north to live in draughty castles and damp, dark shooting lodges. They dressed themselves in tweeds and trudged through the heather, drenched by mists or tortured by horseflies. They were stung, by everything and everybody. From the laird who let his moor for £3,000 and the grocer who charged quite as fantastically, down to the youngest beater with an eye for a shilling, the countryside knew the sporting tenants were their game.

That is not an honest way for a countryside to live. And how pathetic that for fifty years only the rents from the moors kept many estates from total bankruptcy. In days when it did not pay to feed a bullock for the professional slaughterer there was good money in raising a grouse for the amateur one.

The days of the big house parties and the organised shoots would seem to be over. When cattle and sheep are more important than grouse on the hills again, Deeside will be a sweeter and a saner place to live in.

Balmoral—ah, Balmoral. When Queen Victoria had built for herself this huge granite castle after the Scots baronial style she brought to Deeside the magnificence and excitement that surround a court. It is not the magnificence of the purple. At Balmoral the Court is on holiday, so the purple is changed for the tartan and the tweed. Homespun pleasures: ghillies and bagpipers. It is all beautifully managed and admirably sustained, for the House of Windsor have learned the tact that is the trade of princes. When at Balmoral, they do as Balmoral should be done by. It is a castle in a district where the feudal relationship between the laird and his people is not wholly forgotten, and there the King plays the laird, with greater propriety than some of our great territorial chiefs ever managed to attain. There is just the right amount of ceremony. To bring the King from London may require a special train and the dislocation of the whole east coast railway service. But at Ballater there are only the Lord Lieutenant and a few gentlemen to welcome the party: a guard of honour present arms; the schoolchildren and the visitors cheer; and the cars drive off to Balmoral. All decent folk in the countryside feel a little warmer at the heart—the gudeman is hame again.

I have lived in Ballater while the Court was at Balmoral and it was curious how little sense of awe there was at such near majesty. In fact it was the other way about. There were stories, delicious little intimate stories which, if not true, could certainly be believed, because they came from royal servants who were natives of the district. How maliciously backstairs gossip reduced the royal figures to very ordinary stature. It was most enjoyable. Nowadays I sometimes wonder about it. Were those stories officially put about? Was there some official, concealed under an ancient designation, whose job was to provide those instances of frail humanity which can temper awe with love. Because that was the effect of the stories. Ordinary people, tangled in the humiliations of our common life, must have some assurance that those humiliations are part of our mortal bondage and may not be utterly ignoble. They seem to find that assurance in the fortunes and the misfortunes of their kings. The steps of a Throne are a stage on which the dramas of ordinary life are played out, but raised high above the degree of ordinary life. That may be deplorable—we might at least thole our insignificance under Orion—but it seems to be true. We need our kings to live above our means. Some people said that when Edward VIII abdicated, the Throne trembled. What foolishness. The abdication was a domestic drama, of personal inclination against what the elders considered public or family duty. No grown person could have been indifferent to the conflict, for everyone has suffered or will suffer that conflict some time in one of its many forms; it was an ordinary human predicament raised high above ordinary state. It showed that a king was also a man; and therefore that a man had something in common with a king. The community between a ruler and his people is the surest foundation of a Throne, and a well-managed abdication can strengthen it better than twenty glorious victories of arms.

Balmoral is *the* sight of Deeside. When the Court is in residence, dozens of cars are drawn up along the roadside and the passengers gaze down into the castle grounds below. Sometimes they use field-glasses and telescopes as bird-watchers do. On Sunday the royal party go to the service in the parish kirk at Crathie, not unobserved. I am told that the cars of the spectators may extend, head and tail, for a mile and more. The crowd render to Cæsar the things that are his; but, by the smallness of the kirk, are saved from having to render the greater service.

Beyond Braemar, all that is left behind. As you follow the narrow river valley, the high peaks of the Cairngorms stand loftier before you. Beyond Inverey you come to the Linn of Dee, where the young river tumbles over a shelf of rock. Then there is a track over the moor to Derry Lodge and the solitude of the hills. There are many who have gone that way in the foolishness of their youth, bowed down under the weight of rucksacks that contained everything but the grand piano. Many have sheltered from the summer rain in the byre at the stalker's house, sharing the stall with a black cow, a warm but gusty companion. Derry Lodge is the last house on this side of the mountains. The road stops there but the traffic goes on, as it has gone from time immemorial. Two paths lead on through the hills—the Lairig-an-Lui and the Lairig Gru over into Speyside.

The path to the Lairig Gru, worn down by the feet of many generations, winds over the moor till it comes to the Dee, now a cold young stream, and follows it up a long steep glen between Braeriach and Ben Macdhui. At the top, the glen becomes a pass strewn with boulders torn down from the mountainsides. There the Dee rises in two little pools, always, except at midday, overshadowed by the peaks. It is one of earth's desolate places: rocks below, the fields of scree above, the dark shadows, the still cold water, the wind tearing through the pass. It is far away from the mild hysteria that froths around a court. It is far away from the things that occupy our time and steal our lives, far away too from the things we use to distract us from thinking on our mortal condition. Everyone should go to such a place sometimes, alone, and stay there long enough to be loosened from ordinary habits. It may not be an easy or a pleasant thing at the beginning. There is at first a sort of fear in being alone among forces that are vast and perhaps unfriendly. At night there must be some hole to creep into, protected by the rocks, and, even then, sleep is impossible, for every nerve is alert and listening. There are so many little desires and appetites that become nearly intolerable and that become the more insistent because there is no hope of satisfaction. There is a nervous tension all the time, the mind being so stretched that thought is impossible. There is the torture of being broken from the habit of drugs, until the pitch of decision is reached—to go quickly and never return; or to stay. The rewards of staying are incommunicable because they are beyond reason. The unease in the great loneliness is replaced by something that is like confidence, only more instinctive, a regardlessness. It becomes easy to lie down and sleep at night in the heather. When the day comes again, time passes unnoticed in walking, eating and resting; in watching and listening to the beasts and the birds. It is seen that each living thing there has a place and a way of life proportioned between means and ends. Even a human being may be led to consider his own way of life between desires and obligations, time past and time to come. The result need not be remorse nor regret, nor humility nor pride, though all of them may be in it, but there may be some understanding from having seen oneself alone and undistracted; and in understanding, whatever humiliation, there is also strength.

A lady from Chicago once said the Cairngorms were one total mistake. She may have been right, for no streetcar called Desire or anything else ever passes that way. But there is quite a traffic through and across the mountains. Many thousands of people go there to walk and climb, summer and winter. The climbs are said to be excellent— I cannot speak from experience because I have never cared to heave my weight on to the top of a mountain. It has seemed to me not only tiresome but presumptuous and not only presumptuous but exposing the climber to the deadly sin of pride. People tend to collect mountain tops and assume virtue from the number they have stood on. It seems one of the bleaker forms of achievement; but I may be wrong. There is, however, this to be said: from the high tops you can get magnificent views down over the lowlands of Aberdeenshire. To the lowlands let us now return.

DONSIDE AND STRATHBOGIE

If I were honest and brave enough I would say that the Don is incomparably the finest river in the world. Of course I have not seen all the rivers, nor many of them, but even if I saw them all, including the mightiest streams that never were, even Alph the sacred one, the Don would still be first, because it ran through my thoughts when I was a child.

When we drove to the kirk in the gig we crossed it on a bridge as high as a rainbow whence we looked down on water that slapped and leaped among the stones and threw up flashes of light that might have been salmon. When we drove to town we crossed a high, straight bridge over the estuary where at low tide the trout fishermen stood in line with marvellous intrepidity. Once there was a seal that held up his head and barked, and that day I could have told you what songs the sirens sang, even what language Hercules used among the women. The Don was in everything remarkable. People used to drown themselves in it, on purpose (not often, but now and then); and our infant mistress used to row herself across it in a boat every morning, over the dead, drowned men. It had about it something more wonderful than you could ever meet on dry land. And at night, in the utter stillness of a frosty night when not even a blade of grass dared breathe, lying in the attic on the verge of sleep, we heard the noise of its water, insistent, sure and strong, that carried us away. Later I lived for ten years in a cottage by the estuary. Twice a day in those sensitive years, when ordinary events were often charged with a significance not to be expressed in words, I saw the sea tides swell up beyond the bridge and brim the river banks and silently retire. I saw them. I smelled them. I got so that I could feel them and know in my bones the moment they were at the turn, the moment of supreme equipoise among sub-lunary things. By such things we are fashioned, and because of them the heart has loyalties that the head denies.

I must admit now that the Don is not a flashing river like the Dee; it runs out of peat mosses and through loamy haughs; the water is brown, the banks are muddy. But Donside is all the better a place to live on for that. At its best it has a fertile soil with a kindly heart and that can be seen in the face of the countryside. The river basin, which includes the tributary streams of the Ury and the Gadie, is all humps and hollows dominated by the blue hill of Bennachie, 1,700 feet high, with the Grampians standing round to the south and west. This combination of a fertile soil that suddenly runs away to mountain tops is characteristic of the East of Scotland generally and of the north-east in particular. If you look west from Old Meldrum you will see what I mean. It is a country of little hills with shallow valleys between them. Down on the low ground there are fine woods enclosing old mansion houses, and farm steadings set in their good fields. The cultivation has been carried and maintained right over the tops of the smaller hills. Bennachie stands in the middle of all that, suddenly, intrusively, reared up, a mountain of stone with the cultivation running away on each side of it, so that it stands with its feet among corn. There is amenity in this countryside—in the woods of Keithhall and Fintray, the haugh lands of Kintore, the tulip fields at Inverurie, in small manor houses like Fingask and Mounie, in the Paradise woods of Monymusk and the wide and fertile Vale of Alford. And whenever you think you must be coming to the end, another howe opens out before you.

If you go to Huntly through the Glens of Foudland, the road climbs for some miles between arable farms that stretch far up the slopes, especially on the north side. They are not good farms and they are not all well farmed. The cultivation wears a thin, grey look and you might think it would soon give place to the rough, but it continues to the head of the glen, and there from that windy headland you look down on the fine rigs of Strathbogie. There are square miles of farm and woodland between you and the further slopes where the mountains gather blue shadows under the west. It is an inviting prospect—the little hills ploughed over their round head, the small woods, the many farms, the milldams each winking a cyclopean eye in the sun, and always towards the west the intractable mountains. It might be the delectable valley at the end of the world. But again this is not the end. If you follow the Bogie round the Hill of Noth that crouches like a lion in the west, you will discover the farmlands of Rhynie, which are not to be despised though the old song says that "Rhynie is a cauld clay hole." Beyond the town of Huntly you can follow the Deveron into the hills where you might expect to meet the waste in a mile or two. But it is not so. Though the hills stand up on each side of the strath, unassailable by any plough, the lower slopes and the haughs have been taken under hand. I went that way a year ago on a spring morning when the hills were streaked with melting snow, a desolate pattern, and the Deveron was running high with the bree; but along the haughs of Glass, tractor ploughs were turning over furrows that smoked in the sun; and even at the Crofts of Corsemaud a smallholder was scratching the surface of his field with a pitiable implement drawn by an aged mare. It is only beyond that point that resolution had failed at the thought of driving the plough any further. There on a bank high above the stream, the ruined castle of Auchindoun stands guard over the empty hills, but at the gate of the Cabrach, one more and more distant habitation.

There is a great variety within a little space. It is not a long step from Logie to the Glens of Foudland, from the beechwoods at Pitcaple, where Gadie loiters through its trout-ringed pools, to the hungry grasslands above Bainshole where the Ury clatters down like a mountain torrent. That is not unique; the same contrast can be found on the Wiltshire Downs. Incomparable treasures may lie in the valley, a whole Amesbury or a single farmhouse, but up on the long bare shoulder, when the combine driver has gone home, the only human left is an ancient indweller three thousand years dead. Some of our hilltops are monotonous too, but on them the hearths are still warm. Whereas the poor man in England became a landless labourer, in the north he squatted on the waste land high up the hill. That he made into a holding and there a poor man still maintains himself. The unique thing about this part of the world is the tenacity with which the farmers have maintained themselves on the windy braes.

Thus a typical landscape of this countryside would show a long shoulder of ground rising up from a shallow valley. On the lower slopes there would be three or four good big farms of various but kindly land. Further up the slopes, and approached along rough byroads, there would be rather more and smaller farms; and then, hanging on to the very top of the hill, a fringe of little family places without a single tree but surrounded by their arable fields.

This may look like highland country but the society is not highland, for the word as used in Scotland connotes a way of life, the pastoral. Lowland also describes a way of life and the plough is at the centre of it. This may be the peculiar attractiveness of Donside and Strathbogie, that the scenery is often highland but the way of life is lowland. Bennachie is a fine blue peak, the Hill of Noth is intractable and heraldic, but the ploughman has drawn a furrow far up their slopes and the arable way of life has been maintained far along the glens. Bennachie, Culsalmond and Foudland are sizeable hills, but when you look down on them you see they are islanded in cultivation, islanded by the plough. Man has set his pattern very firmly on this countryside.

But then man has been living here for quite a long time. There are many relics which indicate a settled society on these hilltops in prehistoric times. There were camps on Barra Hill near Old Meldrum and on Dunnideer at Insch. Older and of far greater interest are the stone circles of which there are many examples still to be seen in what may be very like their original shape. These used to be called druid temples and dreadful ongoings were supposed to have happened there. Archæologists now incline to think they were devices for fixing the seasons. If they were so, then the inference might be that they were put there by an agricultural not a pastoral society, since it is the husbandman not the herd who needs to observe the seasons. That is only a speculation, but there is one thing to support it—the stone circles are usually found in or overlooking what are now the better farming districts—at Ythsie in Tarves for instance, at the Standing Stones of Dyce, at the Kirk of Bourtie, at Daviot.

I can understand why this might have been a place of early settlement by an agricultural people. The lower hilltops are arable. When the boulders have been removed a furrow can be turned over and the resulting tilth made fertile. A lot of work has been needed to clear the way for the plough and constant care is needed to keep fertility in the tilth. But the soil is willing. Somewhere in its stony heart there is a kindliness. Here man and the soil have arrived at a good partnership. There is no question of mining away the natural fertility, as the shepherds have done on the hills—anyone who tried to mine an Aberdeenshire farm would soon be on the rocks. This is a countryside where you must always be putting in as you take out, but whatever you put in comes back to you. Man, nature and the plough are in a good community on Donside and in Strathbogie.

FORMARTINE AND BUCHAN

There remains the third part of Aberdeenshire—the grim and ancient district of Buchan. By the usual definition, Buchan contains all the land between the Ythan, the Deveron and the sea. A long time ago I called it the cold shoulder of Scotland, and now that I have made my home here I realise how right I was. Only those who live on it can understand how cold a shoulder it is and how wonderful a creature man is to have civilised it.

Buchan is the true lowland plain, and for the purposes of this book I will include the land from Aberdeen to the Ythan. It is a plain as the glaciers made it; not the flat plain of the prehistoric swamps, for it rolls gently and in all directions; yet it is a true plain with only one hill, Mormond, of any size on it. To me it is a fascinating country. Between the Don and the Ythan there are first sandhills covered very thinly with tough marram grasses; then an extent of links that carry fine bents and whins, suitable for sheep, golfers and courting couples; then farmland on a light sandy soil which can be kept fertile if managed with plenty of stock. This is a bare, treeless country, often rising into hills of sand and chingle, but trees do grow in it, as may be seen in the woods of Menie, Balmedie and Foveran. It is more interesting to look at the country along the Methlick road. This climbs a little above sea level through good enough land, until at Whitecairns the bare bones stick through. There and in the district beyond it called the Canna-hars, you get an idea of what other parts of the north must have looked like before they were civilised. There are still a few small patches of wild moss, small patches of unreclaimed moor; fields in which the land has the unsubstantial blackness of peat and others in which the rocks lie here and there among the corn like petrified kine. There is a poverty of the soil and of the spirit hereabout, seen in the steadings of the small farms—grey, bare, bleak and blasted among the rocky fields, without the extravagance of a single tree. It is an unkindly, an unthrifty shank of land. Then quite soon you come into a very different place. At Tillycorthie the road crosses the railway over a high bridge and there, as from the top of a little hill, you can see before you ten miles of country, or imagine it, for so much is hidden in the replications of the ground. Whenever I cross that bridge going north, I feel a lightening of the heart. In the foreground there are the long woods of Udny, but it is not for woods this country-side is famous; they are signs that point to other things. The grass is of a darker green. The corn stands closer and taller. The cows show their udders between their legs. It is altogether a kindlier countryside, and one not desperately scraped up between the stones. At Pitmedden there is a walled garden three hundred years old. Tolquhon Castle is a ruin with enough architectural grace to prove that the land there yielded good rents four hundred years ago. The stone circle at Ythsie may prove that the land there was esteemed in prehistoric times as it is today. Haddo House is a great mansion in the Adam style. It is big; it is noble in its balance and simplicity; and it is not out of place in this countryside. Methlick, which lies beyond its woods, was in ancient days the vale of honey, and the bees still gather honey there.

A mile or two up the hill from Methlick the proper county of Buchan opens out like a backyard of the world. It is a part that visitors usually pass by because it is supposed to be deficient in picturesque scenes and places of historical interest. The only sights are the ruined Abbey of Deer, some fantastic cliffs at the Bullers o Buchan and the convict prison at Peterhead. The genius of Buchan lies in the absence of the picturesque, in what may seem its wholly utilitarian air. It is often bleak; it is always bare; you might think there is little in it to plea-sure the spirit, and you would be right. Yet Buchan as you can see it to-day is one of the triumphant works of the human will; an idea imposed on nature at great expense of labour and endurance, of weariness and of suffering. If ever men and women made a country, it is here between the Ythan and the sea. It was a mighty work, and it is only half done.

When the glaciers had ground their way over Buchan they left the surface furrowed in the most irregular way. There are the water-courses that flow east or north to the sea and the burns that feed them, each in its shallow howe. These have a natural order and relation. But everywhere there are the hollows cut by the glacial traffic that have no intelligible direction, and no relation among each other, for although they may be separated by only a few hundred yards in space, in time they may be ages apart. The soil is as various as the surface. There is stiff clay—I have seen the turnip drills in Slains baked like brick in a dry summer. There is a light soil near Fraserburgh, where crops ripen a fortnight earlier than in other parts of Buchan. There is the Old Red Sandstone near Turriff. There are cups and saucers of peat almost everywhere. The nature of the soil may change from one farm to another; even in a single field you can find different soils of a widely different provenance.

This could not have been very promising material for our

forefathers when they took to arable husbandry, and the records indicate that they did not make very much of it. The state of Buchan in the eighteenth century would seem to have been this—fishermen lived in small villages right along the coast, usually round sheltered coves, but sometimes at the edge of open sandy beaches on which they could draw up their boats. The countryside was bare and wild. Most of it was muir if dry and moss if wet. On the better and drier patches there were farm touns, each rented by a tenant who lived in a small farmhouse, surrounded by his sub-tenants and his cottars. The cultivation was primitive, amounting only to small irregular fields cleared from the waste. The muirs and mosses lay around and between those fields. There may have been a few better patches, as for instance around the Abbey of Deer and Ravenscraig, and perhaps in Fyvie and Ellon, on the Ythan. But the overpowering impression is of a wild, untended country, bare of trees, blasted by winds and chilled by mist, where people scratched a miserable living, eked out by spinning the wool from their sheep; a people oppressed by their lairds and plagued by fevers from the swamps.

In the hundred years between the middle of the eighteenth and the nineteenth centuries, nearly every acre of Buchan was brought under the plough or planted with trees for shelter. It was a mighty labour of which I must give some account later in this book. The tenants and their families cleared away the stones from the face of the land. They levelled the ground. They drained the mosses. They dug miles of ditches. They surrounded their new fields with drystone dykes. They built a stone house, a byre, a barn and a stable. At the end of nineteen years they had a farm, through the weariness of labour, the denial year after year of lightsome games and toys, the direction of all vagrant impulses to the one end of making farmland.

Our ancestors imposed their will on Buchan; and, even after another hundred years of building up fertility, the land is kept in trim only by unremitting care. If discipline is relaxed for a year or two the land sinks back into its original poverty. But in all the worst years of farming there was hardly an acre that was allowed to go back. The land won by labour in hope was kept by labour when all hope seemed to be lost. There is good land in Buchan and there are one or two pretty well-wooded villages, such as Old Deer and Longside, yet the impression persists that the land is bare and near the bone. But people have willed it to be fertile and have made and kept it so. That to me is its very powerful attraction.

BANFFSHIRE

The county of Banff might be called Aberdeenshire's little sister. The two have the same character, the same look; but there is a greater proportion of waste land in Banffshire and the good parts are not so kindly. The coastal plain, having turned the corner, now slopes north to the Moray Firth, with all that is implied in a north aspect. The foothills intrude further into the plain, coming in some places very near to the sea. The better farmlands are confined to a strip along the coast, which resembles Buchan; and to the valleys of the Deveron and the Isla, which resemble Strathbogie. The slopes are steeper and poorer and there is a feeling that life is lived nearer the bone. But the Banffshire farmer had as stout a heart for a steep hill as ever his Aberdeenshire cousin had. On the slopes of Glenisla behind Newmill and along the Deveron above the Bridge of Marnoch, there are places where the plough has been taken to fantastic heights—even further than the present farmers go. You might wonder what soil could lie up there, yet that is not a thing to bet on; better soil and a greater depth of soil are sometimes found on the higher slopes. The upper part of Banff-shire runs away into mountain country where the Avon comes down out of the Grampians through a long highland glen past Tomintoul, a lofty village remote physically and perhaps spiritually among the hills.

Lower Banffshire is the coastal plain where the mountains have intruded very close to the sea. You might say that all between the Isla, the Deveron and the firth is plain by rights, but some unkindly force heaved up Aultmore in the middle of it. This Aultmore is a great lump of high land about ten miles long and ten miles wide which has some outliers taller than itself, such as the Knock Hill to the south and the Bin of Cullen, a blue cone that stands by the sea, on the north. The effect on Banffshire is that the undulations of Buchan are replaced by steeper slopes. There are not the same long bare shoulders of land; though the shoulders are as bare around Aberchirder, they are not as long. But as to monotony there is little to choose; for the slopes of Banffshire being the steeper, they are usually the poorer.

Since we must begin somewhere let us begin at the point most natural to me. Our gateway to Banffshire is in Turriff, an old market town of Aberdeenshire which has crowned the slopes above the Deveron with white walls and blue-green roofs. From Turriff the road goes over the Deveron and up through the woods of Forglen, which nobly shade the sides of the vale, until the woods are left behind and the road passes through a bare country like Buchan. In the middle of it stands that countryside's metropolis. It might have been lifted straight out of the heart of Buchan—the houses bare and angular, stretched out along the road; the kirks, the school, the public house— and the whole thing set on a bare raith of land, with a shoulder of ground along the north. It is Aberchirder, locally known as Foggie-loan, or even Foggie. The name means something. Loan is a narrow by-road, like the English lane. Foggie may be an adjective from either meaning of fog: (a) green grass that comes up in stubbles, or grass of a poor quality found in poor pastures; or (b) mist that rises early at night over land with a cold bottom. The second may be the right one. I guess the mist comes out early over Aberchirder.

The traveller may care to stop and look at Foggie, as I have often stopped and looked; and he, as I, may wonder why enough people live there to make it a village. It is a question that may be asked about many villages between the North Water Bridge and John o Groats— about hundreds of farms, about thousands of them. Why do so many people persist on those bare uplands, those remote unlovely howes? Why don't they all come down and muck-in among the purlieus of Babylon? Of course many young people do leave the countryside as soon as they can, because there is no scope for their abilities or because they wish to see the world, or just to get away from their relations. There was a time when that natural movement became a mass migration because there was no living in the country places. There are still those who leave not from any inward compulsion but through disgust at bad houses and work that is needlessly hard. But there are always those who are tolerably happy to stay; and incomers who remain although brought up in a very different kind of society. Those who stay of their own free will must find some satisfaction, even in unlikely places. In the vast and always shifting friendlessness of the modern world, men and women need to find some place where every tree and well of water grows familiar and where they have a place in the community. In the years we spend between the forgotten and the unknown, we need to have some familiar place in which we have some value, and which has a value to us, otherwise we join the multitudes of displaced persons who drift about the deserts of the industrial world, victims of every substitute for a satisfying life.

We are accustomed, especially in the north, to think that money is the deciding thing. But money is only the symbol and there are still quite a few who think the substance is more important. There was a labourer in a small factory who proved himself a diligent and capable man and was made foreman over the other three labourers. The manager said to him, "Of course this'll mean an extra shilling a week to you, Geordie." Geordie said, "The money'll be welcome, but I'm nae askin' for't. It's the power that matters." That may point to the satisfactions which keep people in Foggieloans. Not only power but the recognition of value. There are salesmen in village shops who would do far better for themselves in a big town. They would be better paid, but they might not have such a place in the community. In the village they know everybody and everything about everybody; they know exactly how to please their customers and their customers come to rely on them. There are mechanics in country garages who might do much better in a big town—but in the village they have the care of a certain number of tractors and motor cars and vans; they get to know them over many years; they have a sort of property in them. When a mechanic sees a twelve-year-old tractor starting its thirteenth season at the plough, he knows that but for him it would have been on the scrapheap long ago. Other people know that too. Though he may be only a man working for a wage, he has his clients who depend on him, and pay him the deference though they may pay his employer the money. These instances can be multiplied in any small community. There is the man who gelds tomcats and the man who is good with roses, the woman who is tremendous at the spring cleaning and the girl who can sing "Trees" as good as the wireless. There are many deadly things in village and country life which is lived under the remorseless eyes of neighbours and relations, but aptitudes that are socially valuable such as singing "Trees" or fixing tomcats do get recognition. Even weaknesses. The village policeman will help the village drunkard home; not only because it would be a great nuisance to lock him up for the night. Mild forms of mania are provided for by trying to remove temptation. If one is not exactly among friends, one's peculiar aptitudes are admitted and accepted. One is a person and of some value in oneself, however small, even if only by weaknesses that make up a nice commodity of scandal. Money may be important, but the thing that matters is the power—being recognised as a person of some presence and value. That satisfies one of the major human appetites.

Some people need to look again at Foggieloan, and if they look long enough they may begin to question the ideas they have come to accept as gospel, about the nature of satisfactions. Perhaps we were the victims of a grand economic conspiracy. In the days when profits were the greatest good and the faster the money went round the greater the virtue, as Thibetans acquire grace by spinning a wheel, we were advertised into thinking that happiness must lie in the multiplication of gadgets and diversions. If people could be made to wish more gadgets, they would work harder to make money to buy those gadgets; then more gadgets would be produced which they could be persuaded to wish for; so they would work still harder which would produce more gadgets. It was an excellent idea on paper; in practice it looked like stretching humanity on the rack of induced desires. Happiness may not lie wholly in the multiplication of needs. It may, however, lie in the satisfaction of a few simple ones. A little more attention might be paid to Foggieloan.

There is a good road from Foggieloan to the coast along a bare slope above the Deveron which gives a full view of the hills of Fisherie and Pennan, a desolate mass ending in the sea at Troup Head. The road down in the valley from Turriff to the sea by Dunlugas runs through a pretty countryside of wood and farmland. At the right time, however, a true tempestuous grandeur may be found there. I have never seen it, but the Rev. Andrew Todd, writing a hundred years ago, described the floods at the Bridge of Alvah:

"This scene, at all times beautiful and romantic, assumes only its character of horrible grandeur when the river is swollen in a flood. On such an occasion, the narrow chasm at the bridge of Alvah, being insufficient to admit the augmented stream, the waters are repelled by the opposing crags and flow backwards for nearly two miles along the stream, and, in many places, extend for more than a quarter of a mile over the adjacent fields. When this mighty lake and the roused up river pour their water over the opposing rocks at the entrance of the gorge above the bridge, and when the tortured stream is thus thrown down with resistless force into the narrow gap beneath the arch, where 'it boils and wheels and foams and thunders through', a scene is presented of such mingled beauty and horror that, to convey an adequate conception of it, might require the combined powers of a Claude and a Salvator."

Eloquent outpourings of words and waters, both of which obviously gave the minister a grand satisfaction. There are perhaps no such floods today; nor such country ministers.

Banff, the county town, stands on the left bank of the river, as it enters the sea, with Macduff on the right-hand side. Macduff is a fishing port and a holiday resort and has been both for a long time. In the days before patent medicines, when mineral springs were popular, Macduff was the Harrogate of those parts, the well at Tarlair being famous for its healing properties. A trip to the well at Tarlair was specific for all the maladies that went under the heading of a decline. If the wife was feeling low after the birth of the fifth or sixth child, the farmer filled the box cart with straw and drove her up to Macduff. Having found her lodging for a fortnight, he stayed a night to settle her in, and, himself, took advantage of the treatment. He drank the unpleasant water. He went and paddled up to his knees in the rock pools. He ate as much dulse as his jaws were able for. Then he went home and returned for his wife at the end of the fortnight, taking the chance to expose himself again to the sea and its saining fruits. That was a long time ago. Other wells became more fashionable, and they in turn were replaced by the patent medicines, the ills of humanity having got beyond curing by water from the rock. But traditions persist; the people of Macduff, determined that their town should always be a resort, built a swimming pool; and Macduff remains a holiday place of the quieter sort, with boats on the stocks and fishermen at the harbour head.

Banff sits like an quiet old lady on the slopes above the sea and the river. It is one of those towns that have age but no resounding history.

The date of its beginning is unknown and of no importance now, for the atmosphere of the town belongs to eighteenth-century Scotland. There are the walls and warehouses at the harbour built of stone, without ornament, but in a simple mass that has dignity and rightness beside the quiet water. The houses of the older town are grey and plain, showing here and there a high gable, or the rounded entry to the court, while one at least has the elaboration proper to a laird's town residence. Others, of a slightly later date, are in the first nineteenth-century style associated with Adam and all his quality, showing a nice proportion of window and an elegant fanlight above the door. Banff has atmosphere. In its best days it was the county town of a small county and it has remained just that. Progress has not passed it by, but has touched it gently, so gently that Banff is not quite of the present day. That impression is increased by the fact that Duff House has its gates in the main street. This huge mansion in the Adam style was built for the Earl of Fife, a great territorial magnate. In its greatest days it was a world's wonder, particularly for its paintings that were ascribed to all the greatest artists, whoever did paint them. One may suspect that Duff House dominated the town—entirely for the town's good, of course—but dominated it all the same. However, time turns all states upside down. Duff House has been given to the town and the town is a little worried by the gift. What proved too big for a princely family may prove too big for a modest county town.

Westward from Banff the coastal plain, wide to begin with, narrows in between the mass of Aultmore and the Moray Firth. The road passes through Boyndie, a parish with an ancient but unconfirmed history. The parish minister a century ago claimed that a decisive battle with the Danes was fought here by the little water called the Boyne, the first time that a battle of the Boyne was famous in British history. He may have been right, because there is a persistent tradition of raids by Danes or Norsemen on this coast. The minister reported too that the grey rat was first imported to Scotland from a ship wrecked on the Boyndie shore: "Three or four of those ferocious creatures were found in the act of killing the sixth of a litter of young pigs; the former five having been devoured and killed. They are manifestly dangerous to young children." Then the road keeps near the coast, gradually crowded in by the Bin Hill and the Hill of Maud, outliers of Aultmore. There is a succession of small fishing towns and villages—Portsoy; Sandend, a little treasure of paint and white sands; Cullen on a beautiful bay; Portknockie, Findochty, Rathven, home of Andro Man, a notorious witch; Buckie and Portgordon, and beyond that the wide horizons of the Spey estuary. Between the sea and the hills, the land is tidily arranged in the northern style with the bigger farms on the better land along the low ground; and then higher up, the small irregular fields grouped round the grey steadings of the

24

family farms. There is substance in the farmlands between Banff and Cullen, for this was one of the first parts of the north to be improved —Lord Deskford having introduced the enclosing of fields and the turnip husbandry about the time of Sir Archibald Grant's work at Monymusk in the early eighteen century. All the way from Banff to the mouth of the Spey there is something attractive about this countryside. The hills, the farmland, the towns and villages along the shore, the blue firth and far beyond it the Sutherland and Caithness Hills: these are the lower Banffshire scene.

The main road goes on to Fochabers past the grounds of Gordon Castle, a vast mansion enclosed in woods and pleasure grounds about the size of a small parish. This was the home of the Dukes of Gordon, and, before them, of Lord Huntly, the head of the Gordon family and the Cock of the North. When the ducal line failed at the death of the fifth holder, the title passed to the Duke of Richmond, who succeeded as Duke of Richmond and Gordon. Twenty years ago, on the death of another Duke, the Commissioners of the Crown Land bought the Gordon estates, and that was the end of another long story. Gordon Castle in its greatest days was more than just another nobleman's house, for the Cock of the North was more than just another laird. His estates were vast, stretching from Aberdeenshire into Moray and from Tomintoul to the coast. These alone would have made him powerful, but he could call on the services of many other Gordons that had established themselves in the north, and held his court at Gordon Castle with a royal magnificence. That was long ago.

There is another road that goes from Portgordon straight into the hills. It winds and rises steeply up to the Braes of Enzie, where the small bare farms succeed each other till the last one crowns the hill. There again one may stop to admire the view across the firth and think again about the matter of satisfactions. What does the boy in the turnip field get there, as he hangs on to a swede with one hand and his cap with the other against the force of a nor-west gale? There must be a something in those chattery fields. The people at least hang on: which is more than can be said of the railway. It is an improbable thing to find, but a railway does run over the hill to Keith—or ran, for the traffic dwindled, the rails were removed and now there remain only broken bridges and tangled embankments, memorials to the days when a railway was the road to fortune. Once over the hills, the road winds down steeply, towards magnificent vistas of hills with mountains beyond them, until it finds real civilisation again at a distillery, with the scattered roofs of Keith in the glen below. Keith, which is the principal town of upper Banffshire, is hardly to be described, for it is not only no town, but two of them with a third, Newmill, close at hand. Keith is sited on both banks of the Isla, which comes from the west to join the Deveron near Rothiemay. On one side of the Isla there is Keith, on the other Fife-Keith; but there is nothing to draw them together into a unity; the place has everything but a centre. It is the market for a great cattle-rearing district: in the days of a free market in meat the Keith butchers were famous for the number and the quality of the beasts they sent to Smithfield. There is also a survival of the textile trade once so common in the north. The firm of Kynoch have an international reputation for woollens of fine texture and design. Keith, like Huntly, is a quiet and prosperous town: and both retain the air of villages that have grown up.

It is natural to follow the Isla as it winds slowly down the haughs to Rothiemay. On the south side the Balloch rears itself up steeply 1,199 feet, but on the other side the ground slopes gently away towards the height of Aultmore. So there is the steep height of the Balloch, with the Isla in the wet haughs under its shadow; and then, gently tilted to the sun, the long, long slopes with the steadily diminishing farms. Here and there small side glens open deeper into those slopes, showing farm beyond farm, to the point where the last ploughman, imagined rather than seen, turns his pair upon the horizon. Beyond the Kirk of Grange the strath opens out, as the valley of the Deveron comes up from the south. The place is full of light and there are flashes of water beyond the trees. At Rothiemay, a picturesque, disordered little village overgrown with trees, the road joins the river, now the Deveron, and both pass down the narrow glen to the Bridge of Marnoch. It is a true romantic passage, especially if it is made by the poorer road along the south side of the river. This road goes through woods, half up a precipitous slope, matched by an equally improbable one on the other side. The river runs in a narrow bed far below, and as it twists and turns, opens up short views of rather alarming beauty, as the precarious road makes sudden dives towards the bottom, to rise again alarmingly. On the south there are the woods and the only company are the cock pheasants displaying their pride on the road; but on the north side the little red tractors draw a furrow down a slope like the pitch of a roof. Men there must grow like goats, come time. Rothiemay Castle stands at the west end of the glen, a square decorated baronial keep among trees, high above the stream; in the middle of the glen Mayen House discloses an unexpected elegance; and at the foot of the glen Kinnairdy Castle stands above the gorge, a little square keep, fantastically high and thin.

At the Bridge of Marnoch the sensible road to Turriff goes by Foggieloan and the bare slopes with their dreich prospect of the Gamrie hills. But there is a better way by Netherdale and the Deveron as it follows another narrow valley to the east. No instructions are adequate to keep a stranger right; he is bound to get lost; but even so he may be fortunate and come to a dead end with the Kirk of Inverkeithney below him on the far bank of the river. The old kirk is a perfect thing to come on unawares, a plain house among trees and gravestones by the riverside, secluded, almost secret under the shadow of the hill. One might expect to find some saintly man in a cell there, spinning by contemplation a thread towards the inner mysteries of godliness. With patience and incidental pleasure, one may find a way out through the woods of Netherdale to Forglen and the woods again and so to the Deveron and Turriff.

The upper part of Banffshire is highland in character. The districts of Cabrach and Mortlach consist of narrow glens confined by high and rugged mountains that defy the plough. Inveraven has the 2,700-foot mountain Ben Rinnes in the middle of it; while Kirkmichael, the innermost parish, ends 3,800 feet up on the top of Ben Avon. The glens are not yet deserted, for the people of those remote parts have a wonderful persistence, but it is certain they were once more populous than now. The Cabrach on the head waters of the Deveron was famous for its cattle; it still produces some; and there may be no good reason why it should not produce many more. The little fields there cry out for lime, and the little farms for capital. This is marginal land, or worse, but marginal land has a value. The same may be said about Glenlivet and Strathavon. In Glenlivet, once part of the Gordon estates, the Commissioners of Crown Lands and the Department of Agriculture for Scotland with the help of the Forestry Commission have begun experiments to find out what can be done in those upland parishes. For instance: what is the best size of holding? Small as at present? Or very large? What is the best sort of management—arable? grass? or which rotation of the two? What is the best sort of stock? Sheep? Cattle? Both? Pigs? Poultry? When these technical points have been decided, there are human considerations. What will induce people to continue living there, or attract new families? The investigation has begun at the right end— the capability of the soil. So much discussion about the state of the Highlands has come to nothing at all because it began at the other end by saying, "People must be encouraged to live in the Highlands. Now how can we find a living for them?" The Glenlivet experiment starts from the very practical question: What is the soil of Glenlivet worth and can it support a healthy community with a high standard of living? If the answer is "No", then it may put an end to a lot of fruitless discussion. If it is "Yes", it may show the way to make the highland glens more useful and more bearably picturesque.

(The Glenlivet scheme met trouble at its beginning. Everyone concerned knew that the people of the glen must be consulted and the scheme explained to them in the hope of getting their co-operation. Unfortunately that explanation was delayed while a survey of the land was made. The farmers were alarmed by the survey and feared that the Forestry Commission were going to take away their grazings.

The newspapers got hold of the story and helped to work up an agitation. The steam-roller of bureaucracy, it was said, was riding rough-shod over another defenceless community; but—the clans were rising. There might be blood on the Braes of Glenlivet—the Braes that are more in need of lime and shelterbelts. Then a public meeting was held at which the representatives of the Crown Lands, the Department of Agriculture and the Forestry Commission appeared—not as defendants but with their case prejudiced. Explanations were made and assurances given that there was no intention to replace men by trees and that the whole idea was to discover the conditions of prosperity in the glen. No blood was shed; the newspapers lost interest; and I assume the scheme goes on. The fuss was deplorable: it need not have happened; but it was not useless. It was one more reminder that, when you are trying to work in a democratic way, the first essential is to take the people concerned into your confidence. Perhaps the Crown Lands officials wished to be able to give the people all possible information when they came to explaining the scheme. But the people did not need any information about Glenlivet—they had learned too much of it the hard way. All they wanted was to know what was going on.)

Glenlivet has always been remote, which had two notable consequences. Many of the people remained faithful to the Roman Catholic Church at the Reformation, as their descendants still do. In the seclusion of the hills they were tolerably immune from the scourge of the over-zealous and they even maintained a seminary that was unsuspected or at least undiscovered by the authorities for many years.

The same remoteness in a later time made Glenlivet famous for the illicit distilling of whisky. Every farmer had his still in which he converted his barley into powerful spirit and then smuggled it over the hills to the south. One authority estimated there were two hundred stills in the glen and on a close day the very air was drunken. The illicit distilling was not confined to Glenlivet and the trade to the south over the Whisky Road was brisk and valuable; so valuable indeed that it attracted people, even more undesirable than Customs officers, who ambushed the smugglers and stole their liquor. Hijacking may have been invented on the Grampian Hills. The trade has now become respectable. Somewhere, perhaps, in the lonelier glens an enterprising crofter makes some malt and brews and distils and stows a few jars under the bed to see him through the winter. None who know the trials and monotonies of a highland winter could grudge him his little consolation. Otherwise whisky is made in distilleries with all the processes under scientific control—and a Customs officer always on the premises. Since the Glenlivet distillery produces one of the finest malt whiskies, expert drunkards may be heard saying of any good spirit that it is "the real Glenlivet". Their opportunities of doing so have grown sadly few since we now send the best spirit ' of the Old World to upset the balance of the New.

When one buys whisky one never knows what one is getting, unless it is of a reputable brand. That it should be so is deplorable, but it is easy to understand. All spirits are basically the same and are very easy to produce. They are alcohol plus certain good or evil substances— or simply alcohol. Now if God intended men should not drink spirits, He made nature very prolific of temptation. Alcohol can be made from any vegetable matter containing carbohydrates—grain, potatoes, fruit, brown paper and string. If the yeasts in the air get at these substances under the right conditions they will produce alcohol without human interference. Nature, it would seem, has a taste for a dram.

The process of making alcohol is very simple. The vegetable matter should be ground small, boiled to get out the carbohydrate and then fermented by yeasts—either those that are in the air or superior ones cultivated for the purpose. The yeast attacks the carbohydrates and breaks them down into carbon dioxide and alcohol. When the fermentation has stopped, the solid matter settles out and a clearish liquor remains. That is not a spirit; it is only a wine or a beer, for yeast is inhibited from working as soon as there is 13 per cent. of alcohol in the brew. That is the limit of the strength of beer or wine— unless spirit is added afterwards. To get something strong enough to be called a spirit, the water must be removed by distilling; or to be more accurate, the spirit must be removed from the water by boiling. As alcohol and its sister spirits boil at a lower temperature than water, they come off in the first vapours, leaving the water behind. So in a still the liquor is boiled in a closed copper vessel ending in a long tube; the vapour that comes off condenses in the tube and comes out at the end as liquor, depending on what was originally fermented. If it was molasses it will be rum that makes the sailor's nose to red. If it was potatoes mixed with old shoe leather it will be a shotgun fired down your throat. After you have got your spirit you can decide what it is to be. Good spirit made from grain and flavoured with juniper is the coarse but quite reputable creature gin. Spirits expertly coloured are sometimes sold as whisky—most disreputable. But there are only two sorts of honest whisky; and only one sort fit to be called the real Glenlivet.

The true highland malt whisky is made from malted barley, pure soft water and the flavour of peat. The distiller makes his malt by spreading out the barley on the floor of his malthouse, where it germinates and puts out a green shoot. The distiller stops this germination by drying the malt in the kiln over a peat fire. He then brews the malt and the liquor goes to the still, which is like a very large copper onion with a long stalk coming out on top. As the liquor is heated the volatile spirits begin to come off. They are not all whisky.

' The first spirits may be powerful but they are very unpleasant; so too are those that come off at the end of the process, heavy oily spirits that would destroy the body and corrupt the soul. The middle cut is the real magic and it is compounded of alcohol and various delicate esters, with the softness of the hill water and the delicate aroma of peat. It is a clear spirit of heroic strength and only heroes and distillerymen could drink it in that state. . . . It should be matured in a cask for at least five or seven years to lose any harshness and bite; for it is not worthy to be drunk till it goes over the thrapple like milk and then glows up like a rising sun.

Every distillery produces its own particular whisky with a subtle flavour that distinguishes it from all others. Or so the experts say: I have not had the opportunity to acquire that special knowledge. It is still possible to get the whisky of named distilleries—Smith's Glenlivet: Glenfarclas; Grant's Glengrant; Glendronach, and so on. But it is not easy, because the public has a taste for blended whiskies that are all alike and is shocked by the difference in the single malt. There is nothing inherently wrong in blending. A reputable blender buys good whiskies from various distilleries and blends them till he gets something that he knows will please his customers. He may then call it by his proprietary name—"Blind Pig" or "Tartan Elephant", "Old Bedlam" or "The Lowes o Hell". In buying a blended whisky one can go only by the name of the blender. The Distillers Company Limited (D.C.L.), who control the greater part of the whisky trade, are too careful of their good name to allow it to be lowered by bad practices. So are the other well-known firms that are not in the D.C.L. Then in some Scots towns there are blenders who have a local reputation and do all they can to maintain it. But the law concerning libel being hard on the truth I cannot help you by warning you against evil practitioners by name. You can only find out by sore experience.

Furth of Scotland, and even inside Scotland, there are some strange poisons put out in bottles under the name of whisky. I once knew a man who made some of them. He was a Glasgow Irishman and distilled his liquor in the worst part of the Cowcaddens—not, as he said, because he liked it, but nobody there would notice one more smell. The recipe he used was potatoes and treacle, which he fermented in a washing tub in the kitchen. The brew was really fascinating; under the scum of yeast it was black and somehow evil. Mike used to call it "The Black Death". He distilled the stuff in a ten-gallon milk can over a gas ring, leading the steam through a twisted copper pipe under the cold water tap, and catching the venomous drops in a five-gill bottle. He did not bother about separating the true spirit from the false. "To hell," he said, "the folk that buy this want a quick knock-out and what'll knock them out quicker than fusel oil?" He bottled everything and sold it at half a crown a bottle at the time when whisky in the shops was twelve and sixpence. Mike was by no means the only practitioner of the black art in Glasgow around 1930. Among them they must have made a few cracks in the foundations of that never temperate city.

There are many stories about illicit distilling, of the tricks people used to cheat the exciseman, and of the remarkable places in which they hid their stills. Only the other day a gentleman of unquestionable veracity, a Civil Servant of high degree who would never speak without first referring to Statutory Rules and Orders, told me, as one giving evidence on oath, about a case of illicit distilling which happened in a northern town and in our own time. The police and the excisemen knew that illicit whisky was being made in the town. For months and years they tried to find the criminal. They watched, they searched; on low moist days they could smell the mash; but no matter how they watched nor where they searched, they found nothing. Then the beadle or caretaker of one of the town kirks died late on a Saturday night. An elder—the exciseman—hearing the news in the morning, went to the kirk to start up the central heating. He went down into the dark and dusty crypt which held the furnace, took off his jacket and opened the door to start the fire. He found there a curious obstruction; and, being of a mechanical turn, began to investigate it. After half an hour he suddenly swore a mighty oath of rage and joy. He had found the illicit still. The beadle had cunningly adapted the central heating system to his own purposes. It is a nice thought that, while the congregation were listening to the Word, the spirit may have been circulating in the warm pipes beneath their feet.

THE PROVINCE OF MORAY

The Province of Moray is one of the kindlier parts of Scotland. It consists of the counties of Elgin and Nairn and is in effect a narrow strip of land along the Moray Firth, backed by high hills and desolate moors. The plain, called the Laich or low country, is greatly favoured by nature and has a dry, agreeable climate. Because of that it is one of the places of old settlement, and Elgin, the capital of the province, is one of the few Scottish towns where you can feel that people have lived with some ease and dignity for hundreds of years.

The Laich of Moray can be approached along the coast from the east, but it is more effective if it is taken by surprise over one of the hill roads. On the Grantown road over Dava Moor or the Keith road over Aultmore, you pass the blasted upland farms on the edge of the moors with the bare hills behind them. Then, at some bend of the road, the prospect of Moray opens before you. Far below the plain stretches from east to west, dotted with small woods and veiled in a light blue mist. Almost imperceptibly the land fades into the blue of the sea, and that again into the darker blue of the mountains of Ross. It does seem a happy raith of garden ground, sheltered a little from those twin scourges, the north-west and the south-east winds. When you go down into the plain the happy first impression is confirmed. Not that the place is really a garden. Along the Llanbryd road the soil is by no means good and runs away to sandy heath and moor. But there is an indefinable something in the atmosphere, a lightness and ease seldom found in the north. And Elgin is not like other towns.

Elgin is a cathedral city; and, although the cathedral has been a ruin for more than three hundred years, it is still the heart of the burgh. The two west towers, all that remain of the original five, rise above the roofs of Elgin as memorials of the noble past; but they are a little more than that; they have some active power on the minds of the living. There is a sense of continuity in Elgin. From the facts that there are in the town many buildings from the older times, and that many of those buildings are piously preserved and used, it is obvious that some people in Elgin have a proper respect for the good works of the past. But Elgin does not live on its past. It has weaving sheds where descendants of the handloom weavers produce woven goods of very high quality and at least one of them has been designed and equipped in the most modern way. Elgin has a cod-liver-oil factory —the pioneer of its kind; and there is tradition again, for, although Elgin is not on the coast, the town council in the eighteenth century spent what was a fortune to them in developing the harbour of Lossiemouth and even put a duty on beer to raise the money. You can buy a packet of patent oats in Braco's Banking under the piazza beside the Little Cross and thus have contact, however attentuated, with Andrew de Moravia, who founded the cathedral. There are few places in Scotland where you may be so conscious of a continuing purpose in human affairs.

The cathedral is a noble work. In its early history it resembles Sarum. The first bishops could not make up their minds where their cathedral church should be. They tried Birnie, Kinnedar and Spynie, but at last they fixed on Elgin, where they built the great house that was to be the lantern of the north: *speciale partie decus, regni gloria, et delectatio extraneorum et supervenientium hospitum, laus et exultatio laudio in regnis extraneis.* Across from the cathedral they built the bishop's palace; while nearby there was the abbey of the Greyfriars, founded by David I. It is hardly possible now to understand the spirit which built these works of the Roman Church in Scotland, and it has been long out of fashion to try to understand. I had been familiar with Elgin Cathedral and had admired it as one should, but I had no clue to the wonder of it until I became one of His Majesty's Royal Engineers. It was my duty then in one of the lost years between 1939 and 1945 to help with the instruction of recruits in building temporary bridges over the Lossie*—a job made difficult by the fact that heavy weights had to be lifted by clerks and shopmen unaccustomed to that sort of heavy labour; and a little complicated by the fact that I did not understand what I was supposed to teach. We had, however, some important aids—motor engines, ingenious pulleys and that sort of thing, including tea brought in a mobile canteen. As the squad heaved on the ropes over the complaining sheaves—grease was in short supply, though we sweated more than enough to grease them—and as they stood round motors that refused to work, I often looked away, as one whose emotions were not engaged by the work at hand, away to the west where the two broken towers still stood up over the roofs of Elgin. I had to wonder then that the great towers were raised with so few mechanical advantages. The builders of the cathedral and I were at the opposite ends of a piece of time. They had used all human knowledge in a supreme work; and I was instructing people how to build without the best mechanical resources of civilisation. It was then for the first time I realised the wonder of the great cathedrals. In 1224 or thereby the domestic architecture of Elgin would not have been distinguished. If historians are right, even castles at that time were seldom built of stone—a wooden keep on a mound of earth was good enough for a powerful chief who had only temporal power. But at that time the cathedrals were rising gloriously under heaven. The cathedral must have towered over the roofs of Elgin, must have towered over the province of Moray. It must have been then the highest expression of all men's thoughts and aspirations in Moray: not a burden put upon them but the kingdom of heaven made actual upon earth in stone.

The cathedral suffered many vicissitudes. In 1390 Alexander, Earl of Buchan, better known as the Wolf of Badenoch, being annoyed with the Bishop of Moray, who had excommunicated him, came up from his hideout in Lochindorb and as a result of his visit

> Brynt the kyrk was of Elgyne
> Be wyld wykkyd heiland men

Alexander, who was the king's son, did penance at the Blackfriars in Perth, and, as some say, also at the Little Cross in Elgin. He also promised satisfaction to the Bishop of Moray, but what restitution, if ever made, is not recorded. The Wolf died shortly afterwards, and was buried in Dunkeld Cathedral. The Church got him in the end when he was too dead to protest.

Elgin Cathedral was rebuilt and survived the first iconoclasm of the Reformation; but in 1569 the Privy Council, being hard up, decided to sell the lead which covered the roof. So the roof was stripped,

* As Lance-corporal (paid).

an impious act condignly punished, for the ship that carried the lead towards Holland sank on the way. The stripping of the roof undid the great house. The people of Elgin petitioned Parliament to replace the lead and Parliament agreed, but the money was never made available. Wind and weather rotted the sarking of the roof; frost got into the mortar between the stones; and gradually the jewel of the kingdom fell into ruins.

But there is a continuity in Elgin. The cathedral decayed; every winter the frost and the rain tore away this detail and that; yet even in its most desolate state the cathedral could be as it had once been, a refuge. In the early eighteenth century there was in Elgin a poor woman called Gilzean Anderson whose husband had been killed as a soldier in the service of the Honourable East India Company. Having nowhere else to go, she made her home in the chapter house of the cathedral, and there under the magnificent groined roof and between the empty windows, she cradled her child in the font. That child, a boy, became like his father a soldier of the East India Company, but unlike his father became a general and, dying, left his fortune to care for the young and the old of Elgin. Anderson's Institution in Elgin is thus the fosterchild of the cathedral nearby.

The cathedral was truly a part of the life of the town, which explains why so much still remains. It explains the work of John Shanks, a glovemaker in Elgin at the beginning of the last century, and a poor glovemaker at that. Either he had a profound piety towards the landmarks that our forefathers have set, or some innate feeling for architectural splendour: whatever the reason, he adopted the ruined cathedral. In the time he could spare from his trade he cleared away the fallen rubble, rescued the sculptured stones and preserved the walls from further decay. In 1825 the Government recognised him as official keeper, and when he died he was buried by the empty walls that had been his greatest care. There might be a statue to John Shanks in Elgin; but, when one considers ceremonial statuary, it is as well there isn't. He requires none anyway; the cathedral is his proper memorial.

Nowadays the cathedral is in the careful and loving hands of the Office of Works. When people make the remarks they are always making about Government Departments, they should except the Office of Works. How many old and noble houses they have rescued from ruin and oblivion. And how rightly they do it. You may walk into the shadow of Elgin's walls, under the immensity of the twin western towers, and there, at once, the great house bends over you. On that green lawn, among the shadows and the shafts of light, through the empty spaces, listening piously for the chanting of the psalms and the creak of blocks raising the carved stone, you may hear the many centuries together and know there is indeed a continuing purpose from Andrew de Moravia down through John Shanks, the poor glove-maker, to the girl who sits in her short school frock, bowed over a list of the English kings, on the tombstone decorated with the figures of a knight, a mace, a halfmoon and a runic cross.

The heritage from old Elgin is not only the cathedral. Across the road there is the bishop's palace, only a token of what it once was, because in the glorious days of free enterprise after the Reformation, the stones of the palace were quarried to make vulgar dwellings, besides dykes and byres and such bestial things; but enough of the palace remains to show what it had once been. At the east end of the cathedral there is Pans Port, one of the gates through the wall that once surrounded it. In the Port you can still see the grooves down which the portcullis ran in the days when a cathedral was not only a refuge from the justice of heaven but a present stronghold against the ravenings of evil men. These today, surrounded by green lawns, have achieved the peace their builders so greatly desired.

Many other good things survive. There is the Little Cross at North College Street where the Wolf of Badenoch may or may not have made repentance for the burning of the cathedral. There is the Muckle Cross in the middle of the High Street, the market cross of Elgin. Of a later date there are the piazza houses. These eighteenth-century houses are among the lost amenities of Scotland. In a piazza you build a covered way over the pavement so that the foot passenger can walk under cover from shop to shop, a very desirable thing in a climate like ours. Dundee had one, at the old townshouse, till it was cleared away, in some idea of improvement. Elgin has three examples. One is the house known as Braco's Banking beside the Little Cross. It has been slightly distorted because the piazza has been taken into the shop, but apart from that the old house has been most piously preserved. The other two examples are both in the High Street, and one must hope that some good citizens will put them beyond the mis-chances of private enterprise and official interference. Up a loan there is Thunderton House, that was once the town residence of a Dunbar, one of the lairds of these parts. Much local history has been decided beneath its high pitched roof and some that was more than local. In 1746 Charles Edward Stewart stayed there in his retreat to Culloden, the last retreat of the divine right of kings. It is now a hotel.

Elgin has also some fine houses in the Georgian style. Anderson's Institution at the east end and Gray's Hospital at the west are in the correct and harmonious style that any architect in those days could knock off between drinks on a Saturday morning. The Kirk of St Giles, islanded in the middle of the High Street, has a plain sort of elegance, topped off by a cylindrical tower. There, as the High Street widens out into something that is more than a street and less than a square, some people find a suggestion of a French *place*. They may be right; but is it not curious that whenever some people find anything attractive in Scotland, they try to explain it by reference to foreign parts? Though few of the houses are at all distinguished, they do sit well together; they make a unity; and at each end the view is closed by a piece of classical dignity—Dr Gray's Hospital and the Kirk of St Giles.

Elgin has many pleasant things for so small a town. Academy Street which runs down the slope from South Street to the railway is a charming example of domestic arrangement. Delightful small houses look on to the narrow road, some of them with stone steps leading up to a door with an elegant fanlight. Every now and then the order is broken by a house or a row of houses set gable end to the road, so that there is a garden wall along the pavement, and a green door, and branches overhanging. It is very quiet, very intimate and entirely a place to live in. That is the real attraction of Elgin—the feeling one could have a good life there. The city has a great deal of the past, from the last stones of the castle on the hill to the houses in Academy Street; and that past is no burden. Elgin has not the dead feeling of a museum of antiquities. There would be many small constant delights for people living there—pretty and curious things that the eyes come on—a detail of a building, ruins across the water, white houses through the trees, poplars gravely bending before the wind, a garden court discovered through an arched close in the High, other closes where the Middle Ages have decayed with all their crowded darkness. There is a pleasure for some people in being reminded of those who have lived before us and in feeling we are their heirs. There must be some in Elgin who feel like that, and who realise that today's prosperity need not mean the destruction of the past. The chief manufacturer has been most active in caring for those amenities of the town. Elgin is prosperous: and there is the heart of the matter—age and vigorous life both together in the same place. The last time I wandered through the streets, while looking over the wall at the Greyfriars, I talked to a farmer from the edge of the town who had carried his trade to great lengths by the most modern methods and ideas. That seemed just right, in Elgin.

In Moray one walks everywhere among the past. On the Loch of Spynie there are the ruins of the castle, once the home of the bishops. Duffus Castle is a short distance away and has been rescued from complete decay by the Office of Works. The Kirk of Birnie, south of Elgin, though older than the cathedral, is still in use. Because of its great age—about eight hundred years—it has acquired particular powers. The country people used to say that if you were prayed for three times in Birnie, it would either end you or mend you. But if you were ended you were buried in the thrice sacred churchyard. In Birnie there is an old bell called the Ronnel. Some say it was made in Rome, of silver and copper. Others think it Celtic work. Up the

Black Burn and a few miles from Elgin the Priory of Pluscarden sits fair in a narrow valley. I went there first about twenty years ago and saw, as I remember so brightly, a group of buildings, rounded and pointed, set on a slope against a low range of hills. Because of the slope the walls did not seem roofless and, walking between the high box verges in the garden, I could not think the Priory deserted. Nor is it deserted now. Cistercian monks have returned and some parts of the building have been completely restored. If there is such a thing as peace, Pluscarden would be a likely place to look for it in.

There is a fine story of disaster and restoration in Moray. Where the Findhorn ran into the sea there was once the barony of Culbin, a valuable estate consisting of a laird's house and sixteen farms, besides the usual crofts and outhouses. According to tradition the land was very fertile, and tradition is probably right, for there is kindly land in that district. The barony of Culbin may very well have been a prosperous and a happy place. But our felicities often depend on the very delicate balances of nature. Along the shore great sandhills had been piled up gradually by the wind and the tide, as can be seen on many other parts of the coast. These were held in place by a sort of marram grass, *Ammophila arenaria*, an austere plant that sends down many roots. The roots helped to bind the dunes and the grass broke the eroding force of the wind. Unfortunately the marram grass was an excellent thatch for roofs and cornstacks and the farm people pulled it in great quantities, thus exposing the sand. In the autumn of 1694 gales of unusual violence began to move the sand eastward over the farmland, burying everything that stood before it. The legend is that everything happened in a day or two: more likely after the first movement the ruin was gradual with every west wind. However it happened, the ruin was complete. The sand overwhelmed Culbin and even blocked the mouth of the Findhorn, which had to find a new outlet to the east. For a long time thereafter the sand encroached and always threatened more good land. Moray paid dear for the thatch of marram grass.

There are plenty of desolations in Scotland, but none quite as remarkable as the sands. On the east side of the river there is the village of Findhorn and farmland and Kinloss aerodrome, a busy, cheerful countryside. If you cross over by boat and walk into the dunes you go straight into a dead world. Some folks say it is like the Sahara; others say it is like the moon: as I have not been to either I can only say that it is utterly desolate. Range upon range of dunes, fantastically ribbed and sculptured by the wind, bear nothing but scrawny tufts of marram grass, and have a lack of any significant feature that wanders the mind and destroys all sense of direction. In some places the dunes are of such fine dry sand that a step at the bottom produces a tiny landslide many feet high, as if the mass were so delicately balanced

37

at the angle of repose that a rougher touch would set the whole thing in motion. In other places the wind has whipped out depressions which in winter are covered with water that trembles under the incessant scourge of the wind. It is an inhuman, an unearthly place: even the birds and the beasts avoid it.

There is no saying how far the waste would have overtaken Moray if something had not been done to stop it. The obvious plan was to replace the marram grass and then find some greater protection. About eighty years ago the reclamation work was begun, and at Binsness there are Scots firs and Corsican pines, some of them planted by Major Chadwick, a pioneer in this work. These trees are well grown, but on the windward side the sand has piled so high against them that you can walk among their tops. Although this early planting showed what might be done, the expense was too great for local proprietors or any private enterprise. Fortunately the Forestry Commission included Culbin among its major works. Now, out of 6,000 acres, 4,000 acres are bearing trees that will bind the sands as long as the forest is maintained.

The Forestry Commission workers have perfected a technique of planting. The first thing is to fix the sand. Marram grass used to be employed, but it grows too sparsely and does not give enough protection for the young trees, only a few inches high. So the forestry workers now thatch the ground to be planted; that is, they put a close layer of brushwood over the sand. Most of the thatch comes from the older plantations—thinnings and lower branches cut in the course of brashing—that is, pruning. These branches often have a fair weight in themselves and if necessary can be pegged down. The seedlings are then planted among them; and the thatch not only protects the trees but, when it decays, it helps to feed them. By the time the thatch has rotted away the seedlings are well established and themselves shelter and bind the sand. It is a wonderful work of re-generation. Throughout the years the trees shed needles which decay into humus, thus changing the top skin of sand into soil. When the trees are felled the roots decay, adding humus to much greater depths. In their maturity the trees drop seeds from which young trees grow up. The process once begun goes on. The second generation still further increase the skin of soil; their roots in turn decay. So in the course of time—generations of time—a new topsoil will overlie the sands. At some far distant day the forest may be cleared and the plough turn a furrow again over the old furrows buried 50 feet below.

Forres, the town of second importance in Moray, is a pleasant place under Cluny hill, with the Findhorn running nearby. It is probably of great age. People say the Romans had something to do with it, which is possible, for some very interesting remains of them were found in caves near Lossiemouth. However, the finding of Roman equipment is no proof that the Romans ever set foot in Moray; the relics may be only loot. Forres is mentioned by Shakespeare in *Macbeth*; it was hereabouts that Macbeth met the witches, and his title of Thane of Cawdor refers, or may refer, to Cawdor nearby. The Romans, the witches and Macbeth and all may be no more than mummers' tales. One relic at Forres is sure enough—a sandstone monolith called Sweno's Stone, covered with decoration in the Celtic style. One may spend a lot of time trying to read the meaning of Sweno's stone, but the decoration, like so much Celtic art, may have no meaning at all, beyond infinite complication, like a canful of worms. Behind Forres the plain rises gently under the woods of Altyre and Darnaway Forest to the high hills and dark Lochindorb with its castle, whence the Wolf of Badenoch descended to ravage Moray. But we are not concerned with such highland matters.

The low lands of Moray continue right across the little shire of Nairn, mighty pleasant with its tidy farms on the light soil tailing away into sands. The firth becomes narrower; the eye is always attracted away to the ships on blue water and to the Black Isle of Ross beyond them. The town of Nairn is not very distinguished, but the surroundings have a delightful quality, in part from the windings of the little river, where the trees hang out gorgeous tapestries in the autumn, and in far greater part from the wide skies and the dry, shining air and the prospect of hills across the water and the massed glories of sunset behind the mountains of Ross.

From end to end Moray is a kindly place, prosperous and yet unspoiled by the grosser works of progress.

INVERNESS

Inverness is the county town of a very large county, and it is often called the capital of the Highlands, but these distinctions would not make a very fat living for a town. Though the county of Inverness is wide, there are more mountains than men in it, and the same is true of the rest of the highland counties. But this part of the world is rich in one thing—scenery. It is a grand place to live in for a week or a month or a summer, and the fortunes of Inverness rest very largely on that. By its strategic position on A9, the road from the south to John o Groats, and the fact that it is the centre of all communications from the north, it is also the centre of a valuable holiday business.

But it is far more than just another town full of trippers, soda fountains and souvenirs, though it has plenty of them all. It is an old town, of perhaps immemorial antiquity. Whenever the Scots kings had any power over the Highlands, it rested on Inverness; and, as central administration grew stronger, Inverness grew more important. After the rebellion of 1745 it gathered economic power. In the days of the banking and railway booms its merchants were able to hold off the capitalists of Aberdeen. It grew by serving and developing the country round about it, and it still serves as a market town, though the developing may have passed into other and stronger hands. The banks, the insurance offices, legal chambers, merchants, warehouses and garages may attract less attention than the tourists, but they are not less important to Inverness. Though there may be little to gather in many of the glens, Inverness manages to gather in a share of it.

As you look at the main shopping centre, you realise that Inverness is and has been accustomed to good society. When the highland chiefs lived on their estates Inverness was a social meeting-place, and many of them wintered there. After it became the fashion to winter in London, the families came north for the summer and the shooting, so Inverness got a summer season. This came to its full glory in the golden years before the great wars, when every piece of moor had its shooting lodge and every lodge its sporting tenant, from London or New York. The golden glow of those happy years can still be felt in the middle of the town. People who could pay £2,000 for a few weeks' shooting, and people who could collect such gratifying rents, had money to spend and were not likely to haggle about prices. The shops that served them have the undeniable air of class that comes from long enjoyment of the carriage trade. They make it quite plain that there is still money in Inverness and not all of it is merely passing through. The business and the administrative parts of the town together give it a substance and a dignity that should save it from the fate that threatens every place frequented by tourists—the greasy slide to Blackpool.

Inverness has a beautiful situation which the people have done little to spoil. It stands at the mouth of the River Ness and the north end of the Great Glen. It has the hills to the south and west, blue water to the north and the broad Ness flowing through it. By chance the sun has always shone when I have been in the town, and the impression remains of hills whose lower slopes are clad with trees and whose peaks are delicately veiled with mist; of the brilliant blue waters of the firth flecked by little white waves; of the river running between the Islands where lovers and old ladies wander among the trees. Or at night, running into the town from the north, I remember the stars in the clean sky reflected in the firth and the river in pure colour and radiance. Then I knew the sirens sang there, though I never exactly caught their song.

Set thus so beautifully among the hills and waters, Inverness demands citizens with a more gallant air than suits a purely lowland town. I would not say that all the people of Inverness walk about as if they were Jacobites at heart and secretly drink to Charles Edward; yet there are those who have a something, just as all highlanders have a something, though they do not always know what to do with it. For instance there are quite a few kilts around Inverness, some of them worn by gentlemen with rather anxious expressions, for the kilt is sometimes more than a garment: it can be a gesture and a protest, and a protest is not an assuring cover for the nakedness of the human body. But when it is worn as a gesture of pride and youth, the streets of Inverness light up and there is music on the hills.

There are two considerations about the wearing of the kilt. First the practical one. It is an excellent garment. It is not only well ventilated but also air-conditioned—that is the only way to explain the fact that it is cool in summer and warm in winter. It is handsome, provided there is a good figure to swing it; and it sets off a well-turned leg magnificently. But it is terribly revealing: it does nothing for the wearer unless he has something already, and if he has too much it emphasises the excess. A fat man in a kilt looks like a sack of meal in a blanket. Men's clothes now are a concealment and an alibi, turning all the diversities of the human figure into packaged goods, but the kilt is a distinction and a challenge and the wearer dare not sag under it. It is incomparable for boys and young men. And it is almost indestructible. You can burn it with cigarettes and stain it with beer, yet nothing shows. When it fades after many years, that only means the colours are less discordant. Kilts are handed down from father to son in old highland families, being sometimes the only ancestral possessions left to hand down.

The kilt is also a symbol and has an emotional significance for certain people. I had not realised that when I was young, for I wore the kilt as a boy and have done at odd times since, when the state of my figure allowed, or the lunacies of military service demanded. Once long ago when I was wearing a kilt I was set on by a female of indefinite age who demanded by what right I carried a Gordon tartan. I had never thought of that before, and the only reply I could give was that I had bought the thing in a second-hand shop for a pound. She asked, was I not a member of the Gordon clan. I said no, as far as I knew I had no connection with any clan. She said, had any of my family been in the service of the Gordons. I said my family were not in the habit of being in anybody's service. Then, she said, I had no right to the tartan, and she glowered so that I was sure if she had not been a lady she would have unfrocked me. I cannot understand such emotion about the pattern of a kilt. But it appears that each tartan is the uniform of a clan. If you wear its tartan you are claiming membership of the clan and must prove your claim. If you cannot prove, you are an impostor, or worse. There may be something in it. People do establish certain rights by use and wont; and it may be that the clans have proprietary rights to their chosen patterns. If they feel that way the rest of us should respect their feelings. One would not go about in the uniform of a Hampshire militiaman, so why go about in the uniform of a Macleod of Macleod? But the question does remain —why should any clan wish a uniform and bring themselves down to the level of those who wear school ties? And why should anyone be concerned to belong to a clan now that the clans have long since ceased to be social units? Perhaps the general disintegration of social life gives the clan feeling an emotional value. But these are things of which no lowlander is qualified to judge.

Whatever be the case about the tartans, the clans have no proprietary interest in the kilt, a garment worn by men in different parts of the world. If any lowlander or Englishman wishes to wear this garment there is no good reason why he should not invent his own tartan. The American gentleman in Compton Mackenzie's *Monarch of the Glen* had a kilt made.

"On the morning of August 28th Carrie awoke to the agreeable thought that . . . it was a gloriously fine day. As a matter of fact it was a fine day, but the rich glow that filled the room was caused not by the sun but by her own husband, who was standing at the foot of the bed wearing a kilt that was not so much orange as flame coloured, a doublet of amber tweed and a heavily brassed leather sporran.

" 'And Kilwhillie said it was all right?'

" 'I don't think he's tickled to death by the orange kilt. He said it was brighter than he thought it would be. He said he'd have advised a saffron kilt, the kind some of the Irish use, if he'd known I was going all-out on orange. He put me wise, too, about the sporran. . . . I thought it would be more convenient to wear it on one side like a trouser pocket. But it seems that for a fellow to wear his sporran on one side tells against him pretty heavily in Highland society. I suppose I'd soon get used to walking about like a kangaroo with a pouch in front of me. . . . I asked him if there was any objection to me carrying an extra sporran on the hip, but that objection upset him a lot. He wouldn't hear of it. Still, there's no question about it, Carrie. The kilt's pretty comfortable.' "

I doubt if the real spirit of the highlander lies in a display of tartan, though a display of tartan can be a substitute for that spirit. Nor do I find it in the bagpipe music, which sounds to me as if someone were blowing up a little phrase with a great deal of breath. Most bagpipe music is like all other folk music: the themes are simple, primitive and often very appealing, but simple and primitive themes appeal only when they are plucked out or blown through a modest piping or twangling instrument. It took Vaughan Williams to adapt "Greensleeves" for a symphony band. Now, whatever you may call the bagpipe, it is not modest. It is the steam organ of an earlier age, the Calliope of the human lung. I admit there is the pibroch, the fugue of the bagpipe. Admit it—that isn't the word: I can't forget it. It was my misfortune to be involved in the *levée en masse* of the European people around 1940, and it was my great good fortune some years later to be attached, for pay, rations, discipline and hope of eventual release, to a highland regiment. It was, if I may say so without seeming ungrateful, a very highland regiment, in that nearly all the details were lowlanders. Because of that they felt it a duty to be more Gaelic than Macrimmon—as, for instance, that all officers must wear the kilt; and that was the one time I wore the kilt against my better judgment, because at that time my figure was vastly administrative. And on the rare occasions when the officers' mess all dined together in regimental state, there must be pipers with the spam and a pibroch before the coffee. Then the pipe major (who was my dear friend and I hope will always make the allowances for me that he made then) used to come in, bearing the hellish instrument on his shoulder, and for the space of three-quarters of an hour used to walk round and round the long table displaying the virtuosity of his lungs and fingers. It was not for me any great ordeal. I had had seventeen years of a Scotch education that conditions you to boredom, and since music was not in my time a subject of higher education, I had still a curiosity about music. Besides I was in a mild way interested in the elementary tactics I had to teach during the day. So when I, as the mess president, sat handiest to the wine waiter, I used to translate the curious sounds of the bagpipe into elementary tactics. That was why the part of the pibroch which used to cause acutest distress to the few musical members of the mess gave me the greatest pleasure. You see in those days I spent a lot of my working time teaching soldiers how to advance upon an enemy, although I had never advanced with any lethal intention myself; and the fashionable method of attack in those days was called pepper-potting. It was a good name if you remember that a pepper-pot seldom gives from more than three of its thirty holes at one time. That was the idea: if thirty men were advancing, not more than three would be going forward at one time. Now in the pibroch there is a movement—if anything ever moves in a pibroch—where the notes, lightly struck by the finger, in no discoverable order, advance upon the ear until all resistance is overcome. I used to think then that if only I could translate that notation of the pibroch into elementary tactics I could retire Wagner's trombones beyond the Rhine with a very small loss of life. Now, looking back on those lost years, I begin to value the bagpipe at its true worth. Not as a musical instrument in the symphony of instruments, but as an instrument of war. Any body of men, led into battle by a pipe band, would fight like hell if only to get away from the bagpipe noise; or with their primitive passions stirred up by those few so simple and reiterated notes. St Cecilia was probably no performer on the bagpipe.

I doubt if the true spirit of the highlander is to be found in the bagpipe noise; to me the great virtue of the true highlander is in his regard for the amenities of life, the amenities between one and another. I remember the children's treat on Christmas Eve in a highland school which went on long into Christmas Day with dancing in the schoolroom and drinking in the schoolmaster's byre. I remember a young stalker called Roddie with whom I found much in common and with whom I exchanged bottles well warmed in the hip pocket. I took a taste of his, and said, "This is not green ginger." He said, "Maybe it doesn't taste like green ginger, but if it is green ginger you wish—that's it."

I remember not so long ago having a meal in a hotel in Inverness with a lady who has a certain something for those who can see it. After the meal we sat for a little time in the hall of the hotel, near a party of elderly men who were about to go their ways after an excellent and protracted lunch. One told, while the others listened, a long and not too presbyterian story. The expressions on the four faces amused my companion, and as she is not an inhibited, well-bred creature, she did not hide her interest and amusement. We left the hotel just ahead of the four gentlemen, and as we were getting into our motor car one of them passed us. Catching my companion's eye, he raised his hat, bowed and smiled, as much as to say, "You are one of us and a very charming person," and then passed sedately on. That, I thought, was a gesture, without a protest, and my sister thought so too. Being a Canadian, she said "There goes a great big butter-and-egg man": and I said, "A real highland gentleman", and each in our own way – meant it as a mighty fine compliment. We both knew it wouldn't have happened in Aberdeen without an introduction.

As with all other towns of the north, Inverness must be considered in relation to its setting. That is a truly wonderful country. To the east the level plain, with its wide skies and long views of the hills across the water, is backed by the moors and the hills that divide the valleys of the Ness and the Spey. To the south the Great Glen, the result of some tremor of the earth that broke Scotland in two, is romantic by its wooded slopes and the shining waters of the lochs. To the west there is the narrow belt of wonderfully good land along the Beauly Firth, and all besides that is mountain and glen, sometimes charmingly wooded, usually austere and sometimes quite fantastic. It is a country of intense light and brilliant colour, glittering under the December snow: every imaginable shade of blue and green at midsummer, and the richest mingling of all ripe colours in the fall. It is as if the land were dyed with the colours of its own violent, improbable history of raids and ravishing and sudden death; of a culture very gracious at its best, that could turn very swiftly to murder of the most brutal sort. It is, too, the country of the Forty-five, the last romantic adventure, a fantastic mixture of regardless loyalty, passion, envy, self-seeking and plain stupidity, which came to its end on Drummossie Moor, where the graves of the clansmen are a pathetic memorial to something which was doomed from the start because it had no relevance to anything but dead dreams. Altogether a very different country from the lowlands, not arable but pastoral and pre-eminently a country for all the forms of sport involving slaughter or self-affliction. It is not by chance that tourism and sport are so important to Inverness.

The season begins about the middle of May and lasts till the end of September. The May traffic is quiet—a few people tramping round the Youth Hostels, motorists on holiday before the roads are too crowded, fishermen making the most of the water before the streams fall too low, and those elderly people that take a provident fortnight out of season at the best hotels. By July the traffic becomes much heavier. Thousands of motor vehicles of every sort follow each other up A9 and are collected in the tangle of Inverness's main street, from which only the skill and second sight of the highland policeman can sort them out. The hotels and boarding houses all the way to John o Groats begin to fill up with family parties; and the golf-courses along the sea, normally occupied by a few old gentlemen and a score of blackface ewes, are made wonderful by strange styles and stranger costumes. August brings the crown of the season, when the best people in London take their holidays and all the highland chiefs are in residence, if they have been unable to let their houses. Then you can see the proud ones who have inherited the earth, or have organised themselves into possessing a slice of it, or are just getting away with something and try to look as if they always had it. This part of the season has its climax in the games meetings, prodigious affairs of tweeds and tartans and shepherds' crooks.

The crowded streets of Inverness are fascinating at the height of the season to look at and listen to. There are tourists of all sorts and shapes: incredibly elegant American babes that look as if they were assembled out of brass fittings on a conveyer-belt; their males who so ably carry on what used to be the English tradition of loud voices and bad manners abroad; poised and charming Canadians on the way to the glens from which their forefathers may have come; Indian princes from the shooting lodges, with the melancholy of those who have all knowledge and have done everything and found it vanity; fair-haired North Europeans and dark-haired Latins; turbaned Mohammedans with suitcases in which they hawk fabrics of Eastern design and doubtful provenance; shepherds off the hills in plus-fours and great boots that strike fire from the pavement; highland gentlemen in plus-fours and shoes, men of long pedigree, well-bred to the point of vacancy; young men heroically beautiful in kilts and young women in kilts, but not so good, being usually quite the wrong shape; handsome young men in shorts and sunburn and young women in shorts, but again sometimes not so good, for shorts and curves go ill together; mothers with small children, hoping that the children at least are enjoying themselves; older children wishing they could get away from their parents for a while; the middle-aged and older drifting along because they must go somewhere; the stout ladies in the holiday clothes they have chosen with such care and infallible instinct for the thing that suits them least; the ladies with parcels of tartan tammies and heraldic china—a whole world on the move drawn into the streets of Inverness. There you can see a little innocent old parish priest from the further Hebrides watch a party of bobby-soxers, elaborately unkempt and dishevelled in sloppy-joes, rucksacks, school pennants and bubble-gum, straight from a high school in the Middle West; and by the look on his face you can guess he thinks Pandora's box has been opened again or the Red Indians have come to town.

The nature of the highland holiday is changing. A generation ago it was a more intimate thing and the visitor did become almost a part of local society. Families went to the same hotel or boarding house year after year, and stayed for a fortnight or a month, or even longer. They were members of the local golf club and tennis club. They played bowls with the natives. Now there is either a new sort of holidaymaker, or the old ones are changing their ways. People prefer to keep moving in search of scenery or whatever it is that makes people endure the monotony of driving day after day, and all day, in motor cars.

And there are the coach tours. All summer from June to September the luxury coaches do the round trip for seven or ten days from the industrial cities of England. It is a mighty convenient way of making a tour: your bag is loaded into the boot; you take your seat, a comfortable seat, along with thirty or forty others; and you have nothing to worry about for the next ten days. Everything has been arranged and the driver has the timetable. While the bus moves, you sit and admire; when the bus stops you get out and admire the reason for which the bus has stopped. A good lunch waits for you at one hotel; a good tea at another; a good bed at a third. It is the sort of service only the very rich used to be able to buy. Only—it doesn't seem to be much fun. The stately bus rolls on, all gleaming cellulose and well-stuffed upholstery, and the tourists look out on the scenery in a rather dazed sort of way, as if they were slightly dead and glazed, as the cookshop people do with doubtful meat. They don't sing or play musical instruments; nor have I ever seen any make even the most modest overtures of love. But that is not for surprise, with the women keeping hard eyes on their husbands, so that the poor fellows hardly dare slip into a bar for a quick one. It seems all a little pathetic to me, because I like to enjoy myself out loud, but it is perhaps the way people wish it—most of them come from the Midlands of England and when they get to middle age the people of the Midlands have a great capacity for not having fun, unlike the grim people of Scotland who contrive to have lots of fun, but never, never admit it.

The bus tour may be a glorious adventure. It may be a glorious liberation from those industrial cities where people must live because they are reluctant to die. But it does seem a very industrial sort of holiday. I mean, when you see a bus tour full of the better-paid operatives from Coventry, you feel that the machine they spent fifty-one weeks in making has taken them for a ride. The bus becomes the focus of the holiday. It is much younger, more polished, more efficient and much more valuable than any of the passengers. The men who drive those buses are very great psychologists: if they were any less, each tour would end in hysteria. But, just as the bus becomes for seven or ten days the home, so the driver becomes the father. He is the one who knows all and can do everything. He takes you by the hand, tells you what and when to eat, leads you into your hotel, tells you when to get up in the morning—he is omniscient and responsible. The drivers are a great race, public entertainers in the best sense of the word, for they can make people believe they are enjoying what is being done to them. Some that I have met are masters in the low art of jollying along. The bus arrives at the evening hotel. The driver hops down, tired after many miles of difficult road. "Wakee, wakee," he cries. "Come along, boys and girls." As a crowd at a fair on a wet afternoon is drawn by the gentleman with the thimbles, so the tourists unwrap themselves from the stuffed upholstery and get down and feel their interest quickened by his patter about double-sprung beds and second helpings. Inside five minutes the thirty-six are on their way to their rooms; the driver and the hotel porter have got the luggage from the boot and on its way after its owners; the driver takes the coach round into the yard and starts to wash it down, after removing the caramel papers, chocolate wrappings, fruit peelings, cigarette ends and exhausted but still adhesive chewing gum, the detritus of a mainly esurient civilisation. However much you love your fellow men and women it is bound to be very hard work. But there is a let-out in most human predicaments. Once I had a talk with a driver about his job. I suggested there must be a certain wear and tear on the spirit. He said, "Oh, I don't know it's any worse than any other job." I said, "You eat with them, you live with them all day, they bother you with silly things all evening." He said, "Yes, but at least I don't have to sleep with them."

THE PASTORAL HIGHLANDS

The time has now come when I must try to show you the lie of the land north of Inverness. That is difficult and I know that I will fail, for I am allergic to highland scenery. I cannot describe to you the mountain parts of Inverness and Ross and Sutherland—the masses of primeval rock divided by the long narrow glens where streams run down over their rocky beds, clear as champagne or a deep-red wine colour from peaty water. Every glen is different and each is the same —a bit of good bottom land at the mouth; silver birch and rowan tangled with dog roses along the river bank; and in the clear spaces a few steadings and small fields of corn and turnips. Beyond those fields the sheep graze on the open hill and pick up a scanty living among the heather and bracken. Further up, the glen grows narrower and bare. The hills stand close with their stony ribs sticking through the skin of peat or heather, or lying in fields of scree where frost has brought down the rocks in ruin. There is a shooting lodge in a quadrangle of fir trees with keepers' and stalkers' houses nearby. Every two or three miles there is the steading of a sheep farm. Then the road, becoming always rougher, ends at the last herd's cottage and only a footpath winds on across the heather by the stream that flows from the coire where the winter snow still lies in June.

Over on the west coast many of the glens have filled with water and lie far into the hills as sea lochs, very beautiful and mighty inconvenient. High over those sea lochs there rise some of the most fantastic mountains on earth—old even in the great age of rocks and of a very enduring stone, they have been moulded by time and the upheavals of nature into incredible shapes. There is one, I swear, that looks broader at the top, like a toadstool, two thousand feet high. But the coast itself has many intimate enchantments. It faces the sun, it is washed by the Gulf Stream, it has little sandy beaches where the waves run softly in on the swell of the Atlantic. Looking out over the sea at the islands that seem to rise and dip in the sunlight, you find it easy to believe in sirens and strange embarkments at this shining end of the world.

The north-west is a desolate and at times an intolerably beautiful country. It is desolate, to me that am accustomed to corn and green pasture, however thin they may have been at times. This is the complete negation of the north-east spirit. Through the northern lowlands it was gospel that every rood of land could be made to bear a crop if a man had time and strength enough. But you can't grow any crop on a field of scree. Even the spirit of the north-east, which is not easily beaten back, would recoil from picking a bite between the rocks like a blackface ewe.

But that is not the greater desolation of the hills. There are glens which were once numerous of people who laboured the land because it gave them some small return. It is unlikely there were as many people as some maintain, whose imaginations fill even the most desolate coire with singing, fiddling and the making of whisky, long ago in a Celtic golden age.

Mr Loch who, as factor for the Countess of Sutherland and her husband, Lord Stafford (before she became the Countess-Duchess and he the Duke of Sutherland), had some part in breaking up the old economy of the Highlands, described the loyal tenantry of Sutherland in these terms:

"When that hardy but not industrious race spread over the county, they took advantage of every spot which could be cultivated and which could with any chance of success be applied to raising a precarious crop of inferior oats of which they baked their cakes and of bere from which they distilled their whisky; added but little to the industry and contributed nothing to the wealth of the empire. Impatient of regular and constant work, all heavy labour was abandoned to the women who were employed occasionally even in dragging the harrow to cover the seed. To build their hut or get in their peats for fuel . . . the men were ever ready to assist, but the great proportion of their time, when not in the pursuit of game or of illegal distillation, was spent in indolence and sloth. Their huts were of the most miserable description: they were built of turf dug from the most valuable parts of the mountain side. . . . They were placed lengthways and sloping with the declination of the hill . . . in order that all the filth might flow from the habitation without further exertion upon the part of the owner. Under the same roof, and entering at the same door, were kept the domestic animals. . . . The upper part of the house was appropriated to the use of the family. In the centre of this upper division was placed the fire, the smoke from which was made to circulate throughout the whole hut for the purpose of conveying heat— the effect being to cover everything with a black glossy soot and to produce the most evident injury to the appearance and eyesight of those most exposed to its influence. The floor was bare enough, except near the fireplace where it was rudely paved with rough stones. It was never levelled with much care. . . . Every hollow formed a receptacle for whatever fluid happened to fall near it. . . . It was impossible that it should ever be swept and when the accumulation of filth rendered the place uninhabitable, another hut was erected in the vicinity . . . and that which was abandoned formed a valuable collection of manure for the next crop."

Captain Henderson, who published his *Agriculture in Sutherland* in 1812, considered that social life was very primitive, but he was not as contemptuous as Mr Loch:

"The inhabitants near the coast live principally upon fish, potatoes, milk and oat or barley cakes. Those in the interior or more highland part feed upon mutton, butter, cheese, milk, cream, with oat or barley cakes during the summer months. They live well and are indolent: of course are robust and healthy. In winter the more opulent subsist upon potatoes, beef, mutton and milk, and at times a little oat or barley cakes. In times of scarcity they bleed their cattle, and after dividing it into square cakes they boil it and eat it with milk or whey instead of bread."

The country, he said, was a nursery of brave, hardy highlanders. Mr Loch, however, was the factor concerned with making the property pay. He could see no dividends in brave, hardy highlanders who lived like gentlemen and harnessed their wives to the harrows. Sheep would pay better than men.

When the agricultural improvers in the lowlands showed that new methods of farming brought a five- or ten-fold increase of rents, the highland lairds naturally wondered if something could be done to make real money out of estates that brought them little beyond prestige. They had their chance, for the Industrial Revolution had created an insatiable market for wool and mutton. Now the little old native sheep that lived in the glens grew fine wool and sweet mutton, but little of either. That great man, Sir John Sinclair of Thurso, who never saw anything without wishing to improve it, including the British Constitution, looked around for a more productive type of sheep that would stand the hard northern winter. He brought 300 cheviots off the Border to his estate in Langwell; and, although everyone told him they would not survive, they increased tenfold in ten years. Sir John was an intelligent man who had an instinct for good husbandry. His idea was that each farmer should have a few score of those ewes to run among the cattle on the hill and to be an additional source of income for the farmers and the lairds. That was, he thought, the proper place of the cheviots in the highland scenery. Other lairds had bigger ideas. A few score ewes on each farm might produce a little more rent. A few thousands in a whole glen might produce a great deal. So the laird gave the tenants of a whole glen notice to quit. Some went quietly in obedience to their chief. The rest were turned out by force and their houses destroyed so that they might not return. No plea of age or infirmity was accepted. In some cases the laird had arranged for ships on which the evicted people were forcibly embarked and sent to make their fortunes in America. The empty glen was then let to a grazier, perhaps from the Border, who paid a big rent to put his sheep on the pasture of the abandoned homesteads. That brought in a mint of money for several generations; but there are no fortunes on the hills today, for the hills are sick and the sheep die. The years of misuse are completing the desolation the lairds began a hundred and fifty years ago.

The sheep farmers neglected what no farmer can afford to neglect for long—the rules of husbandry. Now the first of these rules is that you must find the style of farming best suited to the soil and the climate, so that you improve the land while you make a living on it. Agriculture cannot for long be an extractive industry in Scotland: nor perhaps anywhere else. The old style of farming in the glens may have been very primitive but it was probably sound. There would have been patches of bottom land cultivated with corn. Small pockets of good soil between the rocks on the hillsides were planted with potatoes. Pieces of meadowland were cut for hay. There would have been a few cattle and a few sheep. It is all set down, beautifully, in Osgood Mackenzie's *A Hundred Years in the Highlands*. That could not have amounted to much—little to sell and sometimes little to eat. But there was a rough balance; what came from the glen remained in the glen. In those conditions a poor soil might support a number of families at a low level of comfort and yet not suffer; while some of the land was by no means poor and would have improved by labouring. There was something else: the pasture may have been thin (again, some of it may not), but the old farmers had the means to make the best of it—the partnership of the ox and the sheep. These might have been divinely appointed to graze together. The sheep is a dainty, selective feeder that nibbles at the small sweet grasses. The ox takes everything that comes within the sweep of its tongue. To-gether they will trim a pasture like a lawn, which is a very good thing for the pasture. Thus the old style of farming may have been at a low level, but there was a balance. Sheep farming upset the balance and finally ruined the glens.

The sheep were reared for export. So many sacks of wool and so many stones of mutton were harvested off the glens every year and nothing was returned to compensate. That was bound to impoverish the soil, already poor.

The sheep gradually destroyed the grazings. Because of her selective habits she takes the sweet grass and ignores the ranker growths. If the short sweet grass is scarce she will nibble it to the crown of the roots and kill it. That has a very serious effect on the pasture. If the good grasses are grazed hard and the rank ones neglected, the rank soon drive out the good. That was the great value of the ox—he kept the rank grasses under control and maintained the balance in the pasture. The grazings suffered when he was turned away. Poor grass drove out the good, then bracken began to creep in. Now the ox is not fond of bracken, but he will take a tender frond in a mouthful of better things; and when the bracken grows tall, he treads it down and so weakens it. The sheep can do nothing with bracken except hide among it to die when the flies have struck her. So the bracken increased enormously, smothering out the grass and spreading desolation over many thousands of acres. I am willing to say that the sheep, next to the goat, is the greatest enemy of good husbandry and the worst waster of a pastoral countryside. Her hoof is golden when she is folded on the turnips, but she eats the heart out of any pasture, and she has eaten the poor heart out of the Highlands.

They say that the greatest enemy of a sheep is another sheep. The proof of it is in the Highlands. The sheep became increasingly prone to take diseases. Their fertility declined; also the power of lambs to survive when born. The reason for this is still debated. Maybe the rams had something to do with it. The ewes are born on the hill, so it is desirable to buy in rams for breeding. At first it was probably thought good enough to buy in ram lambs or shearlings (one year old) from a neighbouring farm with a good stock. Then pure breeding and pedigrees became fashionable and pedigree rams of a good line brought always bigger prices. The raising of rams became a trade and a fine art for the specialist. Thus far it was a good thing for agriculture. But then, as some experts say, the breeders went wrong. They bred too fine—a constant danger in all pure breeding; for, in trying to fix certain good points—such as the proud carriage of a head —strength and hardiness may be forgotten. Most pedigree animals now look just a little too fine. Dr Allan Fraser, an authority on hill sheep, argues that a great mistake is made. The rams are bred on the low ground and fed on the best of everything to put them in bloom for the sales. Then the poor devils are sent to gather a living on the hills and tup the ewes forbye. It is, he argues, about all they can do to live, let alone perform their engendering offices. Of course there are plenty who repel his arguments with eloquence and anger. It is not for an outsider to pass judgment or a cow farmer to interfere in ovine matters but—well, there could be something in it: a weakness could be introduced that way.

Sterility and diseases are signs that there is a weakness, aggravated by the fact that the hills are tired and sick. The ruined grazings do not feed the sheep well enough to keep them in health. People have wondered where the germs of each new plague came from. The answer may be that the germs were always there, but a well-fed sheep had the power to resist them. Whatever the disease a hill sheep dies of today, the predisposing factor is usually under-nourishment. The depopulation of some hillsides is now almost complete. They cannot support even the sheep for whom the human inhabitants were driven out. That is something to be remembered whenever landlords or farmers argue that they are the only people who understand that last resource of nations, the land.

Science has been able to help—if not to cure the ills at least to lower the deathrate. Research chemists have discovered vaccines for most of the diseases and the hypodermic and the capsule are more to a herd than his crook. The sheep may be empty of food but it is full of antibodies. That is a great service, but it is not enough for anyone concerned with first causes. Something must be done to rebuild the resistance of the sheep and save her from the alternatives of dope or death. The answer seems to be—restore the old balance on the hills. For the wool and mutton that go away, put back lime and fertiliser on the low ground. Restore the cattle for the health of the grazings. That is being done successfully by some who have the enterprise and the money. Where the plough can be put in, the grazings have been reseeded and properly eaten by sheep and cattle. Winter keep—silage, turnips and oats—has been grown on fields won, laboured and made fertile many hundreds of years ago. Where the plough cannot be put in, the bracken is cut; or where that is too expensive, the weed is left for the hoof of the ox to tread and weaken. The hills begin to recover virtue when the balance has been restored. Like so many other good things in farming, this work can be seen if you know where to look for it. Lord Lovat has now a herd of some hundreds of cattle on the open range behind Beauly. Colonel Gibb is proud of the turnips he grows at Gruinard. Mr Miller of Dale behind Halkirk is reseeding the moor. There are others who do valuable work, against the wise advice of their neighbours. The value of their work cannot be assessed by any accountant. They are repairing the evils of a hundred and fifty years.

The glens are desolate to me but not because they are so empty of people. They would not be any more pleasant if they were full of crofters scratching a subsistence in between bouts of hard liquor and pipe music. Civilisation is more than a counting of heads and will not flourish on an overburdened soil. We are told again and again that in some glen there were once two thousand people where now there are twenty. It is difficult to see how such a mass of people could have got a living, or got it for long. One may suspect that, when the landlords encouraged the people to emigrate, or forced emigration upon them, they were merely forestalling nature and cashing in while there was something left to cash. That does not excuse the landlords—nothing but the elevation of greed into a gospel can ever excuse them. If they forestalled nature they did it to defeat her unconscious purpose, the keeping of a balance. That to me as a lowlander is the true desolation of the Highlands. There must be a community between man and nature, a very close community, for nature includes men, though they often do their worst to disown her. Men, when they act with right reason and within the discoverable laws of nature, can achieve a new balance to nature's advantage. It is the sadness of the glens that men and nature are no longer co-operating in a fruitful way. Sheep infected with ticks on grazings infected with bracken are the signs of a disordered community. If only the plough were breaking the sour pastures and cattle were back on the hills, and a few families got a decent living in rebuilding the fertility of the soil, there would be no need to regret the clachans that have fallen back into the soil from which they were dug.

THE LOWLANDS OF ROSS

The narrow strip of lowland country through which A9 runs is very different from the interior of the north-west. There are few more charming or fertile corners of Scotland than the shores of the Beauly Firth, from Inverness round into the Black Isle of Ross, where A9 runs under generous woods by well-cultivated fields between the blue hills and the blue water. If there is an Eden upon earth I guess it's somewhere about the Kirkton of Bunchrew. This part has an air of richness: in the first part of summer it is almost lush, an uncommon quality in Scotland. In the beginning of June the road is banked high with white and purple hawthorn that makes the still air heavy with its scent; and in the beginning of July the banks are starred with pink dog-roses, while the cottage gardens are riotous with lupins in daring combinations of colours. As the road turns north round the top of the firth, there is a very charming prospect of low hills to the west beyond Beaufort Castle, with the mountains behind them—and that is the best way to see mountains, in the distance over fields of corn.

From Beauly A9 goes through the Muir of Ord to Conon Bridge and Dingwall. Above Muir of Ord there is an interesting example of a crofting community in the many small places strung out along the hillside. The rule, perhaps universal, certainly holds good here, that the poorer the land, the smaller the farms; and the quality of the land here can be judged by the acres of whin and broom whose golden flowers could be seen from Inverness in the month of May. For a contrast, east of A9 there is the Black Isle of Ross, a place of old settlement and modern fame. It is a peninsula between the Beauly and Cromarty firths, with gently sloping fields to the north and west and steep, round hills along the east and south. It is reputed to be one of the best farming districts in Scotland, and there are indeed some fine big farms in it, but I suspect its reputation is a little overblown. The amount of really good land is small and a good deal is inferior stuff up on the hills. If I had my choice I would prefer Easter Ross, especially around Nigg across the Cromarty Firth, or the southern shore of the Beauly Firth. Still the Black Isle is kindly and I would not trade a hundred acres of it for a whole highland country.

The Black Isle has an old-established atmosphere; its historical relics show there must have been a fair degree of comfort there in the olden time. The villages of Avoch, Fortrose and Rosemarkie that look south-east across the Moray Firth from the shelter of the hills are sunny places with sands for children to play and old men to sleep on. Cromarty at the north-east corner is a little old town with an atmosphere not of this day and generation. Situated on a spit of low ground where the entrance to the firth is guarded by two massive hills called the Soutars, Cromarty seems to lie right out on the water, with the sea on one side and the wide blue firth on the other. It would have been born of the sea as a fisher settlement and developed into a port in the days when roads were impassable. Certainly it had been a place of consequence some hundreds of years ago, as the stone houses in the Scots style show. In this it resembles the old towns on the coast of Fife—Largo, Aberdour and Culross. It is famous by two great but very different men. Hugh Miller who was born here was an outstanding example of a type common in Scotland during last century. The son of poor parents, he became a stonemason and laboured in his trade, but he had the passion for knowledge and the enquiring mind. As was right enough in a stonemason, he became a geologist and graduated into a writer and finally a newspaper editor. His autobiography *My Schools and Schoolmasters* was a book everybody read and which many still praise when they remember it. It is a good and honest account of life at the beginning of last century. Most of it is beautifully written in a simple, clear style which makes an immediate effect. Nothing intrudes between the life he describes and the readers' experience of it. Page after page has that classical beauty of things once deeply felt and recollected in tranquillity and set down in an objective way. It has nearly everything, but it lacks the one thing that might have been supplied by the other great man of Cromarty. Sir Thomas Urquhart is one of the great figures of the world, less for what he did than for what he was. He did much, including the translation into English of *Gargantua and Pantagruel*, a work in which the translator seems as great a spirit as the author himself. He must have had a touch of the Gargantuan; he was a vehement, noisy man of passionate loyalties and contradictions; a royalist who died of laughing when he heard about the death of Charles II. If only Hugh Miller had had some of his passion and extravagance and outrageous Scots laughter his books might be lifted up more often from the bottom shelves. To be honest and good may be enough for life; it is hardly enough for immortality. Even to write well is not always enough for that. Yet I guess there will always be some to find Hugh Miller, as I have done so late.

Cromarty is out of the modern world in spirit, and also in space. It is a good twenty miles thence to rejoin A9 at Dingwall through the pleasant farm country on the north shore of the Isle. Dingwall is the market for a good district and the administrative centre of Ross-shire.

It has no large industries to give it size, although local government is quite an industry itself. It is a nice little town, especially when seen from the east, where a long line of poplars stand between it and the water. At Conon Bridge, nearby, there is a charming example of the old Scots inn, where a traveller is still kindly entertained.

Strathpeffer, a mile or two away, had a considerable reputation as a spa in the years before the wars. The waters there had a slightly unpleasant taste but were good for the ills of the flesh, especially of the flesh that had been too well fed. Thousands went to take the cure. They drank large measures of water at the pumproom, played bowls, sat in the sun and listened to the music and drove to see the Falls of Rogie, Castle Leod, the Falls of Conon and the mountain scenery of which Ross-shire has so much. It was an intimate place: the same people went there year after year and made friendships that were annually renewed. It was very popular among the farm people—to go to the Strath was a mark of prosperity, and if you could afford it, it was almost a social duty to go there: you owed it to your reputation as well as to your rheumatism. The Strath is hardly as popular today. The waters have not lost their power and people suffer as many ills, but there are more fashionable therapies than drinking unpleasant water and the old-fashioned quiet holiday is gone out of favour. These times call for faster music, stronger medicine. Strathpeffer remains sedate, Victorian and just a little dowdy, although there is at least one large and handsome hotel in the modern style. To me, revisiting the place after thirty years, there was something attractive in the want of fashion. I remembered the place as it had been—the boarding-house breakfast of ham and eggs, toast and tea; the ritual procession to drink the waters; the games of bowls and tennis in the warm gardens; the smell of wooden pavilions and rubber shoes on a hot day; the walks over the golf-course and the vistas of, to a boy, endless and irrelevant mountains; the little spring upon the moor where a drink cost nothing and tasted even worse than the official stuff at the pumproom; the drive with strangers in a horse-brake to see the falls, and the games invented there while the elders admired a small stream falling down an inconsiderable height; the boarding-house teas with wasps in the jam; the long twilit evenings while the mists came down, and the gulls squeaked louder; the concert where a fat man in a kilt made speeches between the songs and two bagpipers played duets like all hell let loose in that small space. Not a great deal worth remembering after thirty years, but I remembered perfectly although so many exciting and expensive things are clean forgotten. Perhaps it was a good thing that we had to make our own pleasure, every day distilling some essence from that quiet place. There may be a lot of pleasure there yet for those who have the right temper to find it. A little more bright paint might put them in the mood.

There is a choice of roads from Dingwall to Bonar Bridge. A9 keeps to the low country and the shore of the firth past Evanton, Alness and Invergordon by the good farmland of Easter Ross. It is one of the plans for bringing fresh life into the Highlands that there shall be an industrial area developed round Invergordon, a plan that has official, though perhaps not very enthusiastic, support. The idea is not impossible. When the hydro-electric schemes in the glens are completed, there should be plenty of power at a cheap rate, but power is only one consideration. Trades consequent to the Fleet being in are likely to flourish round Invergordon, but as to the rest—now that a plan has been produced the matter may be allowed to rest there, for it seems to be all in people's heads and nowhere else. The surer hope of a good life is in the fields of Easter Ross, where the fine herds and crops have all the marks of a sound economy. The shorthorn bulls of Calrossie and the seed potatoes of Nigg are worth a whole bright world of good intentions.

Tain that lies in the north-east of the district is another old burgh from which the importance has gone, but which was a place of consequence in its day and still retains that indefinable quality—character. It has a main street with some buildings in the regular eighteenth-century style. It has also a townhouse that is a notable piece of old Scots and new. The square tower is old, surmounted by a pointed spire and at the four corners by round turrets pierced by shotholes. The rest of the building belongs to a much later time and was built in keeping with the tower. It is not a bad exercise in copying the past, but to balance the turrets it has got a number of little things like pepper-pots that are useless and ridiculous. Across the firth there is another old town, companion to Cromarty and Tain. Dornoch was once a place of great state. The Bishop of Sutherland had his cathedral and his castle there; and later it was the county town. Now the county officials have gone to Golspie. Dornoch has lost the tide and lies stranded between the firth and the sea, in a corner of an almost deserted county. The Cathedral and the Bishop's Castle are still in use, though a little fallen from their former state, the cathedral being used as the parish church and the castle as a hotel, but both of them satisfying, each in its own way. Sitting over against each other in the middle of the town they make a perfect medieval unity. Dornoch itself is a period piece, the tiny burgh with its big hotels and its famous seaside golf-course, remote from the world on a sandy shore. When you walk through it at seven o'clock on a June morning with the sun warming the cathedral walls and opening the flowers in the castle garden, Dornoch seems a little unreal, as if it had been imagined for the setting of some romantic tale. There are not many such in Scotland.

It is one of the attractions of this eastern shore that each part is best seen from its neighbour and across blue water, as Easter Ross from the Black Isle and Sutherland from Easter Ross. The best prospect of Sutherland is to be seen from the Struie road that runs over the hills from Evanton to Bonar Bridge. Far below there is the narrow Dornoch Firth with the high hills of Sutherland beyond it. Then towards the west the firth narrows to a river which soon opens again into the Kyle of Sutherland. It is a confusion of waters and mountains, mist, sunlight and wandering showers, as if the world were newly made that very moment and man had as yet no place there. That goes for much of Sutherland, where civilised man will never have a place.

Anyone interested in the mutations of time could do worse than turn west at Bonar Bridge to have a look at Lairg. The Countess-Duchess of Sutherland cleared away many crofters from the Sutherland estates for their own good and hers, and the sheep grazed over the small pastures that the crofter's wife had laboured and the crofter's cow had husbanded. The hoof of the sheep was golden—for a while, but the land began to miss the crofter's cow and the crofter's wife. By 1877 James Macdonald, special reporter of *The Scotsman* in Aberdeen (an agricultural reporter whose descriptions of the northern counties in the *Transactions* of the Highland and Agricultural Society are of the greatest value to anyone who wishes to understand why things are as they are today), put it so:

"[Some sheep farmers] are beginning to find that their farms will not carry so many sheep or keep them in so high condition as 15 or 20 years ago. Considerable portions of the grazings are becoming foggy and rough and of little value as sheep pasture. We could point to one or two hirsels which carried stocks of from 1,000 to 1,100 over winter some twenty years ago and which will now scarcely winter 800. The cause of this, we believe, is the covering of the land for so long a period exclusively by sheep, without any cattle being allowed on it. . . . The experienced sheep farmer says, 'The land is getting tired of sheep and is needing to be cropped and thereby sweetened by highland cattle'."

That is what the experienced sheep farmer is saying today as if he had newly discovered the fact.

The sheep paid well but they were not the final answer. Another Duke of Sutherland found, about 1870, that £25,000 a year went off the Sutherland estates to buy oatmeal for the people and turnips for wintering the sheep. He decided to encourage arable farming, and engaged Kenneth Murray of Geanies in the Black Isle, a very experienced improver, to report on the possibilities. Murray recommended that a start should be made near Lairg along the shore of Loch Shin and the River Tirry. In all 1,175 acres would be improved and the cost be £25,037, including roads and buildings. Murray estimated a new rent of £1,205 as against £150 the land was then yielding, or a return of more than 4 per cent. on the cost of the work.

The Duke, unable to let the work by contract, took on the job himself. Beginning with Dalchork he had the land drained and began to plough it with steam tackle. One may wonder what the natives thought of the steam plough, for that cumbersome outfit was the first application of mechanical power to cultivation. It consisted of two steam engines of the sort that used to work threshing mills up to a few years ago. The engines sat one at each side of the field and pulled the plough by winding up a wire rope. The plough was a very solid object on wheels with two sets of mouldboards, one at each end so that it did not have to be turned at the headlands. This incidentally is the latest idea in the design of ploughs and a few can be seen, drawn by tractors, with one set of boards in the ground and the other in the air, as if, according to Dr Allan Fraser, to plough heaven and earth simultaneously.

At the beginning there were many difficulties with the plough, mostly in the way of breakages when the boards hit the earth-fast stones. But the Duke had a great interest in mechanical things (he subsidised the building of the Highland Railway and had a train of his own), and by perseverance and unlimited money he overcame the trouble from stones by fitting a large disc coulter on the front of the plough. When the disc met a large stone it rode over it and lifted the plough clear over the obstruction. The plough must have been a noble piece of work, a match for any modern prairie-buster, for it could plough a furrow two feet deep. Besides the large disc in front it had a hook like the bill of an anchor which followed the mouldboard and loosened up the subsoil. The hook was known as the Duke's Toothpick. That plough, kept steadily at work when the weather allowed, broke up 1,829 acres in four years. Steam engines were used for all the work of clearing and making the land, a wonderful contrast to the laborious methods used in other places where so much was done by hand.

"The Shiness valley presented a novel scene of activity. When the operations were in full force no fewer than fourteen steam engines were 'puffing' away at one time, and several hundred workmen and many horses busily engaged. Drainage, ploughing, clearing off stones, harrowing, erecting fences, making roads, building houses, were all in progress at once, creating a stir and bustle which, in a valley hemmed in by hills on all sides, could not have failed to impress the visitor as marvellous."

The spectacle cost the Duke a pretty penny, but there is no point in being a duke if you can't have fun. This great enterprise did not bring the return it deserved for the great depression came about in 1878 and lasted for sixty years. Looking at those lands today it is difficult to believe they were ever the scene of such an exciting adventure.

There is no end to the problem of keeping people in the glens. In more recent times, the Department of Agriculture set up a number of smallholdings near Lairg—almost, as it were, a return to the old crofting society before the clearances. Unfortunately, the history of new smallholdings in the Highlands has not been much better than that of the old ones. Some of the smallholders do well enough, but others seem to have inherited the temperament that Mr Loch deplored, although they no longer carry out illicit distillation. One may guess that smallholders in the Highlands are as great a problem to the Department of Agriculture as their ancestors were to the Earls of Sutherland and suchlike.

North from Dornoch, Golspie is a plain little town, strung out along the shore with the Duke of Sutherland's castle of Dunrobin on the height above it. Beyond Golspie the farmland is crowded in between the hills and the sea and you may feel you are coming to the end. Then suddenly you come on a town with factory chimneys and a coalmine. Brora has a coalfield with a pit that has supplied the local coal for a century. There was a theory that Brora stood at the northern end of a field which must lie under the Moray Firth, and there was a time when landlords in Banffshire sank workings in the hope of finding the other end. They were disappointed. Brora with its woollen mills and distillery remains an economic sport, a small island of industrialism in a pastoral country.

CAITHNESS

The arable land disappears altogether where Helmsdale sits under the shadow of the Ord of Caithness. In that precipitous little fishing village you feel you have indeed come to the end of something. But A9 sets off across the black mass of the Ord where Langwell Forest ends in a precipice above the sea. It is a hard climb from Helmsdale, one to trouble the minds of those who travel in old motor cars, and it is made the more alarming by an optical illusion in the first part of the road. Round the corner from Helmsdale the road seems to run downhill, yet the engine labours as if it were climbing. It is an alarming thing for any motorist who doubts the power of his car—I know because I have experienced it and I have seen my car run backwards up the hill with the engine shut off. People say the downward slope is an illusion, but I am inclined to think it is the work of the devil for whom the Ord would be a suitable dwelling. The climb over the Ord is not as hard as it looks and the prospect from the top is magnificent in desolation. There can be few places in Scotland more bare, windy and inhospitable to man than the miles of Langwell Forest with its deep ravines cut into the noble mountains of rock that stretch away towards the Atlantic. Those hills are not very high, but there is something in their shape and the steepness at which they rise that gives an impression of very immediate and even overpowering mass. I should not like to be alone there at the moment of twilight when hills step forward in the clearness of the air. Nor should I like to live in Berridale which sits at the bottom of a ravine. It is a beautiful, sheltered village, savagely adorned with the horns of dead stags, but with such a deep and dangerous descent on either side one might feel halfway to hell. Beyond Berridale, A9 continues over the moors, the wide and windy spaces that stretch away to the ragged line of mountains on the border of infinity. The stranger may still feel, as at Helmsdale, that he has come to the end of something.

The feeling may be justified, for Caithness is different. Caithness is unique. So are the people: and they might well be, cut off from the rest of humanity by the sea and the Ord. At first sight, and seen from the moors, the arable east and north of Caithness resembles the Buchan district of Aberdeenshire. It is obviously a part of the lowland plain, quite different from Sutherland across the Ord. And again as in Buchan there are many small family farms, with some fine big ones on the best land. There is a third likeness, an almost complete absence of trees. The fishing villages along the coast make a fourth. They are less tidy and bien than, say, Inverallochy and St Combs, but the kinship is plain to see. There are many parallels in those two shoulders of land that lie into the cold North Sea.

There are differences though they are not so easy to describe, and I have never been long in Caithness before I was saying, "This is nae my countryside." There is one obvious immediate difference —the land is less well laboured, except in the very fine districts of Bower and Watten. At the worst in the crofter districts along the coast south of Wick, there is the agricultural squalor usually associated with crofting—a lot of bad pasture, a handful of ewes and an un-thrifty cow. Elsewhere the standard is much higher. There are small farms on the Causewaymire between Thurso and Latheronwheel, places discovered rather surprisingly on the moor, that have a good stock of ewes, poultry, a few store cattle, and no doubt a pig— enough to make a decent living. But there could be so much more. The pastures have a permanent look—the look of being permanently tired through undernourishment. If they were laboured and fed and reseeded they would carry more stock and feed it better. I am sure that any farmer from Buchan would soon have the plough in, and, although he might not do much good, he would at least go through the motions. There are too many daisies and buttercups in Caithness, usually a sign that the plough and the lime cart are rested.

Once while trying to find those elusive differences between Caithness and Buchan, I happened to come on an experiment being made by the North of Scotland College of Agriculture, a few miles from Halkirk on the Causewaymire. There about 70 acres of land that had once been cultivated but allowed to fall back into bad pasture had been ploughed, limed, manured and reseeded with good grasses and clover. It was an island of green in the surrounding grey and brown. A flock of 400 ewes with their lambs were pastured on it; and, as is usual with sheep, had been unable to keep it down—the ryegrass running up to seed showed there was room and need for cattle as well. The value of that grass in such a place can hardly be calculated. The sheep had a wide range of natural pasture where they could find maintenance; the new cultivated grass provided a supplement that could make all the difference between life and death. For instance in the spring it could put the ewes in good condition to bear and suckle their lambs. The effects are cumulative and cannot be set in figures by an accountant.

As I was admiring this work of regeneration, I was joined by an old man who knew the district well and was willing to talk about it. When I asked him if there were not other grazings that could be improved, he waved his stick in a wide arc and said, "Ye can see them everywhere." It was a subject about which he had strong feelings. "The people," he said, "don't labour the land enough; not like their forefathers did. Somebody laboured hard enough years ago when they cleared the land and ploughed it. Now nobody has ploughed it for eighty years and it's full of sour grass as thin and tough as fine brass wires. Let them labour the land and the land'll pay them." He waved his stick at the countryside so fragrant with the smell of heath, and he was a fine sight in his indignation; a big old man with blue eyes and long hair, like a Viking retired from the sea. I think there was more to his words than the natural superiority of the old. The grey muirland looked as if it could well bear the plough in the places where it was not sodden peat. I am, of course, committing the pathetic fallacy of ascribing to nature feelings that were only my own, but I would say the muirland was crying out for the plough. That was the difference between Caithness and Buchan. The soil of Aberdeenshire may often cry out, but not for labouring.

The impression given by even the arable part of Caithness is of grass predominating; and—in July—of overgrown grass at that. For, while the bullock is the foundation of farming in Aberdeenshire, Caithness lives by the sheep. In Thurso mart alone I have been told nearly 100,000 lambs are sold every autumn. The comparable figures for cattle are 1,400 store beasts and as many younger ones. The disparity of these figures can be seen in the pastures where the sheep nibbles away the sweet grass and lets the rest go by her. It is very rare to find a pasture eaten to a level sward and white with clover in the month of July. In that month anyone looking over Caithness might say:

> On acres of the seeded grasses
> The changing burnish heaves.

But the Caithness farmer finds that the sheep are well pleased and leave him a profit and sees no reason to change his ways.

After all, he may be right. It is very easy to make any sort of land produce more. It is very easy to make three blades of grass, and a lot of clover, grow where only one blade grew before. That is only the beginning. The stock may not like the new grass. They may not thrive on it. I have provided milk cows with beautiful lush pasture of the highest pedigree and the beasts despised it, in favour of the weeds and the coarse grasses at the dykesides. No part of farming can be taken alone—grass must not be cultivated without close reference to the beast that must eat it. If the stock are healthy and prolific on an old system of management one may very well be reluctant to meddle with it. Scientific discoveries made by specialists, while seeming of very great value, may raise great difficulties before they can be fitted into a scheme of farming practice. The Caithness farmers have avoided the major troubles suffered by those whose grazings are on the hills. Their land has heart in it and the fertility has not been mined away. It is a more balanced system altogether, and more in keeping with the principles laid down by Sir John Sinclair more than a hundred years ago, that the sheep should be a part, but not the whole, of farming.

Caithness does not really resemble Aberdeenshire. It is unique. The lowland part is flat, homogeneous, has not suffered that harrowing by the glaciers. It has a different atmosphere. Men have not so imposed their will on Caithness, as a whole, however beautiful they have made Bower and Watten and Olrig. The people who reduced Belnagoak and Oldwhat to order would have carried the corn far over the Caithness moors and kept it there. I guess there is better land under the skin of peat in Caithness than much of the uplands of Banff that once built a classical mansion for the laird and kept the farmer in more whisky than was good for him, though perhaps less than he needed. I wish they had done more with Caithness. But then Caithness has the sheep and the sheep is always the enemy of the best husbandry, unless well bound into some scheme of arable farming.

The people of Caithness are different from any other people in Scotland. They are not highland, not Celtic, not Scots. In the great days of the Norse people, Caithness was colonised from Scandinavia and that strain remains, unique. A gentleman of Wick I once talked with on the bridge there said that there were no people like the Caithness people. I said, "We think the same about ourselves in Aberdeenshire." He said, "But in Aberdeen it is quite different. Kincardine merges into Aberdeen and Aberdeen into Banff and so on all the way to Sutherland, but between Caithness and Sutherland there are the blasted miles of the Ord and the Den of Berriedale which prevented any comings and goings. So the people of Caithness have grown up a race apart with peculiar virtues and peculiar——" But I stopped him there so that I might speculate on the nature of their peculiar virtues.

The coast of Caithness does resemble the coast of the north-east.

There are the same great masses of cliff, the small bleak fisher villages, the occasional silver sands and the long prospects of the sea. It is an attractive shore along the Pentland Firth between Thurso and John o Groats. There the land runs out in great headlands, Duncansby Head and Dunnet Head, but between them there is a low shore and sandy beaches that seem protected by the shoulders of rock—though that is perhaps all in the eye of the beholder. This low shore has, in at least one place, a look more of the west than of the north-east, where a crofting settlement stands almost at the water's edge and the little steadings spread out on the flat land might be a fleet of fishing boats at anchor. Those beaches look into the sunset and the long midsummer light of the north. They look on the islands that lie in the afterglow across the water—Stroma and the Orkneys and the Pentland Skerries, the remains of a ruined land over which the tides race and battle through the firth. They look on the traffic of ships among the islands and on the hard passage between the North Sea and the Atlantic. So they have a quality of light and space and wonder; they are not lonely shores though they seem to be at the world's end.

Many people visit this part of the country every year, not for the sea air or the scenery, but for John o Groat's, that is said to be the most northerly house on the mainland. Why they should do so is a matter for speculation. There is, of course, a good hotel there, but even a good hotel would hardly draw so many people over so many long Scotch miles. I can understand why the touring buses go—John o Groats is a very definite point and the things must turn homeward somewhere. But that people who are their own masters should go there voluntarily in motor cars, on cycles and on foot—that is beyond me. I know because I went there myself. I travelled with a feeling of mild expectation. I arrived, looked at the dunes, the rocks and a trawler having a bad time in a choppy sea, and then went quickly towards the refreshments. There were many others like myself, several busloads, many carloads, who had arrived at last, and walked about the dunes, photographed each other, picked up sea shells as mementoes and wondered how soon they could get a cup of tea. At the scheduled time the bus drivers collected their parties and drove them away, having given them one more thing to speak about when they got home. I also turned homewards, feeling I had done something I could speak about. I had been to the most northerly dwelling on the Scottish main. It was a little something—not as great as the discovery of American perhaps, but certainly one that distinguishes me from all the people who have never been there. Those small distinctions are very precious. Besides it may satisfy a primitive sense of wonder to have reached a point beyond which you cannot go. There is also wonder in finding even there the afternoon teas and the tartan souvenirs.

Wick and Thurso, the two towns of Caithness, are very different from each other—one being of the sea and the other of the land. Wick is probably an old settlement, but it is a fairly recent town built up on the herring trade. Again Sir John Sinclair was at work. He saw that the pursuit of herrings could make a living for the poor crofters, so he brought over Dutchmen to teach the craft. The trade developed very quickly, for eastern Europe was hungry for herrings. Wick became a chief centre for the catching and curing. The season was short, but it was a stirring one. Drifters came from all the herring villages to fish from the port; and, when catches were good, landed vast quantities of herrings. Most of those were salted and packed into barrels on the quayside and shipped to the Baltic. There was money in the trade, sometimes a very great deal; and, if the merchants usually got the best of it, the fishermen did have a share. Although Wick had perhaps more licensed houses than any town of its size, men were ten deep round the bars when the boats were in—men from all the herring ports and the middlemen who hang on to the trade like barnacles to a boat. Those days passed away in 1914, and the herring trade is almost gone from Wick. There is still some white fishing, which is a decent, steady trade. And Wick is a decent, steady town. As a revulsion from the days of the roaring saloon, the majority of citizens voted the town dry and kept it so for many years, which was a great incentive to travel into the surrounding countryside. Wick has got some public houses again of the more civilised kind, where customers must sit down instead of standing till they fall. It is unlikely that the herring trade will ever return. Wick is a quiet place in spite of having an airport, and it looks as if it had seen livelier, though not necessarily better, days. The decline of herring has been offset by the prosperity of farming, and in the end there may be no great reason to regret the loss of a seasonal trade which turned over huge sums but did not leave so very much in the town.

Thurso, standing on a bay and at the mouth of a small river, looks inward to the land. The old High Street which curves down to the river has the air of a small seaport, a touch of Cromarty. There is some white fishing and valuable hauls of salmon are taken out of the river. But the main part of Thurso looks like a market town. There is a nice little square, called Sir John's, with memorials of the Sinclairs set among flowers. There are at least two good hotels. There are some decent old houses down towards the river. There are even some trees round Thurso Castle. As it looks over the green fields of the strath, with its back to the sea, Thurso might be in the deep country, though the wide bay and the magnificent headlands are over the rise of the hill.

The arable part of Caithness stretches for some distance along the coast west from Thurso. The road which runs that way, being on the higher ground, gives wide prospects over the grazing to the Pentland Firth and the distant hills. But the hills come closer to the sea until at

Melvich the crofts are crowded on to the cliffs. To complete the impression of Caithness, the traveller should leave the coast road a mile before Melvich and turn south along Strathhalladale to Forsinard and Helmsdale. The narrow strath with its river lies far into the hills, a lonely place, one of those that gives you the idea it will end round the next bend of the road. Yet it is inhabited for miles—a sheep farm; another; a few crofts; a church; a school; crofts; a sheep farm; so on and on. The hills rise up on either side bare and empty enough, but wherever there is a piece of bottom land, there is the steading of a farm and a family. They must find some real satisfaction to keep them so far away from the discomforts of civilisation. Indeed the soil must have something in it more than peat and stones. By the side of the pool I have found a mass of yellow irises in full bloom, obviously rooted in some kindliness of the soil. Then at Forsinard in the middle of the empty moors there is an excellent inn, though one might wonder what custom it gets in that loneliness. The railway from Helmsdale crosses the road at Forsinard in its long sweep through the wilderness. When I went that way at the end of June the crossing gates were shut and I thought it a long chance that the infrequent train and the infrequent traveller should coincide. But when the stationmaster opened the gates for me, he explained that, although trains were few, road travellers were fewer, so they kept the gates shut all the time.

It is a long way from Forsinard to anywhere, certainly a long way down into the strath of Helmsdale. The single track of road, with its passing places nicely poised on the edge of a sudden crop, climbs and winds and descends to wind and climb again and then descend into the narrow strath. There again people live where the pasture is green. Some of them live there for only a few weeks in the shooting season, but farmers, herds and keepers live there all the year. It is a very narrow valley between high hills, but it has been laboured and would repay labouring again. It is not any sort of progress to waste the little wealth our forefathers created at such great pains.

No more about the lie of the land. There are many miles between the North Esk and Strathhalladale. There is a diversity of land which is shown in the diversity of farming; and there is a diversity of people, caused partly by the soil and partly by migrations in far-off times. There is also a likeness common to all the districts and the people who live in them. Agriculture of some sort is the chief and often the only industry, and the people depend on agriculture even though they may not be directly engaged in it. Taken one part with another, the soil is not rich, but it is willing; and the people have learned to care for it so that it keeps them in some small degree of comfort. It should do, for they made it.

CHAPTER II

THE MAKING OF THE NORTH

I N order to understand the face of the north-east we must look back two hundred and fifty years. Travellers from the south in the early eighteenth century reported that the land was a bleak wilderness of moors and mosses through which abominable roads led by small farm settlements to villages infested with children, dogs and lice. Of course travellers in those days were fortified with a fine contempt of the north, and travellers always exaggerate their discomforts a little for the sake of effect; but, when all possible allowances have been made, the impression does remain of a treeless land where people lived in a very primitive way, scratching a living among the stones.

We can get a very good idea of what the countryside was like from the estate papers of Monymusk in Aberdeenshire, recently edited and introduced by Professor Henry Hamilton. Monymusk had belonged for a hundred and fifty years to the Forbes family, a rather obstreperous clan; but in 1713 Sir William Forbes, like many another country gentleman then and later, was overtaken by his debts and forced to sell. Monymusk was bought by Sir Francis Grant, a lawyer from Banffshire, who sat in the Court of Session as Lord Cullen. Sir Francis soon repented of his bargain and finally handed over the estate to his son Archibald in return for an annuity. It was a fortunate act for Monymusk and the north of Scotland. Archibald turned out to be one of those people who know good ideas when they see them and can put those ideas into use. It happened to be a time of new ideas in agriculture; and he applied them to Monymusk and led the farm people of the north-east out of the Middle Ages.

There was plenty to do at Monymusk. The house itself, according to Archibald Grant, "was an old castle with battlements and six different roofs of various heights and directions, confusedly and inconveniently combined, and all rotten, with two wings more modern, of two stories only, and half the windows of the higher rising above the roofs; with granaries, stables and houses for all the cattle and of the vermin attending them, close adjoining." The immediate surroundings were rough: the heath and moor reached "in angles or goushets to the gate", by which I imagine there were angles of cultivated land between those gussets. This was unfenced, so "the cattle and their dung were always at the door". There was a stream before the house, but it did not add much charm, for it "ran in pits and shallow streams often varying channel; with banks, always ragged and broken". It would have been a favourite place with the cattle, who would have done nothing to improve it. There must have been many lairds' houses like that in Scotland two hundred and fifty years ago. Just as the prosperous merchant still lived above his shop, the laird still lived above or next to the cattle that were his wealth. The big houses were in a stage somewhere between the fortified farmhouse, where everything could be gathered in for safety, and the gentleman's country residence, where the cattle were dispersed to kennels and home farms for amenity—"along with the vermin attending on them", by which, I hope, Grant did not mean the grooms and cattlemen, but we can't be sure.

There was a home farm, but it was not yet what came to be known by that name in the late nineteenth century, when the home farm was one of the forms of conspicuous waste that marked the gentleman. The eighteenth-century laird was also a farmer, and a good part of his living depended on his efforts in that trade. When examining the eighteenth-century portraits in the smaller Scottish mansion houses I have sometimes been puzzled by the fact that the ladies look a trifle plain—and somehow familiar. When you have taken your ideas of the eighteenth century from Gainsborough and Reynolds, it is difficult to place those ladies—hard-wearing and hard-working, of iron frame and character, who look as if they could have drilled a staff of domestics but and ben the house. I realise now why they look familiar; take away the titles and the antique dress and they might be farmers' wives of the kind you can meet today in the hardest parts of the north, that still make butter and rear chickens and work from dawn to dark, outside and in. It is difficult to imagine life at a distance of two hundred years, but life for the gentry in 1713 may have been very like life in a big farmhouse in our grandparents' time, when the farmers drove about to kirk and market, took a part in public affairs and spent the evenings at cards and toddy while their wives raised large families and drilled a staff of cheap domestics.

Grant certainly thought himself a farmer and the home farm was a source of income. It was called the Mains, which is the style of the county. Sometimes it was worked by the laird himself; sometimes let off to a tenant. And the cattle strayed right up to the door of the big house. Nobody would have thought to keep them away. They were sacred. They were real wealth and their dung at the door may have had a savour of goodness.

The heart of the estate was the Kirk Town of Monymusk, a quarter of a mile from the house. It was a small village of about a hundred inhabitants, with a very old church, a school and a meal mill, and all very miserable. Grant described it—"the farme houses, and even corne millns and mans (manse) and scool, all poor dirty huts". The walls of the houses were built of rough stones packed with earth and clay and topped with one or two feet of turf. The couples of the roof were five or six feet apart and were fitted to posts built into the walls and bolted with wooden pegs. Branches were laid across them and these were covered with turf, pared very thinly with a flaughter spade, laid on like tiles and overlaid with heather or thatch. The lum (chimney) was a wooden box let into the roof, through which the smoke sometimes found its way out. The windows were very small and usually only the top part was glazed, the lower having wooden leaves. But not all the houses were as grand as that. One at Platecock, occupied by William Dickie, cottar and labourer at the Mains, had no door, no window and no lum. It is not surprising that, as Grant said, those houses were "pulled in pieces for manure or fell of themselves almost every alternate year".

As to the rest of the estate: scattered throughout it were "touns" or townships, each consisting of about eight houses, with or without lums. A toun was in fact a farm—even today we still speak about a farm steading as the farm-toun. The simplest sort of toun was a farm leased to one tenant, usually for five years. He then sub-let portions to families, who paid a rent, partly in kind and partly in service. Those sub-tenancies were held at the will of the farmer, and the number on a farm might vary from year to year—there being no great expense in building a new house, nor great capital loss in throwing an old one down in the midden. Besides the sub-tenants there may have been cottars, who had a house but no land, though they may have had the grazing of a few sheep or even of a cow.

It is not possible by looking at Monymusk or any part of the arable north to get an idea of what the countryside looked like in the eighteenth century. Perhaps a poor crofting township in the West Highlands is the nearest thing to it in the physical condition of the soil. The farmer cultivated where the going was easiest, the two decisive factors being water and stone. Nothing could be done with bogs and mosses; as for the earthfast rocks, the farmers piously left those ancient landmarks where the Almighty had set them. So a farm was a number of irregular patches of cultivation among the waste; and, even in the arable, great boulders lay like prehistoric monsters among the corn. As the standard of farming was low, in a wet season when the weeds choked the crops it would have been difficult to tell where the arable ended and the waste began. The land was in a very poor state, and uneven, due to the clumsy ploughs in use. Those ploughs were hauled by teams of twelve owsen, an outfit no ploughman could turn in a tidy headland, so the furrows were drawn along the field in the shape of a capital S—as it were preparing to turn all the time. Then the serpentine ridges became very high, for the furrow was always turned up towards the crown of the ridge, which stole away the soil from the deepening hollows between. To our idea one of those tilled fields would have looked like the results of some extractive industry and the weeds between the ridges would have completed the sense of destitution.

All the methods of husbandry were primitive. The farmer divided his land into four parts. The best, which was usually nearest the steading, was called the infield. It got the farmyard manure and was cropped with rye, oats and pease, year after year. That does not look like good practice. Even with tractors and ingenious cultivators and chemical sprays we find it difficult to keep land clean under successive corn crops, so we may guess that many more things came up than the farmer sowed, and the return of grain must have been by that the less. Those old infields are still the best land on many farms, due to their greater age of cultivation. The second sort of land was the outfield. It was cropped with corn as long as the farmer could reap from it a little more than he sowed. When exhausted, it was left to recuperate under a crop of weeds and natural grasses, helped by the cattle that grazed and dunged it, till there was a sod to plough down and nourish a few more crops of corn. The third sort of land was the meadow— the permanent grass so dear to many English framers—and it was perhaps no poorer than some that is cherished today. The grass that the cattle could not eat in the flush of spring was cut for hay to keep them alive during the winter. The fourth sort of land was the rough grazing which lay all round, the untamed waste, covered with rocks and whins and broom, or soggy with peat, where the cattle foraged for a bite.

That was the aspect of the northern farm. The farmer's house and steading, small dark buildings, whose roofs waved shaggy and green in the growth of June. Scattered around, the smaller houses and byres of the sub-tenants; and the hives of the landless workers without door or window or lum. Nearest to the buildings, the infields under a tolerable crop, enclosed by hurdles or low turf dykes; beyond them the outfields, in which the proportion of weeds to corn showed the stages towards exhaustion; on the damp meadows the husbandmen leisurely cutting the hay and cursing the horseflies; and somewhere on the waste the cattle and sheep herded from the corn by a ragged boy. No drains, few ditches, no hedges, no trees except a rowan to keep off the evil eye. In a wet season the land was drowned. When the herd fell asleep the cows ate the corn. The road a dirt track in summer and a continuous bog in winter. Altogether the impressions are of a subsistence farming by a peasantry who had neither the skill nor the incentive to improve their condition.

We may be sure that life was not very spacious in the touns, but it is never safe to condemn old times because they lacked some of our amenities. The value of a life to an individual is still decided at the final count by the spirit or want of it in the individual himself.

Comfort, no matter how well stuffed the cushions and ingenious the springs, cannot minister to an uneasy mind. People in the Middle Ages suffered a great deal in winter in their damp, dark houses, where they were always cold, often hungry and slept six in a bed on the floor. When spring came they were released, reborn. New life ran in wonder through their blood, so quickly that they made love in every thicket, and composed, as it seems spontaneously, verses in praise of love, as clear and triumphant as the songs of mating birds. Some of us who have to spend a small fortune on drink before we can feel anything except a chronic foreboding among our suites and sanitary ware, might be glad to endure such a winter for the passions of such a spring. When you were sure that the May flowers would follow the April rain, that the sun in Sirius would burn the distempers out of your body and the sun in Leo bring the harvest to the sickle, that vines would ripen for winemaking, and every bush bear fruit and the oaks and beeches rain down their nuts for the pigs to fat on, you could thole a long winter in Paris or Sussex with the promise of such release and ripeness. But our forefathers in the north were perhaps less fortunate. Our spring comes late and our summer has no great abundance. Two hundred and fifty years ago when crops were much later in ripening than they are now, the corn often was not gathered when the snow came at Martinmas and ruined it. There was always too narrow a margin between subsistence and hunger. Life in the farm touns must have been too often dark and damp and anxious. No doubt the people made the most of it. A good harvest meant plenty of strong, thick, purging ale: there was a roaring in the touns all night and the ministers prepared strong portions of hellfire as an antidote. Our forefathers could enjoy themselves tremendously when they got the chance, but I fear they did not often get it. And when they did it was snatched from fate, not the rich and certain gift of fruitfulness.

It is tempting to think of the rural north in those days as a sort of "deep south", with the farm touns equal to the sharecroppers' cabins and the keeps and castles in place of the planters' mansions. But the analogy will not work. The American deep south is a social condition produced by the decay of a rural society. It was a paternal society founded on slavery, but it did have an elegance of living and thought. At its best it produced Randolph, Jefferson and Lee; and Monticello was beautiful no matter what it was founded on. Well, the story of the rural north was different. It had not decayed from anything—unless we can believe in some Gaelic golden age when the bagpipe was a musical instrument and the rocks when smitten poured forth whisky. There had been the Church, of course, which had created, by faith out of poverty, the austere Cathedral of St Machar at Aberdeen, the modest little Abbey of Deer and Elgin Cathedral, the glory of the kingdom. There were a few great houses—Fyvie, Huntly, Aboyne,

Darnaway and Cawdor, where the lines of the grim Scots keep were lightened by notions brought from France. But what did it all amount to? There were King's College and the cathedrals; a few noble figures such as Bishop William Elphinstone, Patrick Forbes of Corse, George Jameson the painter and Arthur Johnston the latinist—those few to set against the temporal lords, ignorant and contemptuous of the civilising arts. Even Urquhart, the translator of Rabelais, was not enough to fill the old time with the traffic of the mind and spirit, though he was the noisiest man in Europe.

There is an interesting comparison with England. When the Industrial Revolution came to the south, it wrecked a large part of the countryside and destroyed some good traditions. In many parts of England you are surprised by the want of any relation between the past and the present. How could the descendants of the people who built Broadway and Corfe Castle, Burford and Lavenham, have built the industrial towns? After the Queen Anne and Georgian brick, how could an architect plan the Prudential Assurance building in London? Whatever the good done by the Industrial Revolution, and it was considerable, there was a certain loss of colour and grace that had flowered in the mediæval dirt. But it is difficult to see that there was any great loss in the rural north. We had no Broadways. Whatever was built was certain to be a little better than the house at Platecock without door or window or lum.

In 1713 the north was getting ready to say goodbye to the Middle Ages. For instance, the lairds still had their feudal powers. There were civil powers that a man like Grant exercised in his baron's court through an official called the baron bailie. This court decided all issues between tenants and between tenants and the laird. The measure of justice may have been variable. The laird had also a jurisdiction in criminal affairs—the power of pit and gallows. He could uplift criminals and either confine them in his dungeon or hoist them at the end of a rope. Again, a great deal would have depended on the individual. There is at least one story which shows that the power, though great, could be used with mercy. The laird of Waterton, near Ellon in Aberdeenshire, had arrested a tenant, and confined him in his dungeon. Waterton, being a kindly man, soon decided that the criminal had been punished enough and ordered his servants to set him free. The servants came back and reported that the prisoner refused to leave because the dungeon was more comfortable than his own house. Then Waterton said, "Well, just set the yett (door) open and see that the bodie gets his diet regular." Could anything better show forth the virtues of the old order? It is the only story of its kind that I know.

There was also the power of the kirk, in all matters of human conduct. It has been fashionable lately to describe the Calvinism of the Scots kirk as intolerably austere and repressive. That may have been the theory: as to the practice—I have my doubts. The love of denunciation and hellfire has a suggestion of the orgiastic, as if the preacher revelled in the sinfulness of the sin he damned. And the effect on the congregation? I doubt if anything could have repressed the Scottish peasantry for long. There was, however, one thing due for a change, the kirk's power of interference in people's private lives. In every parish the government of the kirk was in the hands of the minister, assisted by a number of elders. The minister and his elders were embodied as the session, a court which regulated the conduct of everyone in the parish. Anyone who was thought to have transgressed had to appear before the session and suffer its judgment. For serious offences, such as extra-marital propagation, the sinner was made to sit on the stool of repentance in the kirk on Sunday and make confession of guilt before the whole congregation. With the endless and boundless temptation to interfere which elderly gentlemen can seldom resist, the session may have been the really repressive part of the kirk. May God deliver us from the power of little men backed by some peculiar interpretation of holy writ.

Though the kirk may not have been able to restrain the begetting passion and the love of drink, it had mastered a far more dangerous enemy: witchcraft and the cult of the devil. The primitive beliefs in any district are far older than any organised religion: they are part of our inheritance and have some emotional validity for most of us. It is likely that there have always been wise women and soothsayers in all primitive communities, as there are today in ours. But it does seem that Scotland was abnormally plagued with them in the sixteenth and seventeenth centuries. There grew up a distinct cult of the Devil—not Auld Sandy, the rather humorous old Scots devil—but the Beast with the smell of brimstone and the goat. Men and women convened in secret places, renounced Christianity and swore allegiance to the Devil, who usually appeared in person—or some person—to receive them. The witches were organised into covens which met regularly to do the Devil's work in their countryside. They ruled by fear and their influence was great. They had the power of the evil eye and every misfortune to man or beast or the crops in the field was attributed to their offices. In the seventeenth century witchcraft had gotten such a hold over the common people that both kirk and state were forced to attack it in their own defence. By the end of the century they had mastered it: the covens were broken up and the witches discredited. But neither sermons nor Acts of Parliament could clear from the minds of common people the superstitions that were so old and powerful. Only new ideas and new knowledge could do that—and both were on the way.

Saying farewell to the Middle Ages, the north had little to lose and very much to gain. That is our misfortune: if there had been more to lose, a more gracious use might have been made of the gains. The way ahead was clear for a most remarkable advance in material things, turnips and straw and the like. That advance was inspired by a few lairds, of whom Monymusk and Lord Deskford were the first; and it gradually appeared to the common people as a vision of plenty let down out of heaven inside the four corners of a lease. In the next hundred years, things were done in the north that would be a world's wonder if they had happened four hundred miles further south or anywhere across the sea.

THE IMPROVERS

Grant began the work of improving Monymusk with the Mains which was under his own hand. The first job was to lay out regular fields and enclose them. That entailed a great labour, for the earth-fast stones and the surface boulders had to be removed and the wet patches drained. However, there were plenty of workers available; and, although they may not have been willing, the authority of the laird and Grant's own powers of persuasion set them to the work. They removed the stones and built them into drystone dykes enclosing the fields. They dug ditches to carry away the surface water and tap the springs. They levelled out the serpentine ridges and laid the new fields as flat and regular as nature would allow. They thus made the physical conditions in which a new sort of husbandry could be practised.

There were two problems for the improver. The first was how to keep the land clean and so reap better crops. The second was how to feed more cattle in summer and bring them successfully through the winter, in good condition. Nothing very remarkable could be done about the weeds: the art of controlling them is still a question of management and of doing the necessary cultivations at the right time. The regular fields and better surfaces did make cultivation easier, but something more was needed. That succession of ground crops must be broken by an interval for cleaning the ground. It is very difficult to weed a grain crop or clean it mechanically after the corn is well up: the weeds grow with the corn and ripen more quickly, so that they have given the land another seeding before the corn is cut. It was necessary to find some way of getting at the weeds and destroying them. Grant found one answer in the English system of fallowing. A dirty field is ploughed, but, instead of being sown, the weeds are allowed to grow, and each successive coat of weeds is destroyed by cultivation and the sun throughout the spring and summer; thus the number of viable seeds in the ground can be greatly reduced. The fallow is a useful system, though hardly a perfect one, because it is rather an admission of defeat: and to a Scotsman it has one horrid fault—the land bears no useful crop in the fallow year. Grant used the fallow, while he looked for something better—a crop that by its very nature would help to clean the ground. He found the turnip.

If there were any justice, the turnip would have a statue in its honour in every market town of the north, for it became the heart of northern farming. It was not new in Grant's time—it was grown in gardens and sometimes eaten raw as a fruit at gentlemen's tables. In Holland it was grown as a field crop for cattle, and Grant had the courage to try it at Monymusk. It took kindly to the north and the people of the north slowly realised its enormous possibilities. As it could be hoed and kept free from weeds all summer, it was a cleaning crop, allowing the operations of a fallow but leaving a most valuable increase at the end of the year. It solved the farmer's other problem of how to carry his stock through the winter. That was very agreeable. It was now possible to get fresh meat all the year round; and at the same time to increase the breeding stock. More cattle in the byre meant more dung in the midden to be applied to the land in spring. More dung under the corn grew into more luxurious straw for the cattle to tread next winter; under the turnips it produced more keep. The northern farmer discovered that there is a law of increasing returns—the more stock the bigger the midden; the bigger the midden the better crops; the better the crops the more stock you can keep. There may be an end to that process but none of us are in sight of it yet. Only economists have reached the peak and found diminishing returns on the other side. The humble root is not an inspiring plant; generations of farm loons have cursed the pulling of it on frosty mornings; but in every country kirk, before the minister prays for them that are set in authority, he should call on the congregation to rise and all together say, "Praise God in His mercy who sent us the turnip."

The rules of northern farming soon became clear; and not invented but inevitable, as the only way in which the land could be made fertile. There may be land in the world that has a great store of natural fertility, but we do not find that sort of thing in the north. We must put in before we can take out: the soil is a medium—sometimes a dour one—where the farmer converts dung into herbs and grasses by the processes of nature. Our ancestors two hundred years ago began the long, slow process of building up fertility by ploughing in the middens to aerate and quicken the clay, and, on the poorer parts, to provide some humus to keep the stones apart. The three essentials were straw, turnips and the feeding bullock, so every farm must have its field of oats, of turnips and of cattle. There was a further consequence. If there were more cattle in the byre all winter there must be more grass for them in the summer. Instead of leaving exhausted cornland till the weeds covered it, Grant sowed out good grasses and clover, making a lea that would give good grazing for two or perhaps three years, and a good sod that would enrich the ground when ploughed under. It was a simple, obvious system, with the authority of a revealed religion. Oats, turnips, oats, then three years of grass—an harmonious system in which all the parts helped each other and which had as its first principle the steady improvement of the land. It set a pattern on the north which has not changed and few would dare to change without long thought and precaution.

Grant's work at Monymusk took him a lifetime, for progress was slow at first. However, he was determined and persistent. Using the lessons he had learned on the Mains, he took other farms into his own hand, improved them and let them to suitable tenants. In some cases he found tenants fit to do the work themselves and encouraged them with long leases at low rents. So the medieval order of the farmlands was redrawn. The new tenant took all the farm into his own hands, levelled and enclosed the fields, and built a house and steading of proper size and comfort. The sub-tenancies disappeared, but many of the sub-tenants became tenants in their own right on smaller farms which they undertook to improve. Some of the smallholdings were only a few acres—insufficient to support a family—but they had a social purpose. The man had the dignity of being his own master as long as he cared to work at home; and the large farmers were glad to employ him whenever he cared to work for a day and a dinner. Most of the large estates were redrawn on those lines—so many big farms; so many small ones; a few crofts for the day men. And then there was the cottar at Platecock who had no door, window or lum—he got no land and had no rights in anything but his labour. Still, his condition improved. Better cot houses were built on the new farms for the married ploughmen, tied houses they held for the term of their service. They probably slept better; and as meal, milk and potatoes came to be recognised as perquisites, they may have eaten better too. It is impossible to make any social change without leaving a few sore hearts, and no doubt there were some or many who resented the changes, but the improvements left no common feeling of injustice such as followed the Enclosures in England and the Clearances in the Highlands. Both those movements drove people out of the countryside—making in England rich but silent fields, and in the Highland desolate, empty glens. The improvements in the lowland north nourished the land and kept it full of people for more than a hundred years.

The spread of improvement was slow, although Lord Deskford applied methods similar to Grant's on his Banffshire estates; and it was not until the end of Deskford's life that another famous name was heard in the north. Round about 1775 a man from the Lothians called James Anderson took over the farm of Monkshill in Udny—1,300 acres of unimproved land. Anderson was a remarkable person. Because of the early death of his parents he became tenant of the family farm beside Edinburgh when he was fifteen. We might consider that too early an age—but we might be wrong. The chance to work at his own job in a responsible way can hardly come too soon to a youth who has some talent: there is far more danger in forcing him to waste his formative years on quite arbitrary academic disciplines, which are often death to the enquiring mind. Anderson's mind was not discouraged; he went on enquiring to the end of his days. Feeling the need of exact knowledge to replace the traditional wisdom of the old farmers, he attended lectures in chemistry and other sciences in the University of Edinburgh, where exacter knowledge—under such great experimenters as Dr Joseph Black—was replacing the theories of the medieval scholars. Then he applied that knowledge to his own farm with very satisfying results. It seems very strange that any farmer should leave the Lothian plain for a moor in Aberdeenshire: perhaps Anderson was influenced by the fact that his wife was a Seton of an old northern family; perhaps his intensely practical and adventuresome mind was attracted by the size of the job. However it was, he came to Monkshill and methodically raised it into a state of high fertility. His influence was great—far greater than that of Sir Archibald Grant—and extended furth of Scotland. Even George Washington was glad to ask his advice about the management of Mount Vernon. But that is not to say that he was a more remarkable man than Grant. Perhaps the times were more propitious. Anderson was a writer as well as a farmer, and he was writing at a time—the turn of the century—when the reading public had enormously increased and an expanding market gave lairds and farmers every encouragement to copy his methods.

There was a text that Anderson was always preaching on—the greatest need of agriculture was the development of towns. A farmer would have no great incentive to grow big crops unless there was a good market where he could sell them—and a good road to that market. Land improvement was geared to industry—only the multiplication of looms and forges could speed the plough. The force of Anderson's argument could be seen within a mile of Aberdeen. As soon as the town began to expand, farmland became an excellent investment. The ground to the west of the town still lay as the glaciers had left it, covered with boulders. Now the demand for food made it seem worthwhile to clear the land. This was done as a speculation and at what was considered enormous expense—but the stone was shipped to London for building and paid some of the cost of the clearing. The new fields soon brought rents that even today would be considered handsome. So Anderson was working in a favourable time. The local markets grew; then contact was made with the new industrial areas. Increasing droves of cattle moved south to market at Falkirk Tryst and thence into England. Corn moved down to the ships at Aberdeen and Newburgh and Banff, to feed Scottish mechanics and English horses. The rate of development quickened in gear with industry until it became quite as remarkable in its way as that which changed villages into towns and towns into cities of unending night. In the thirty years after 1801 the population of Aberdeen grew from 18,000 to 58,000—which curiously enough was just about the average increase for industrial towns. Three times as many people to feed—and often at a higher standard of living: that was surely incentive enough, and it drove people to almost incredible labour. How can we assess now the weariness that went to enlarging the stony limits of the fields? Remember the small patches of cultivation, the infield and outfield among the waste. Working outwards from those, year by year and generation by generation, men, women and children dug out the stones, hauled them away on sledges and built them into the dykes that still enclose the fields. It was a monstrous labour. Some of those dykes, hundreds of yards long, twelve feet broad and six feet high, look like things on which a Pharaoh might have tried his 'prentice hand. When the stones were removed the ground was often so rough that it had to be levelled by the spade before the plough could go in. In many cases water was the obstacle, particularly in the old peat mosses where the fuel had been cast, leaving haggs five feet deep, black and dangerous under a cover of moss. The tenants of those unkindly acres dug miles of ditches to run off the water, and again the spade was needed to level out the inequalities for the plough. The man-hours used up on that work would stretch far into eternity. When all that had been done, the result was not always a field in which crops would grow. It might be hungry sand or spouty clay, a dead, inert mass with nothing in it to feed a plant; or peat too acid and unsubstantial for cultivation. The hungry sand had to be fed with dung or turf, and the sodden clay aerated. The moss was consolidated with hundreds of loads of clay to every acre. All the land needed lime that had to be carried long distances over abominable roads. The sum of it all is beyond reckoning. When you travel through the north and see how the cultivation has been carried right over the brow of the little hills, and remember that the work was done with the spade and the mattock, you must surely realise that there were once great men in the land.

The momentum of improvement carried people to fantastic things. When all the likely land had been taken up, young men were driven by a sort of land hunger beyond the reasonable limits of cultivation. For a long time, men with no capital except their own strength, had squatted on some rough moor, had cleared a few fields and built a house and steading. Then the laird agreed to give a lease—at a rent which made certain the poor man would work hard all his life to retain what he had created. So far, the land had been good enough to make that injustice tolerable. Now the squatters were forced up the hillsides, further and further up, till it seemed that the Mither Tap o Bennachie and the Tap o Noth would come under a six-course rotation. But there is a limit to human endurance. As you walk across the lower slopes of the hills you may find a heap of stones that was once a house, and trace among the bracken the rectangle that was once a field. They are melancholy things, witnessing that courage, determination and all the ancient virtues are not enough to bring life out of a stone. A hunger for land drove the people there, and the insatiable hunger of the soil drove them away again. Those ruins are at the stony limit where a human tide spent itself before it began to ebb away.

After the fields came the steading and the houses. There were two periods of building on the farms. When the land was improved, the old thatched buildings were replaced by modest new ones. Then in the good times which ended in the late 1870's there was a considerable rebuilding. Little was done in the next seventy years; and nothing that changed the plan made a hundred and fifty years ago. The northern farm steading, infinitely repeated with small variations, is in the form of a rectangle, with one side removed. One side is a byre; the second a byre and barn; the third is a stable and cartshed. In the middle is the midden, the storehouse of fertility. Other accommodations had to be found: a turnip shed, for instance, which may be at the angle where the two byres meet. That is where it should be, for convenience in barrowing the turnips to the cattle—fifty feeding bullocks will eat 1 cwt. of turnips a day each, which means the cattleman has to roll 50 cwt. in his barrow, and every yard saved will lengthen his life by a little so much. However, people did not worry very much about saving life or labour at a time when both were so plentiful; the turnip shed might be tucked away in some curious corner and on a lower elevation. The barn usually had a threshing mill driven by a water wheel to which the water came from a mill-dam fed by a stream, if there was one, or by drains from the surrounding fields. If there was no water—and many parts of the north-east are very dry, having a rainfall of thirty inches—the mill was driven by horses pulling on levers round a circular course outside the barn. That turned a shaft connected to a driving wheel inside the barn which turned the mill. The barn itself was on two floors. The sheaves were pitched in through a door on the top floor and fed into the drum. The straw was delivered below at one end and the grain at the other. Then there was a granary, usually on the top floor, beside the place where the sheaves came in. Therefore, all the grain had to be carried up a ladder in four-bushel sacks weighing a hundredweight and a half. That also was a certain waste of labour, especially when the rats got into the granary, which was always.

The cartshed usually stood open in plain arches, for there were no doors, and as each arch held two carts, they were an indication to strangers of the importance of the farm. They still are. If you see three arches, you know it was a 3-pair farm—about 200 acres. If five arches the farmer can have an overdraft of £5,000 for the asking. There was a loft above the cartshed and stable. The largest part of it held hay, which was thrown down to the horses through square holes above the forestalls. It was a private and comfortable place for courting. The small part of the loft was partitioned off as a chamber called a chaumer—French *chaumière*—for the unmarried workers, who slept there two in a bed. It was sometimes so cold in the winter that the young men took their boots into bed with them, else they would have been too hard to put on in the morning. A staircase of squared stone led down from the chaumer—sometimes: for at many farms the only access was by a ladder up from the stable through a trapdoor. There might be other offices somewhere—a shed with a door to it, in which the farmer kept his gig; a workshop, called the shoppie, which held small hand tools, such as forks, scythes, blunt chisels, rusty saws, nuts, bolts, staples and those useless parts no farmer can bear to throw away; a henhouse, cleaned out once a month; a pigstye cleaned no more frequently; and a wooden doocot hung at a gable end. Somewhere there was a pump and a horsetrough beside it. Then to one side, or at the back, there was the cornyard, filled with stacks of corn all winter, and with dockens and nettles in summer. That was the plan of the northern steading, and you can see examples of it everywhere today, hardly changed in any material particular since they were built a hundred years ago.

The fourth side of the rectangle is filled by the farmhouse, usually a little distance away (the further the better if the midden is a copious one). There are two styles of house and both are a development of the but and ben of Sir Archibald Grant's time. The but and ben had two proper rooms—a kitchen and, beyond it, the bedroom for the master and mistress. The older children and domestics slept in the loft above. Now of the present styles the first is an ampler form of the but and ben—the single storey with attics lit by skylight windows. The second is of two storeys and skylit attics. Both are comely in their original state. But alas builders discovered how to put dormer windows into the attics, thus in effect changing the one storey into two. The effect may be all right inside, but it makes the house seem to have horrid bulging eyes, as if it had been stricken with a rectangular goitre. There are thousands like that in the north. Going still further, the builders sometimes threw out bow windows on the ground floor, which were not bows at all but nasty angular projections for the display of Nottingham lace. Thus the modest face of the house was completely undone. The titivators seem to have found an unassailable dignity in the old two-storey house. They may have thrown out a bow window here and there (the very word shows the want of civility in the act), and an occasional farmer has ploughed back the wartime profits in a sun parlour, but it has beat them to syncopate the plain harmony of two windows below and three above, with sometimes a gracious fanlight above the door. So much for the front. Many farmhouses, especially the small ones, are in the simplest form: that is, on the ground floor they have a kitchen at one end, a sitting-room at the other, looking to the front, with a small bedroom behind looking to the back. Upstairs there are two or three attics: or, if it is a two-storey house, there are three bedrooms with a loft above them. On the larger farms, a kitchen wing has been added at the back, making a ground plan like a capital T. The front door is in the garden; the back door in the farmyard; and a long passage separates the place where food is prepared from the place where it is eaten. These are simple styles of farmhouse building, and there are very few farmhouses in the north that differ greatly from them.

Improvement increased the rentroll of an estate fivefold in a generation, so the lairds found a wonderful change in their condition. In the old and unregenerate days they had been rich in many things —privilege, services, corn and cattle—but they had always been short of hard money. As the nineteenth century grew a little older, services and rents in kind were converted into cash and the lairds had real money to spend. Every one, even though he had only a thousand acres, built himself a mansion house and planted a wood to shelter it. The owners of great castles might content themselves with a new drawing-room wing and a few acres of gardens. Others smothered a plain square tower in a confusion of baronial masonry. Many abandoned their small old houses and got themselves something handsome and commodious in the classical style. One of the prettiest examples of the old and new can be seen at Raemoir House, near Banchory, where the old Ha' House stands, well preserved, behind the modern one. Meldrum House, at Old Meldrum, is a beautiful example of an old house added to. Both can be seen at any time, as they are now hotels, and very good ones at that. Those who were fortunate enough to employ Simpson of Aberdeen got a work of real beauty, as in Park House and Tillery. Gordon of Haddo built a magnificent house at Kelly in the Adam style. But there were no ugly houses, for laboured ugliness had not yet become a mark of wealth. The new mansions were at least decent to look on. The rooms were large, lit by several tall windows and nicely proportioned—every country builder had an instinct about the proper relations among length and breadth and height which make a space for living, instead of a box with doors and windows. As you walk through the gracious rooms and along the sunlit corridors where each window has a vista nicely contrived of lawns and woods and a hill beyond, while the sheltered air flows round you with a scent of roses, you know the amenity that a little wealth could buy. Those houses perfectly express their time, which was comfortable, expansive, confident, a time of high prices, high rents, loyal tenants and cheap servants. They have as little relation to the present day as they had to the condition of the people whose labour made them possible. They exist in a timeless world like all good art and good workmanship. That is perhaps fair enough, for they were built for people who thought they had inherited the world and taken possession of eternity.

I doubt if the mansion houses did the countryside much good, but generations have blessed the woods that were planted round them. Archibald Grant was the leader in this as in so much else. He planted by the million and lesser men followed with their thousands. If you stand on the top of a hill and look across the country you can pick out the lairds' houses by the woods, now old, but no less remarkable than they were when newly planted. How desperately our country needs them. When the farmers had done their work, the land lay under crop, yet that new tidiness and order would not have concealed the nakedness of the land, and may indeed have made it more defenceless when the plough had ripped it to the bone.

You can see what I mean if you stand above Cairnorrie, which is the gate to central Buchan, and look towards the north, over the howe and up the brae and on and on, across the small irregular fields of corn and grass and turnips, to the last braehead that meets the sky. The corn is pale gold there in harvest and the grass is sometimes green, but nothing generous, the increase stands in a thin covering to the lean earth. You see field after field, and to every six or eight a small steading and a grim grey house with one tree at the gable end. It is a utility landscape of the very barest kind, with no refreshment for the eye or rest for the spirit.

Then turn to the south and you see the woods of Kelly around Haddo House, containing green fields in their arms on the forward slope, then cresting the braes and falling away into a mysterious middle distance of treetops before the woods rise again on the furthest slope. It is best at the lip of harvest, when the cornfields have turned, and the well-managed pasture fields are still a growing green, and a blue haze lies into the gussets of the wood. Then the eye can rest on the treetops and the mind wonder what beauty lives below them— what elegance of stone and lime across the plane surface of the lawn; what ornamental waters where the swan floats double and *Hæmatopus æstralagus* cries "killee killee" out of his orange bill; what hot deep silence in the thickets, where the heron, all wings and neb and blue-grey nothingness, sinks down to her nest with a horrid squawk; and how many small boys find more wonders there than Tartary could offer to a grown man. In a countryside like ours, we need the mystery of the woods. A few trees along a dip in the road is a rest to us; even a rectangular planting of ungracious fir is a benefaction. No wonder that we love the old woods and when they are cut something of our youth, something protective, dies with them. Let us remember the lairds who set them there a hundred years ago.

Along with improvement of the farmland there went an improvement of the farmstock that was to make the north famous across the world. As to the original breeds of cattle there may be some doubt, but there was, particularly in the Buchan district, a race of small black Polled (hornless) cattle; and throughout the north, and far more numerous, a Horned breed, black, brindled or dun. In the early days of improvement the Horned won great favour, for they were good drovers. In those days the cattle from the north could not be fattened at home from the want of keep and so were driven south to Falkirk Tryst, where the north of England farmers bought them, and they made the journey very well. As Dr James Barclay has written about them:

"A drove of some hundreds of these cattle—with their nice springing black-tipped horns, their small heads, broad between the eye and with short muzzles—had a very taking appearance. They were large and strong in the bone and as a race inclined to be narrow across the back, though the great depth of chest by which they were characterised perhaps made this narrowness more outstanding than it otherwise might have been, the chest being much deeper in proportion to the circumference. A great point with fanciers was the shape of the horn which was long and arched inwards, of a pure white colour with tips of black . . . a waving tuft of black hair on the crown of the forehead (was) indicative of a pure descendant of the breed. . . . As a breed the Horned cattle were marked by great hardiness of constitution and were long livers, while the cows were both prolific and great milkers."

But they disappeared. According to Dr Barclay, the last representative died about 1888. She was bred at Cevidly near Alford and owned by Mr Ronald at Pitbee in Pitcaple. When she died she was twenty-five years old and had produced twenty-three calves. As a dairy farmer I wish I had a few so long lived and prolific milkers today. The most famous of the breed was the *Kintore Ox*, bred by the Earl of Kintore. He won first prize at the Highland Show in 1834 when seven years old, and was toured about the country as one of the wonders of the age, being 28 cwt. The Earl sold him for a hundred guineas. But the *Kintore Ox* was more than a wonder: he was a portent. His mother was one of the Horned breed and he had her head and horns; his father was a Teeswater bull, and the name Teeswater introduces another story.

The Horned breed were native to the unimproved north and perfectly adapted to their environment. They were hardy, did well on
a spare diet, but probably did not make a lot of beef. As soon as the
improved farms gave a lot of good keep, the farmers looked for an
animal that would turn the keep into good flesh, more generously
and more quickly: an animal that could be finished at home. So the
emphasis changed from ability to travel to capacity for making flesh.
Barclay of Ury (a great sportsman who could use his head as well as
his feet), brought up bulls from Tees-side, of the Teeswater stock,
that were notable for size and responded well to feeding. Those ancestors of the English Shorthorn were mated with the native cows
and produced a cross that could make plenty of flesh and make it
quickly. The *Kintore Ox* was the result of that first crossing; and,
although a freak, he was probably just an excessive effect of hybrid
vigour. But that vigour, shown more modestly in other cases, attracted
most farmers. The Teeswater strain gradually overcame the Horned
breed and even threatened the Polled cattle of Buchan. However, the
Buchan breed managed to keep a place, for they too responded well
to good feeding. So by the early years of last century the north had
two types of beef animal. Prime Scotch meat was becoming famous
and some of the best of it came from the north.

During the century those Horned and Polled sorts of cattle, no
doubt a very mixed lot that would have puzzled a Mendelian, were
taken up by specialists, who evolved a standard type for each, and
started herdbooks into which no animal was admitted unless it conformed to type. Thomas Bates of Kirklevington, an Englishman on
Teeswater, bred a strain of Shorthorn that became extremely, fantastically fashionable in the middle of the century. When the fashion
wore off (and farmers are as susceptible as girls to changing fashion) it
was realised that Bates had produced a dual-purpose type, for beef and
milk, that, like most dual-purpose articles, was not perfect for either.
That was the English Shorthorn.

Meanwhile Amos Cruickshank was producing a Scottish type. Amos
and his brother Anthony, who was an Aberdeen hosiery merchant,
took a lease of the farm of Sittyton, near Aberdeen, and there Amos
for fifty-seven years worked out a breeding policy which added much
to the happiness and the dinner-tables of mankind. Amos was a
Quaker and showed in all his dealings the staunchness of that quiet
sect. He had an idea of the sort of animal he wished to produce. His
customers for bulls were the tenant farmers round him, and they
required a beast that would do his work and pay the rent. The bulls
must leave stock that were strong and vigorous, carry a lot of good
flesh and mature early. Pedigree was desirable but performance much
more so. At a time when breeders were mad on pedigree he looked
at the animal first and then at the family tree. He managed to breed

what his neighbours required, but it was a long time before he got near to his ideal. His success came—almost, it seems, by accident. Having searched England for a new stock bull, in vain, he wrote to a friend asking if he had or knew of anything that might suit. The friend replied that he had a good old bull that might serve until something better could be found, and Amos could have him for thirty guineas. Amos bought the bull unseen and so *Lancaster Comet* came north on a journey that had wonderful consequences. The chill winds of autumn in Aberdeenshire soon extinguished the *Comet*, but he left a son that Amos called *Champion of England* and that wholly justified the name. *Champion of England* was considered far from perfect, even by his owner—he lacked refinement and style. But he had the qualities that Amos was looking for—vigour, strong constitution and rapid growth, and in due season he showed he could transmit those qualities. That of course is the chief purpose of a bull—to transmit; though some or many breeders have sometimes or often forgotten it in the search for prizes and applause. Amos did not care about applause. He proceeded to get the *Champion's* character into the whole Sittyton herd, by close in-breeding, which, as happens when the stock is good, reinforced the desirable qualities. Sittyton's reputation began to rise. American buyers found the hardy bulls did well on the pampas and the prairies; they bought and bought again. By 1895 when he died Amos saw the *Champion* strain beginning to dominate the breed. His work was carried on magnificently by many breeders, of whom the most famous was William Duthie of Collynie in Aberdeenshire. It is interesting that Duthie withdrew very early in his career from showyard competition, which was either superior sense or superior showmanship. Perhaps his stock were too strong to take prizes. Whatever the reasons, it paid: in 1920 he sold a draft of twenty-four bull calves at an average of £1,400. Prices have risen since then: a few years ago a Pittodrie bull went to the United States at £14,500, and bulls bred by Mr M'Gillivray at Calrossie in Ross-shire have had a wonderful and consistent success during the last twenty years. In 1950 a draft of fifteen Calrossie bulls at Perth in February averaged £2,523. Amos Cruickshank would be surprised at such figures. He might even be horrified. He might have reason to be.

The old Buchan Polled breed were ennobled through the work of an Angus man, Hugh Watson of Keillor. Watson started farming in 1810 with six of his father's best and blackest cows and one bull— which indicates that the Polled breed were not wholly of Buchan— and he increased his stock by buying in heifers that conformed to the originals. His work was carried much further by William M'Combie of Tillyfour in Aberdeenshire. In 1867 M'Combie exhibited *Black Prince* at the Smithfield Fat Stock Show, where the beast made such a sensation that he had to be taken to Windsor for a command performance before Queen Victoria. Some time afterwards the Queen visited Tillyfour. M'Combie, who was a character, paraded the whole herd past her singly; and, so that a good show would be even more impressive, had some of them go round a few times, like a stage army. Sir George Macpherson Grant of Ballindalloch on Speyside built up a famous herd from a cow *Erica* of the Keillor stock and a bull *Trojan* from Tillyfour. Of those three herds that did so much to form the breed only the Ballindalloch one remains. The name Polled was used until late in the century, when it was changed for the more distinctive Aberdeen-Angus. By that time the breed had quite re-established itself in the north: though Aberdeenshire had the leading Shorthorn herds, the Aberdeen-Angus were the feeders' fancy, being supreme for the very best quality of meat. They are smaller, finer in the bone, more delicate in the flesh and altogether prime. For years the champions at the fat stock shows have been of pure or cross Aberdeen-Angus. Like the Shorthorns this breed has made great favour abroad. They have never made the high level of price that the Shorthorns have done, the record being 8,500 guineas, but that is plenty.

They were great days when the breeds had been well established and prices rose steadily at the sales. The prizes of success were large and the competition for them was great. At shows and sales the fortunes of the leading herds were followed by ordinary farmers with the passionate concern they now show in the football games. But in spite of rising prices, few breeders made much money at the end of the day: the expense of buying in stock bulls takes the bloom off the profits and a loss of favour can mean a shocking loss of capital. Most of the breeders would have done as well by sticking to commercial cattle, though, of course, they would have missed some fun or anticipation. As prices have risen into the hundreds and the thousands it has become fantastically expensive to start a herd with fashionable stock and useless to start one with anything else: and it is also highly speculative, for you may spend many thousands, yet never breed anything that takes the eye. The pedigree business is in the hands of a small number of successful breeders, some rich business men trying to buy their way in at any cost, and very welcome indeed, and a few who carry on in a modest way for the fun of the thing. One of those last stated his attitude very well. A neighbour was teasing him about his pedigree cattle and said, "Why do you keep them? There's no more money in them than in my feeding beasts. All either of us gets out of them these days is the dung." The breeder replied, "Well, my pure beasts gie as much dung as your commercial anes and besides I've aye an outside chance o a winner."

The pedigree breeding has done good. It has evolved two excellent sorts of beef animal. The improved bulls graded up the commercial herds and so helped the ordinary farmers. Whether the effects have been wholly good is another question, but there need be no surprise about that, for few things are ever wholly good. There is always some price to be paid for improvement. Animals bred fine tend to become too fine: as they become more valuable they are in danger of being pampered. There can be a loss of vigour and constitution. Old cow families as well as old county ones can become degenerate. So there is a need in every other generation of an Amos Cruickshank to go back to first principles and, disregarding fashion, breed for the power to survive.

As regards general farming in the north, the pedigree trade was not of any great value during the bad times. Even the prime quality meat did not pay, for the fine Polled cattle were expensive to finish, both in food and labour. Farmers turned more to big rough cattle that could be brought into market condition on the grass. That shook the faith of the old-fashioned farmers when quality no longer paid. It seemed a sorry end to so much skill. As indeed it was.

I sometimes wish I could live for a little while in the years between 1850 and 1875, when there was confidence, peace of mind and a large ease in the countryside. I may seem to overpraise that time, forgetting the occasional bad harvests, the cattle plagues and the hard life of the labouring men: perhaps not—since a mind at ease can endure casual misfortune and the steady draught of labour. The countryside was a good place for many people eighty years ago. For the lairds a very good place, when their steady rents gave them the means and the leisure to practice conspicuous waste, with their gardens and stables, their shoots and dinners and parties, their seasons in town, their tours abroad, their adventures in politics, and now and then a few years of viceregal state in Dublin, Delhi or Ottawa, with a more than regal magnificence—was ever dung more pleasantly transmuted? For the successful farmers a very good place, when the profits of good years easily stood an occasional misfortune, and they had always a ten-pound roast on the sideboard and bought their whisky by the jar. For the ploughman a good enough place because though the wages were small, they were regular, and an enterprising man could always better himself in the towns. The great work of improvement was finished and it must have seemed very good—the mansion houses now sheltered by the woods; the farms and steadings, all built of stone and lime, secure against wind and water, and at their best unequalled anywhere in the world; the land well drained, enclosed in the miles of drystone dykes, managed with skill on a system that steadily improved it—the labour of the generations had been greatly blessed. The times had matured and their temper in the countryside would have been that proper to a vigorous middle age when everything has been made secure. Trust in the six-course rotation and take your pleasure where you can find it. O happy state. O paradise. But of paradises, there are, alas, two kinds.

The year 1878 is usually quoted as the date when the fortunes of British agriculture sank below the waves of cheap imported food. Grain and meat began to pour in from the New World, making that fine old individualist the farmer face something he had never faced before—competition, which he did not like then and has never learned to love, however much he praises it in the people he buys from. The imported food might have done much less harm to farming if there had not been a slackening in the demand for British goods abroad, through competition from the United States and Germany, which forced down wages in the manufacturing towns. The artisan in Glasgow or Leeds would have bought prime Aberdeenshire meat or Down mutton as long as he could afford it; but when times were bad, he made do with anonymous quadruped from the pampas and the prairies. As James Anderson had pointed out a hundred years before, the prosperity of agriculture depended on the towns, and in the long run always will depend on them.

There is no point in telling again the story of those unhappy years when the hope of good times was always deferred. In many parts of England the days of farmers' glory came miserably to an end, among the docks and the nettles, the cornlands abandoned, the clover supplanted by bent and fog, proud ewes displaced by the hungry phthisic cow: until, in the last despairing act of husbandry, the dogs were put down and the hunter sold. Not even a good war could save many of the old yeomen. The brief prosperity of 1914–18 was an unthrifty thing. Ten years later English farming was worse off than before and square miles of Norfolk could be had for a penny by anyone who would undertake to keep the weeds down. The thistle, the dock and the nettle crept out from the disordered hedges and buried the plough that had been left to rust in the headland. Farm buildings and the hamlets where the workers lived were mouldering slowly back into the untended earth. A social order was dying of conditions over which it had no control because it could not, or would not, understand them.

The north did not share the physical ruin of the south, and I have often wondered why.

Once I thought I had discovered the reason. In the winter of 1940 when the mornings were cold and rime lay opaque in the valleys of the Wiltshire Downs, we used to climb up on to the long grey shoulders of the land where a little thin wind blew over the graves of ancient men. There we dug holes and filled them up again, so that democracy should not perish, until it was time to go back to camp. We descended from the Downs into a dry eroded valley, where the grey grass gave place to rotting stubble and thistles raised their tattered flags. Hedges sprang up, unkempt and broken. A little clear stream, a little ghost of a stream, whispered at the side of the track. Down, down we came to a pasture of thin grey grasses where a few melancholy beasts stood at a gate. Down, down we came to signs of more recent cultivation—a rusting plough abandoned in the middle of a furrow months ago, a black gesture of despair against the cold sky. Then, there below us was the farm. As I remember, cowsheds and stables of brick and thatch stood round a square cobbled yard. The walls had been washed cream; doors and woodwork painted black. At least, one guessed about the doors, for they were gone. By the openings one could say, "There on the right were the three hunters and the stout cob. There in the centre were the work horses. The hole between them was the harness room. And the other buildings—but how can a barbarian from the north guess at their purpose?" We could guess that the square yard, where the docks heaved up between the bricks, was once kept clean by some old man no longer fit for the plough. Beyond those buildings there were the ruins of the barn. It must have been a noble building, timbered and thatched, ample to hold the produce of many acres at 120s. a quarter. A deal of craft had gone to the fashioning of the beams ; a deal of art to their placing; and how much pride. But the glory was fallen. Where the thatch was blown off, the rain had got into the beams. Joists had rotted—even the noble oak—and fallen apart. The great barn was sinking back into the earth, which sent up rank weeds to receive it.

The house sat alongside the farm buildings, joined to them by a track beaten through the weeds. It was built of stone—of which stone I would not know, but a soft stone where the yellow lichen grew as if it remembered in a cold climate the suns of all its yesterdays. In shape it was not distinguished, being long and low; or it may have seemed all the longer because it was not high. It seemed irregular because there were three mullioned windows on the ground floor and the front door was necessarily offset between two of them. There were four little dormer windows above with small, square panes, the sort that have a mighty powerful effect on anyone who remembers childhood as a golden age. The house was ill tended. The wood needed paint; mortar had crumbled from between the stones; the mullions of the windows had been gnawed by the frosts of so many years. Yet the house bore on its face the marks of love and a good life, as an old woman does, all passion spent. It had been cared for, once. You could see the marks of love upon the wall where the clematis had withered; and in the garden, though the chicken runs made deserts of dung and feathers on the waving lawn, and the great apple tree had cankered. The garden was a herbarium of decay, the old blackcurrants were stricken with big bud, the old raspberries contracting in the grip of virus; old infertile pears stood by a wall that no longer supported them; rose bushes had reverted to the briar; the dock, the nettle and the deadly nightshade proclaimed a total anarchy. It was ruined and wild—too wild, as it always is where man has laid his hand for a long time and then withdrawn it.

In the centre of the garden I found a delightful little thing. It would have been a lily pool. There was a square pavement of Cotswold stones surrounding a depression filled with weeds, and in the middle of the depression a square plinth on which—as I imagined—there had once sat a nymph in yellow stone, or a marble god was poised; for in those days taste had not declined to the whimsicality of gnomes and rabbits. A path lined with boxwood carried round the pavement, making on the side towards the house a semicircle for a stone pillar that had been the base of a sundial. But it told no hours. Time, as measured by men, and setting the pace for their ambitions, was no longer heeded in that garden. ·

I tried to imagine what the house and garden had looked like when the place was kept in order, and the quality of the life that had been lived there. Then I began to see that it must have been a little different from life on a comparable farm in the north. Lairds might make lily ponds and set up sundials; especially sundials, for they could be sure that, however many shadows passed, their family would remain; but that a northern farmer should waste time thus—I could not imagine it. I began to realise what a long memory the English farmer must have had; and how complete his faith that, however bad things might be this year, they must soon come right again. I saw how much older those parts of England were than the north of Scotland—I mean that farmers there had enjoyed a spacious style of living while my ancestors were still scratching among the stones with a pointed stick. Tradition was in the pulse of their blood; change was nothing more than the gradual progress of the seasons and as natural; and their condition in life must have seemed as settled as the Downs that sheltered them. How could they understand that the monopoly on which their living was founded was gone, and how could they adapt themselves to the new conditions?

When the hard times came, the northern farmer was in a better state to meet them. They were only a reversion to what was still quite well remembered, for the poverty of the old farming was only a few generations away. Though prices fell, the land was not allowed to go back. It had been so recently won for the plough at such great labour that the habit of work was strong in the people. They could not abandon weakly what had been made at such expense by generations so near them. They worked hard and lived carefully: they did their best by the land and it responded by keeping them through the worst of times.

I would not like to say that the northern farmer understood

immediately that times had changed. And I certainly would not say that he altered his style of living in the spring of 1879. He no more than the Englishman imagined that low prices would remain for sixty years, and he did not allow them to spoil his fun. Our grandfathers were tremendous fellows. They ate and drank enormously. I, born into that society, remember very well the generation that took the knock of 1878 and survived it. As a boy I sat in at their parties in the northern farmhouses when a dozen people faced a twelve-pound joint with a roast duck at each corner of the table and two more in reserve on the sideboard. I can remember the evenings at cards, when the greybeard sat by the master's chair and the tumblers of toddy reamed and steamed till breakfast time. Markets were markets then: farmers bought and sold without any restriction or control; and in the same spirit they drank when the market was over. Wise people kept off the roads on a market night from fear of drunken farmers racing home in their gigs; but later on they would hear the quiet steps of a pony picking her way home with her master sound asleep and snoring. They had inherited a fine world and they allowed no temporary mischances to spoil their pleasure in it. But—they were tremendous fellows. If they went home roaring drunk at midnight they were at the stable door at yoking time and very much the master.

However willing the spirit and however strong the flesh, money is the lifeblood of a capitalist society, and the money slowly dried up in the countryside. All through the first three decades of this century there was a steady attenuation of rural life. A fall in numbers was to be expected. Even the very modest degree of mechanisation meant that fewer hands were required at the corn and potato harvests. Mass-production in the factories was bound to undercut the local tradesmen. The gay and garrulous company of village tailors and soutars dwindled away before the competition of Leeds and Leicester. More young people had to leave the countryside if they were to get a living. It was nothing new that young people should do so. When a good strong wife was likely to rear eight or ten children it was obvious that they could not all stay at home. Even with the small birthrate today some must go away, and that is right, for it would be intolerable if no country child could get away from the land. Even in the great days of the improvement, thousands of young men and women had gone south—to Aberdeen, to Lanarkshire, to the railways; and later to the Dominions. Migration is a normal and healthy thing in rural life. But in the early years of this century the export of bodies was going too far. The young people were leaving not only because they were too many but because there was too little even for those who remained.

By the 1920's the poverty had begun to show, at the edges. It could be seen in the mansion houses where the old servants were paid off, or not replaced; where the stucco began to peel from the walls, and weeds crept up the avenue, and the coping stones lay as they had fallen from the policy walls because there was no longer an estate mason to replace them. Life still went on in the big house, but economies were made, in things that were not of immediate necessity. The poverty could be seen on the farms: small repairs neglected and gradually becoming major problems; fences, dykes and gates—small matters of pride and good husbandry—now clumsily patched, inadequately mended; and the workers' cottages decaying at the very time when standards of housing elsewhere had risen. A consequent poverty could be seen in the villages. The joiner, the mason and the slater could not thrive when there was little building and few repairs. Hard times. Hard times. Oh, don't think that they were taken sadly: that is not the way of the north. There was plenty of complaining in public, but those that had to have it could still get their dram on market day— many drams on many market days. There was a roaring in the pubs on a Saturday night which might have convinced a stranger that all was well. Perhaps the drink created an illusion that all was well, but it was only an illusion, for some things were very, very bad indeed.

Living in the poorer parts of the north between 1925 and 1936 was bare to the bone. On many of the small family farms I doubt if the people ever had money through their hands, good spending money in effective quantities, from one year's end to another. They sold their fat beasts at the mart when they bought the new stores to feed, and the price of the one about squared the other. They sold their oats, and got enough to pay the rent, the seedsman and the smith. The wife sold butter and eggs to the travelling merchant—or, to be exact, exchanged them for groceries and clothes. They were almost back to the subsistence farming of their ancestors, although they were producing far larger quantities of far better food. It was a perverse, disheartening, situation, but—and this is the great thing about farming in bad times—there was always the subsistence.

The ploughmen were the greatest sufferers. Those men, who carried the weight of agriculture on their shoulders, found their wages go down below the level of human decency. In the worst time some of them were seen in their village not above twice in the year, for the good reason that they had not a sixpence in their pockets to spend. And those were the fortunate ones who had work. At the potato lifting in those days you could hire men for 3s. 6d. a day and their dinner to gather potatoes, first-class workers, men who had been foremen on big farms. The full degradation was seen in the clothes the children wore to school, patched until the patches would not hold together; and the boots in which they had to tramp and wade the by-roads—it was only in a Christian country that people were expected to attain virtue so young through physical suffering.

One thing shines out supernal in that sorry time. Whatever suffered in the countryside, it was seldom the land. I can remember very well a company of agricultural experts who made an extensive tour of Britain in the 'thirties and their surprise at the condition of the north. The farm equipment might be in a bad state, but the arable land everywhere was well tended and in good heart. The grain and root crops were tolerably clean, and there were few old, exhausted pastures. They were men of intelligence who could see how constant a discipline our soil required, and they were full of admiration that the discipline had been maintained, often by what to them were antique methods and in the most depressing circumstances. The care of the land was a sort of religion, perhaps nearer to our hearts than anything the churches teach, for there is something inveterately pagan about the north. The care of the land was a religion and the six-course rotation was its gospel. Profane in most else, the northern peasant was true to his faith, with a devotion that the priests of more sophisticated creeds might have envied. How happy I am to say that in this case at least virtue has brought a great reward.

The north survived the bad times through the tenacity of the men and women who worked on the land. I have said nothing so far about the lairds; for about most of them there is little good to say. They failed, and in most cases failed completely, in their obligation to the land. Now, in saying that, I am not erecting some cross of my own design to crucify the dead on. The lairds themselves in the last fifty years have talked enough about the sacred bond between the landlord and the land and have cursed both loudly and long the politicians who ignored that bond. We must do them the justice of looking at them from their own point of view.

By tradition, the leaders of the countryside, they did lead in the improvement of agriculture. Their motives were not entirely altruistic, but that is no discredit to them, for an enlightened self-interest can be of great service to the community. They did give the first impulse to the work that was carried through by the labour of several generations, and they got a reward that may have been out of proportion to their services when their rentrolls increased fivefold in thirty years. In some cases the tenants got a proper share in the result of their labour. On the Haddo estate of the Gordons in Aberdeenshire— then miles long, across several parishes—a man who had spent nineteen years on improving an old bog got another nineteen years, or thirty-eight, at a modest rent, to repay him. But in other cases a man who had spent nineteen years on improving his land—the miles of drains, the miles of drystone dykes, the levelling, the trenching, the digging of foundations, the raising of walls for byres and stables, the hard darg day in, day out, year after year—when he had returned every spare penny of those nineteen years to the land, was told he

93

must pay the full rent the place would bring in the open market, and that in a time of land hunger, when rents were sometimes uneconomically high.

The lairds did well out of the improvements and we need not work up a rage against them, for the weary bones that earned the money should be well rested now. It is when we consider their own claims that we see how they failed us. They claim to be the natural leaders of the countryside and the conservers of its resources. If they were so once, it was a good thing they gathered in so much money during the good times, for they were the trustees of the future, the responsible men who could be trusted to see that the surplus of today would be available against some distant necessity. It did not work out quite that way. I was brought up on an estate in the north where the old laird, as he was called, had a great sense of duty to his tenants. He used to go round and read the Bible to them in their houses. He died after 1878 and left a very large sum of money to found a mission in a big town. About forty years later we would have been grateful for some of that money to mend our steading roof. But what money the old laird had not spent on good works, the young laird spent on his expensive pleasures. And that has been the story of so many estates. The lairds may have been trustees but the bad times discovered them as defaulting. When the night grew dark they had no oil in their lamps.

I can't dismiss them thus as if I were a presbyterian full of complacent godlessness. I have myself a leaning to foolish virgins. I can be thrilled, as many a decent hard-working tenant in the north was thrilled, by the extravagances of the young men bred in those gracious houses. There is a certain something, a recklessness of the spirit, that the northern farmer or ploughman could recognise and respond to. I can remember an old farmer speaking about a man of ancient family who had inherited a great estate in the north and had flung it away with both hands in the high Edwardian holiday. One day this nobleman met the farmer on a grazing high up on the hills. They sat down together and shared the flask and talked about old times when they were boys together, playing football on the village green. The nobleman said, "Dammit man, life has some rare mischances. Here's me: forty years ago I heired all the land we can see"—the two old men looked from peak to peak and up the valley and down the valley and across the further slopes where good cornland climbed to the moor or slipped away into the unfolding of a fertile strath; and both looking with the eyes of love and knowledge, could count over the quarters and the good ewe lambs that paid the rent at Whitsunday and Martinmas, and it was more thousands than a man could tell between waking and sleep on a wakeful night—"It was all mine; and now, Davie, I don't even own the clothes I stand in, for I haven't paid the tailor, and I never will." No good man grudged the lairds their magnificence while the going was good. No honest man grudged them their gambling, their drinking or their fancy ladies: those that are set above us should always have great vices and get away with the things we should like to do but dare not. Charles II and George IV had no need to fear a revolution: they at least were worth the common man's money. Nell Gwynn went to bed with a whole nation by proxy. When the owner of an estate staked it all on the turn of a card or the form of a horse, it was to many of his tenants like a fairy-tale—and fairy-tales satisfy some undying sense of wonder in us. But that can hardly be an excuse for the unwary virgins; not when they set themselves up as our trustees: and we must treat them on the grounds of their own propaganda. They speak now as if they had been the bankers of the countryside: but when agriculture cried for an overdraft they defaulted.

The system of personal ownership was probably the devil in the piece. The laird had so many expenses—his position, his social and political ambitions, the endless drain of little charities, his pleasures, the irresponsibilities proper to a gentleman, and the responsibilities—sons to be settled, daughters to be married, so many gusty piggies feeding at the dish and so difficult to deny one, so easy to borrow while capital remained, and so hard to save when there was no policy. Seven daughters could be as bad as seven wet harvests, and a day at the races worse than the year of the short corn. At the heart of it there was a confusion of mind as to what the laird owed to himself and what he owed to his estate; and too often he excused as due to his rank what was just his personal inclination. Or, at other times, he did what he wished to do, regardless of cost while the money lasted, and then thought up excuses in his old age. The lairds now argue that personal ownership is the only system which will give the continuity and the personal touch that is desirable in the management of land. Well, the personal touch is valuable in any contract—but it cannot be ensured by primogeniture. Too much depends on the interests and the character of the heir. If we could have a sex-linking of landlords as we have of productive fowls, then I would agree, but human affairs are not so wisely conducted. Personal ownership must depend on the person owning. If the heir has no understanding of or true interest in the land, how can we be sure he will not give away the reserves of an estate to endow a home for retired variety singers?

At this point someone is sure to say, "It's the Death Duties that ruined the landlords." That is the usual excuse, but it will not stand: the landlords had galloped far down the road to ruin long before the Death Duties were invented. And there are ways of dealing with Death Duties by those who are wise enough to take them.

When the hard times came, very few of the lairds were able to lead or even to help their tenants. As we will see, agriculture was in a difficult but never a hopeless position. It was due for a change in methods and ideas; and to make that change quickly with the least possible suffering to those involved, two things were needed—leaders and money. If the landlords had been what they claimed to be, they could have provided both.

They failed—though here and there a laird made an appreciation of changed conditions and treated landowning as a business. They survived the worst times with the equipment in a condition that gave the tenant some encouragement. There again the law of increasing returns worked quite plainly. When the capital equipment is kept up, it attracts the best farmers, who can pay the best rents, and at the same time improve the land. There is nothing a good tenant likes better than a capable laird. The capable lairds were scarce when they were needed most. Agriculture was crying out for the Grants and the Deskfords. Too many lairds were now too far away from the land to understand it, and too poor to finance it. Even their great houses that had been their pride now became a burden. Some were sold to be hotels, some bought by public authorities and some slipped back to a condition that Sir Archibald Grant would have recognised—where the laird made a poor penny off the cow tethered on the croquet green, the goats stabled in the back kitchen, the angora rabbits in the servants' hall and the bins of the cellar empty except for a moulting wyandotte and a china egg.

THE NEW IDEAS

It was a good thing that the northern farmers could stand on their feet, even though they were only standing still. I think it is fair to say that in 1928 most of them were still farming by the ideas of 1878. They reared calves or bought in cattle from Ireland and Canada to be finished off in the byre on turnips, straw and cake. They grew a lot of oats and a decreasing amount of barley. Dairy cows were kept near the town to supply the local demand, and potatoes were grown there for the same purpose. Good oats and prime beef—these alone were worth the consideration of a good farmer; while the best-known men adventured in the highly speculative breeding of pure stock, often winning great fame, and seldom making money by it. The rotation of crops was sacred. The three-year-old grass was broken up for oats, followed by turnips, followed by oats or barley undersown with grass and clover which gave one year's hay and two years' pasture. The turnips fed the beef cattle in stall; the cattle trod the straw and made the dung on which the fertility of the land depended. It was a simple system: it was, as you might say, classical, for the rules were strict and there was no scope for the extravagant imagination.

Success or failure—survival, perhaps—depended on the individual's skill within narrow limits, on nice appreciation and adjustments, on an instinct for the right time to sow and reap and buy and sell. But it was a sound system that carried the north through sixty hard years and steadily increased the fertility of the land.

Having spoken fine words about the turnip I must now praise another friend in the time of need. We owe a very great deal to the wild white clover which was brought to the north about 1910 and soon improved the pastures beyond all calculation. The wild white clover is a wonderful creature. It is an excellent food for cattle because it is rich in proteins and also because it makes its best growth at midsummer when most grasses take a rest. That is only one part of its value. It is a legume, which means that it can take nitrogen from the air and store it in its roots. When it is ploughed down, the nitrogen is set free to stimulate the succeeding crop. The plant made a great difference to farming at the time when it was needed most. The weak part of the six-course rotation had been the third year's grass, which was usually so thin that it was valued at no more per acre than the rent the farmer paid for it. Now the wild white clover is persistent and has a colonising habit. Once established it spreads. It creeps into every vacant space and so it crept into the six-course rotation. By the third summer the grass might be thin but there was thick sole of clover to feed the cattle and the pasture had some profit in it. There was more to it than that, for there is always a chain of effect in agriculture. The clover, by covering the ground, kept out the undesirable weeds and so made the land cleaner; and, when ploughed down, enriched it. The wild white soon became as sacred as the rotation; and it remains sacred even to those who have now abandoned the rotation.

There was another factor of some importance, though it was seldom appreciated at the time. The farmer's market had been spoiled by cheap imported food, but he too was a buyer. His prime cattle had for long depended on cotton cake and linseed cake from abroad, and the undigested parts of that food gave a great value to the dung in the field. So while the feeder got less for his meat he also had to pay less for the cake. The balance may have been on the wrong side but it was not as great as it might have been or as some pretended. Then, while the price of oats had fallen, the man who kept a lot of pigs, or poultry, or dairy cows could buy feeding stuffs all the more cheaply. The farmer's income had certainly fallen but so had the price of everything he bought. Though he had to sell in a buyer's market he also bought in one. His great problem was to adjust that fact to his own advantage. Not only that fact but many others. Looking back with all the wisdom that comes after the event, we can see that times, though often hard, were never hopeless. Of course, it was not easy to see that at the time. The characteristics of the northern farmer during the first thirty-six years of this century were a solid faith in the traditional ways and a deep resentment that they paid so badly. That most of them came through those bad times more or less solvent was due to the ability of their servants and themselves to work hard and live near the bone.

Fortunately there were others who were unwilling to sit down patiently and hope for the return of old and better days. They correctly appreciated the fact that as prices fell the costs of production could fall too. If old methods would not leave a profit, then new methods must be tried: if old sources of income failed, then new ones might be found. These men did nothing spectacular—nothing to equal the transformation of a century before. But at the time when the lairds had abdicated, these men—most of them tenant farmers—tried to lead the industry out of its troubles. They succeeded in showing the way by lowering the costs of production and growing what would pay best without regard to tradition.

They did it by taking more land, which lowered their overhead costs. Suppose it needs £300 a year to keep a farmer and his family on a 300-acre farm, the oncost is £1 an acre. If the farmer takes another 300-acre family farm, they need not eat or drink any more, so the oncost falls to 10s. Over 1,000 acres the oncost is 6s. So there, on one item, is a saving of 14s. an acre. If the acre yielded 7 quarters of oats, it meant the cost of producing each quarter had fallen by 2s. And that was sometimes enough to change a loss into a profit. There were other advantages. It usually costs more to do a little labour than to do a lot—the more acres to crop, the lower the cost for each acre. Then you can buy a large quantity more cheaply than a smaller one, and, curiously enough, you may sometimes sell a large quantity at a better price, because there is a lot of two-way traffic in farming—the firm that buys your grain may hope to sell you fertilisers. There were many advantages in working on a bigger scale—each of them small, a sixpence here and there, but in the sum considerable. People who could command capital, or charm it out of the banks, were able to use those advantages. Farms were becoming difficult to let, especially the larger ones; in many cases the buildings had gone completely out of repair and in others people were afraid of the capital and the work entailed. Lairds were very glad to let them at a very modest rent to anyone that had the capital to collect farms. This did not develop on any great scale. It did become fairly common for an able farmer to have two or three farms. A few had half a dozen extending over 1,500 or 2,000 acres. One did, indeed, become a collector in the grand style and farmed 6,000 acres scattered throughout a dozen parishes. Such a way of doing was a wonder in the north—the wonder being where those men could get the money. It was really quite simple, as one of them explained: "When I began I was frightened to meet my banker. Now he's frightened to meet me." The hardest part was to persuade the banks to begin lending money; but, once they had begun, they were afraid to stop in case they lost the lot. The banks had no need to fear. Their money was well invested. Those farmers, tenant farmers, were the true successors of Sir Archibald Grant, who also had trouble with bankers in his day.

The new improvers found ways to increase their production per acre. Plant breeding stations were bringing out new strains of oats and barley that ripened earlier and gave heavier yields. Where the old potato oats gave a return of 6 or 7 quarters an acre, the new strains could give 10 or 11 quarters, and at almost the same cost of cultivation. Later on in the 'thirties the new strains of barley bred in Scandinavia yielded 8 or 10 quarters against 4 or 6. In the days when oats fell to 18s. a quarter a 6-quarter crop was worth £5 8s., and a 10-quarter crop was worth £9. And the difference between those figures was the difference between a loss and a profit: for the costs of production were about the same, £6 an acre.

The new improvers found the way to reduce the cost of producing beef. The prime northern heifer was an expensive beast to feed, expensive in labour for she had to be tied up in a stall through the winter, and expensive in food for she needed the cotton or the linseed cake. By the late 'twenties she could not pay her way. Meantime William Findlay, the Director of Field Work in the North of Scotland College of Agriculture, had evolved seed mixtures that greatly improved the pastures, on which a bigger and rougher type of animal could be got into market condition. These animals were not prime quality and real artists would have been ashamed to send them to the mart. But they often left a profit.

Northern farming was too rigidly based on beef and corn—new sources of income were needed. Potatoes for instance. The north had never been a potato-growing country—at least not an exporting country—perhaps because we do not get the heavy yields common in Angus, the Lothians and the Fens. Geography is against us— but it is also in our favour. The potato is a delicate creature subject to many virus diseases which are spread by the aphis fly. If the Fenland farmer saves his own stock and plants it for two of three years, the potatoes will be completely infested with the viruses and the crop be quite unprofitable. Therefore, he tries to buy a new stock at least every second year, from a district where the viruses are not so common or the aphis so plentiful; and he is willing to pay a good price for that seed. Now the aphis is not too happy on the windy braes of the north, it will not fly in a wind, and the wind is always blowing on our uplands: so it is possible to grow a healthy stock of seed here. A few farmers, realising this, began to develop a trade, before scientists could tell them why their seed was superior. Though they had occasional disasters they had more successes. As the trade developed, the Department of Agriculture took an interest. First they started a scheme of inspection to ensure that the seed was true to type—so that when the buyers paid for Majestic, he got Majestic and nothing else. The grower had to go through his fields and remove all the rogues—every stem of a different variety that might have strayed in, and every stem that was not true to type. In recent years the inspection has become more thorough, as the scientists have demonstrated the nature of various diseases that appear on the stem and the leaf. Now the farmer must remove every stem that is affected with any virus or other disease, with a very small margin allowed for human fallibility. If the field then passes inspection the grower gets a certificate of health and purity and so earns a much better price in the market. This was a new source of income to the north, and one that suited it, for the growing of good seed needs the care and attention that are inborn here; and the smaller yield is offset by the much higher price. Many thousands of tons of potatoes now go south every year.

When beef ceased to pay, the improvers looked at their byres and asked, "What about milk?" It was a pertinent question, for milk was one thing that did not come in from abroad. Of course the north had never been dairy country. There were dairy farms round the towns. And there was also the town dairy where the cow was an urban dweller, getting all her food brought in from the country and having perhaps one small field for exercise. It so happened that the town dairy was losing favour with the public health authorities, for the milk was sometimes dirty and the byre was often an offence to the neighbours. That made a chance for the outlying farms, and some of them were changed over from beef to milk. Though the work was hard, the money was steady and more farmers changed over, till the supply broke the market. At last the dairymen formed a producers' agency which found a market for the surplus, and in 1938 the Aberdeen pool was sending some thousands of gallons of milk south every day, even so far as the Midlands of England. There was not a fortune in it, but there was a living.

The hen, the humble hen, proved herself a real friend in need. There had been some hens on every farm from time immemorial. By my great-grandfather's last lease he had to pay six fat hens every year, as rent, along with some other and larger considerations; and on a big estate the henwife who took receipt of those fowls for the laird was a woman of some small power and large self-consequence. The fowls on the farm were the housewife's perquisite, scrounged a living at the kitchen door, disgusted the farmer and died in debt. They lived a happy, careless, natural life in those days, laid a modest number of eggs, then went into a long moult and spent some months in quiet introspection. But when times became bad, their value was realised.

Many farmers' wives got no money for household expenses; they had to keep the house on their eggs and butter, which they exchanged with the merchant when his van came round, as they still do. That forced them to look for a more productive hen and to keep pure strains bred for laying. Most farmers had no patience with all that, but the wives persisted until they had a balance of cash in their favour when the merchant came round. They were then in a very strong position, as the more manly enterprises had a balance on the other side. The farmer had to admit the hens as a valuable part of the farm stock, finally taking them to their bosom and thinking it no shame. There can't be shame where there is a profit.

The new improvers were among the first to see the possibilities of the hen, especially if kept in very large numbers. If there was money in 300 there would be far more in 3,000. There are, however, difficulties in handling a large number of living things. The more birds per acre, the greater the danger of disease. There was a time when the hen seemed to have a fatal fondness for dying. Fleeing from disease some people took refuge in the ark. This is a small henhouse with a run attached, the whole thing easily portable, all in one piece, and holding about twenty-five birds. Each ark is moved once a day so that the birds have fresh grass every morning and do not remain long enough to foul it. They eat the fresh grass which is good for them and they leave their dung which is very good for the land. Here and there you may see the arks in line across a field, and if you look back you will see where they were ten days ago by the deep strong green of the grass. By this system a man or woman can manage 2,000 birds and the danger of disease is much reduced. Its one disadvantage in the north is seen when there is a heavy snowstorm and the farmer has to dig the arks out of three feet of snow.

The logical development of large-scale poultry-keeping for eggs was to house the hens indoors in separate cages where there would be little danger of infection and they would always be protected from the weather. Besides they would have no scope for wasting energy and food. A hen shut in a cage only a few inches bigger than herself must concentrate on one activity—laying eggs; and the keeper gets nearer the ideal of putting into her just as much protein, carbohydrate and calcium as will produce an egg with a utility shell on it. The tending can be highly mechanised under that system. In the last year or two, trays holding food, water and grit have been made to travel along in front of the cages, so that they pass every bird once in an hour and take two minutes to pass. The bird has two glorious minutes of eating and drinking and spends the next fifty-eight in anticipation that grows from the pleasant to the frantic as the trays come round again. Underneath the wire netting on which she sits a mechanical scraper removes the droppings to the midden. The attendant has a store of food at one end of the building to fill the trays as they come round. The water troughs are filled through a ballcock arrangement as they pass a certain point. If there is a weakness it is that the attendant has to walk round once a day to collect the eggs; and what it lacks of nature might be corrected if a mechanical rooster accompanied the food and water. This system gives a large number of eggs with the least trouble to the parties concerned. Some people do not approve of it. They argue that a hen kept in such unnatural conditions cannot lay natural eggs. I find it difficult to imagine an unnatural egg, yet it is possible that some vitamin might be lacking—possible, though not probable, for the vitamins get into the egg from the hen and if a hen is lacking vitamins she is unlikely to lay eggs. But this argument about natural and unnatural is brought up against all our methods of farming. And right enough, for arable farming itself is unnatural. Still there may be something in it. No bird that has been in a battery may be used to lay eggs for hatching: the inference being that her year in the factory has ruined her constitution.

Those were some of the methods tried to make farming pay in the worst times and they succeeded—modestly perhaps, but it was success. It must seem strange that they were not more generally adopted. In spite of those demonstrations that a change might pay, the majority remained faithful to the old ways and prayed successive governments to make them profitable again. They did not like the things they saw. Those 12-quarter crops of corn—how were they got? —by fertilisers out of a bag—sucking the land dry; burning the guts out of it. Potatoes too, they were an exhausting crop—even more exhausting to the farmer than to the land. And the dairy cow—all that milk was milking the land. These things might pay for a while, but no good would come of them. How could it—there were too many college notions going round, and what could folk in a college ken about farm work? And so on and so on. It would be an interesting exercise for someone to sort out the emotions which lay behind that body of criticism. Two are fairly easy to distinguish. There is the fear of a new technique very common in people who have an uncertain command of an old one—or perhaps do not command the technique they use but are commanded by it, which is probably the state of most farmers anywhere at any one time. They have learned their methods by rote without understanding the reasons behind them and are scared to depart from them in any way. To them, the idea of change is truly terrifying. There is a second and more honourable opposition. Some who have completely mastered their craft—say, the feeding of cattle —think it is the highest study of mankind and any departure from it a fall from grace. It was such a master who, seeing a magnificent herd of dairy cows on what had once been a good feeding farm, shook his head and said, "Eh, man, the pity of it."

The battle between tradition and change really came to a decision through the tractor. The first sight of the machine in large numbers in the north was during the war of 1914–18, and it was taken to be just another of the deplorable but temporary conditions of war. For a few years after 1918 the tractors almost disappeared: then they slowly made their way back again. As long as they were only substitutes for a pair or three horses, drawing tools designed for horses, they made little way. When manufacturers designed tools to exploit their immense capacity, the advance was irresistible. As with every good new thing in farming there were unexpected advantages. For instance the tractor brought a new theory of ploughing. Horses could plough only a fairly shallow furrow in our hard land, and for a hundred years farmers had been working the top five or six inches of the soil, while the sole of the plough gradually consolidated a hard pan under that six inches, often impermeable by water and the roots of plants. The tractor could draw a deeper furrow and so break up the hard pan, allowing better drainage and a deeper tilth for plants to feed in. That seemed a good thing, but it raised a tremendous controversy. It was one of the commandments of good husbandry that the subsoil must never be brought to the surface, being sour, inert, dead; and nothing would grow in it. If you brought up an inch of subsoil you would repent it for a generation. There may have been something in it, there usually is in all those traditional ideas, even though it is not very much. A lot depended on what your deep plough did—whether it brought the subsoil to the surface or merely stirred it.

However, there should have been no debate about one of the effects of deep ploughing—the death of the couch. This weed spreads by means of rhizomes under the surface and in favourable circumstances, such as a corn crop, makes a dense mat of roots that possess the field and greatly depress the corn. The time to deal with the couch was when the land was being made for turnips. During the late spring days, the land was grubbered and spring harrowed to bring up the rhizomes, which were then gathered into heaps and burned. Sometimes this had to be done three times before the ground was tolerably clean, and three times in a spring the fertility, the meagre fertility, went up in smoke. Besides, the improvement was temporary: small pieces of root had the power to grow again and all that cultivating left plenty to carry on the race. There is a better way. A plough that can bury the couch under six inches of soil kills it dead and for ever. The deep-digging tractor ploughs were soon smothering this ancient parasite; and by the presence of its long feathery heads flaunting over the corn you can tell the farms where the hard pan is still unbroken and the weeds unbowed. However, even that evidence is not enough. There are still many who must feel that the hard pan is the only sure thing between them and Hell.

The debate—Horse *v*. Tractor—helped to fill up the awful spaces of the rural night for twenty years, but it has been decided now, and that because the horse deserted his supporters. He did worse—he died of grass sickness. The provenance of this disease is unknown, though a virus is now suspected: the results are too horribly familiar, being almost always fatal. The death rate increased every year to such an extent that an unfortunate farmer might find himself left without a single horse. Tractor salesmen had then one incontrovertible argument —whatever could be said against the tractor, at least it did not take grass sickness. Men bought tractors out of sheer necessity and then slowly learned to use them, and the north is now perhaps the most highly mechanised part of agricultural Scotland.

In the years between the wars the northern farmer was greatly reinforced by the scientists, though he was rather unwilling to accept their help. The North of Scotland College of Agriculture at Craibstone, near Aberdeen, had carried out a long series of demonstrations in the field under Sir Robert Greig and William Findlay which had an increasing effect by example on the more intelligent farmers and through them some small effect on the rest. Then the Rowett Institute was set up next door to study animal nutrition under Boyd Orr. At the other side of the town the Macaulay Institute was founded to study the soil and all the questions that arise from it. Those institutes were regarded sometimes with suspicion and sometimes with contempt, but they could help farmers when they got the chance and they did slowly build up confidence in the public's mind. Of course the people they helped most were the people who needed it least—but that's the way of the world: knowledge spreads down through the people who are anxious to take it.

When the war came, northern agriculture was in an interesting state. Sir Archibald Grant could have gone on to many farms and felt quite at home. He would have been delighted with the binders and the lissom ploughs and the wild white clover. The perfection of the black heifers and the yields of corn would have set him calculating a rise in rent. The pious observation of the old six-course would have assured him that his generation had discovered an eternal truth. He would have had no difficulty in speaking to the farmers, for their ideas were essentially the same as his. A few here and there among the backhills he might have found just a little old-fashioned. He might have been distressed by the disrepair of some steadings, but must indeed have been touched to find some ploughman's cottages, built by his fellow lairds in 1770, still tenanted by ploughmen after a hundred and seventy years, little changed by the passage of time, except that they had become less wind and water tight, which was only to be expected.

On other farms he might have felt himself a stranger in a strange world. He would have seen byres full of black and white Friesian or red and white Ayrshire cattle, byres cleaner than the house of Monymusk in his day, byres hygienic, byres aseptic, byres in which dung, instead of being God's benison, was something to be hurried out of sight of the sanitary inspector. He might have gone into a shed and seen fifty tons of potatoes sprouting in boxes; in another shed have seen 15,000 eggs hatching in an incubator; in another 400 pigs fattening under one roof. He might have looked in the stable and seen three tractors but not a single horse; into the house and seen the farmer at the fireside in his slippers selling 500 quarters of oats to Glasgow by telephone. That would have been very strange to Sir Archibald at first. In the end, however, he might have felt he was again in his accustomed place, at the head of progress.

By 1939 there was rather a gap between the best of farming and the average. Great things were done during the war and are still being done. The average has improved; and so has the best, and the gap between them is now even greater.

The best farming has made wonderful advances—I really do mean just that. There are farms in the uplands that thresh out 12 quarters of oats an acre in a good season, and where common eight-day cows average over 900 gallons of milk a year. Yet the over-all increases are not big, which indicates that the majority have not progressed like the few. If you examine the farming of the north in detail you will see all the last hundred years living together. This is particularly true on the marginal lands of which we have so many, far up the slopes of the hills or in backlying parts where the heart is cold. The farms there show all the signs of a drought of landlord's capital. The houses and steadings are old and in bad repair. The farm roads are atrocious. Fences and ditches have been neglected. The couch waves insolently above the corn. The land needs lime. You might wonder how anyone could make a living there on the outside edge where the corn is thin and the grass is grey. But now and then you may come across a farm that is like an oasis in that desert, green and virile. There are probably a few acres of potatoes grown for seed. The oats may be of a black variety that go to England for seed at an extra ten shillings a quarter. There may be 400 hens and perhaps a few breeding sows. And everywhere the signs of good husbandry— fields limed and fed with dung and fertilisers, crops sown and planted early, pastures strong and well eaten down so that nothing is wasted. What is the secret? Money? Perhaps, but more likely management. Where the best modern knowledge is put into use, even the stony limits will fill the basket; which seems to prove what some have argued, that we have more marginal farmers than marginal farms.

The contrasts are even greater on the good land, especially in the matter of permanent equipment. Many farm steadings have been untouched in seventy years except for the most urgent repairs. They are badly designed, badly lit and very wasteful of labour, now the farmer's greatest expense. During the winter they sit in six inches of mud. In summer they have a very uncertain water supply. The farmhouses, built to hold twelve children and two maids, have long dark passages, innumerable stairs and back kitchens stretching away to the end of a woman's temper. The workers' cottages would be considered bad in a city slum, being small, dark and damp, with the pump maybe a hundred yards away in a turnip field and the original dry closet long since perished in the winter storms. Not a very inspiring set-up for men or masters, in the general discomfort and waste of labour.

In the same parish you may find a farm on which the neglect of the last seventy years is now being made good. Old buildings have been altered to make easier working. New ones have been built—perhaps courts for 100 dairy cows or 100 feeding bullocks. Sheds to store implements. Sheds for potatoes so that they can be dressed in comfort, even though the weather is bad. Electricity for light and power. The yards covered by tarmac or concrete, and lit by lamps so that you don't have to slither in darkness and six inches of mud at five on a December afternoon. The farmhouse—perhaps the old kitchens abandoned to the beetles and a pantry made into a kitchenette behind the dining-room. The workers' houses enlarged and every house with a bathroom and electric light. All these things, or some of them, as time and money allow. And machines for lifting, conveying and loading, to save the solid, expensive drudgery which the worker detests and the farmer cannot afford.

There is an excessive contrast between those two examples—fantastic but no exaggeration. It may explain the gap between the highest level of production and the rest; or the gap may explain the contrast in equipment: I think the truth is that the two act upon each other. The money for the improvements must come out of the higher production: and when the improvements have been made the production rises higher still. The best houses and the best working conditions attract the best workers. The farmer who has bad cottages and a bad steading is thus left with inferior men and his handicap increases. He has every reason to curse the lairds who betrayed their trust a generation or two ago.

When you look over a well-managed farm I think you get the feeling that great things can be done yet. It is not so much that any one sort of production will be marvellously increased. For instance it will be some little time before hens are bred to lay two eggs every day, or the average yield of dairy cows be 2,000 gallons a year, though an occasional one already gives over 3,000 gallons. But small advances in everything with good management can give a most impressive result.

A great deal may be done with grass. The plant breeders have fixed new strains of pasture grasses that have more leaf and less stem and so give us more food to the acre. The people who study the habits of a grazing animal notice that she is a very untidy feeder: she picks a mouthful here and there, then lies down to chew it—and spoils the part she lies on. They also suspect that she is a glutton and eats more than she needs. So they have evolved systems to ration the grass. Some let their cows on to a piece of lush grass for maybe ten minutes three times a day, then keep them on a bare piece while they are lying down or just standing around admiring the scenery. By grazing each plot for ten days, or more or less according to the season, and then top-dressing it with fertiliser, they can keep a dairy cow on half an acre each all summer. When the grazing is uncontrolled about an acre is required, and if the pasture is unimproved, perhaps two acres. So if the best grass is combined with the best management the saving is easy to calculate. A 40-cow herd would have needed at least 40 acres of pasture in summer. Now it may need only 20 acres. The 20 acres saved can grow barley, perhaps 30 tons of barley—and just think of the whisky that would make.

Or the same extent of grass can be grown and cut at its richest growth and ensilaged to make winter food. I do not know how silage is made, though I make some hundreds of tons every year. If you put green grass into a hole in the ground it ferments and amino-acids are produced that are the basis of protein, the body builder. If the air is then excluded the fermentation stops and the mass inside the pit suffers no further change. You can take it out at any time within the next twenty years; and, if you have been lucky or clever, you have a food that smells like a brewery, looks like plug tobacco, is rich in protein, and delights the heart and the belly of the cow.

Even better, the grass can be dried in a current of hot air, and either baled or ground down into meal. If it has been cut at the right time the grass will give a meal at least half as rich as the cotton cake we can no longer afford to buy from dollar countries.

There are so many possibilities. The further we go the more we realise that we just do not know what our soil can do, and the more we suspect we are only scratching the surface.

Northern farming is in a fascinating state—such variety, such contrasts. Out of all its contradictions two things appear quite plainly. It needs a vast amount of capital to restore the equipment and more good farm managers or fewer farms.

I have indicated already that the hard times were never disastrous. It might have been better for agriculture today if they had been much worse. Then the people who would not change their ways would have been forced out and their places would have been taken by livelier men. The first-class managers are managing too few acres.

Agriculture is becoming more and more an exercise in logistics, putting man power, engine power and scientific knowledge working nicely together to get the best results. The number of people who can do that is bound to be small. There are farmers today who have doubled the production of 2,000 acres, and could do the same for 20,000. And there are among the workers young men who could do the same if they got the chance at the right time. I know that the traditional road for the worker is to save until he can take a small farm; and, after another fourteen years, take a bigger one—and by that time he is a little tired, and so is his wife. That is a wasteful process, because it means he is working with his hands in the best years when he should be working with his head. If there were more large units such a young man could be given a manager's job as soon as he showed the ability to hold it, and from that point his own ability would be the only limit to his advancement.

We have come two hundred years from the days of Sir Archibald Grant, and what a lot has happened to our northern farming in that time. There has been a tide in its affairs, now high, now low, now high again. Vitality is returning to the countryside. The dairy cattleman is now paid as much as the parish minister. There are no ragged children at the school. All the vitality will be needed, for the re-building of rural society is only begun. I have no doubt it can be done. When you look across the arable parts of the north, at the small irregular fields won so recently by the mattock and the spade, and now so fertile, you may have confidence that people who have so imposed their will on nature will maintain themselves in their own place whatever fortune may come.

CHAPTER III

ABERDEEN

ABERDEEN is a city in which nearly two hundred thousand people live and most of them earn a tolerable living. That is, perhaps, the most remarkable thing about the place. For Aberdeen is well beyond the northern limit of industrial Scotland, far from the coalfields and the iron foundries, and one of the largest cities to be found so far north. It has had no great mineral resources and it has not developed through any one specialised trade—as Dundee exploited the manufacture of jute. When you look across from Kincorth at the shining walls of Aberdeen, and notice how infrequent the factory chimneys, you may think the town has no visible means of support. How then is Aberdeen the third city in Scotland—a position it held for long, then lost, and now has won again?

It is the strength of Aberdeen that it has grown naturally out of the north-east. This cold shoulder of Scotland has only three resources: the land and the sea and the people that live by both. The interaction of these and the town of Aberdeen have made the north as we see it. The town and the country have acted on each other and helped each other and gone forward steadily together. In medieval times Aberdeen was a seaport; the market in Aberdeen encouraged the development of farming; and in the eighteenth century the Aberdeen merchants often financed the improving of the land. The growing of flax and wool on the farms helped the textile trade in the town, and when textiles declined, the white fishing brought much greater wealth. Aberdeen has grown naturally out of these resources, the land and the sea. Both require a certain perseverance and fortitude, but they do yield a small margin of profit to people who know how to make the best out of what they have. That seems to me the secret of Aberdeen—of its strength and of its weakness. When people have been making the best of it for a long time they make something of themselves. There is the third and greatest resource of Aberdeen— the character of the people.

When you look across from Kincorth at those shining walls, the many kirk spires and the few chimneys, you may indeed wonder if Aberdeen has any means of support, except a hope of the life to come. But the best resources of the town are not machines in factories; they are under the hats and the bonnets and at the fingertips of the Aberdonians. Perhaps the people themselves are the machines; that is something we will come to.

In order to enjoy the unique character of Aberdeen, it is necessary to consider its past—but briefly.

Now two rivers, the Dee and the Don, come to the sea in this part, with about two miles between their mouths; and a ridge of ground divides them, rising and widening towards the west. Twin rivers produced twin towns. Old Aberdeen or the Aulton* grew out of a settlement of salmon fishers on the Don at Seaton. Aberdeen too was probably a fisher village. The two settlements, some distance apart and on opposite sides of the hill, became two burghs distinct and separate, with no great love between them, and as such they continued for centuries. But the Aulton was badly placed, for the Don made a bad anchorage and Aberdeen captured all the trade. While Aberdeen grew steadily into a modern town, the Aulton remained behind in the Middle Ages, till the greater swallowed up the less, so that they are now one and indivisible.

Aberdeen must be an old town—just how old no one can say, for it is likely there would have been some sort of settlement at the mouth of the Dee in time immemorial. In the end of the thirteenth century, when Edward I was trying to take Scotland under the English crown, a Frenchman in his army reported that Aberdeen had a good castle. Even then it was accounted the third town of the realm, after Edinburgh and Glasgow, and probably flourished on the coastwise trade. When more settled times came, the town grew steadily, as towns did in those days, by developing the resources around it. That is something we are inclined to forget, now that towns seem too often a monstrous burden laid upon the countryside; hungry bellies that have eaten up the green fields. The older ones were true market towns with the merchants at the centre of the economy. The medieval merchant, like the medieval town, must be given his due. The old writers have little good to say for him, because he had a habit of cornering goods when they were scarce and so making too great a profit. But he must not be wholly condemned by a few shortcomings. Trade like chastity is an honourable way of life, subject to great temptations. Though agriculture and fishing were in a primitive state they did yield a surplus, for which the merchant found a market and brought back things the north-east could not produce. The merchant also found a market for the skill of the hand workers. As Aberdeenshire was far more pastoral than arable, there were many sheep of the little old native breeds whose wool was spun and woven

---

* There is some debate about the name Aulton. It could be auld toun—the old town—or it could be from the Gaelic, meaning the town of the high ground. The second would be reasonable, since the Cathedral and the Chanonry were built on high ground above the village of Seaton, but etymology is a difficult science. A clergyman seeking a derivation of Bennachie, our local mountain, said that it was surely Bend-up-high, because in shape Bennachie looks like someone touching his toes.

in the district, and the cloth had to be sold though the weaver went in rags. Aberdeen had a trade in rather coarse woollens. It was famous for stockings. The countrywoman knitted stockings so fine that a pair of them could be drawn through a thumb ring, and the Aberdeen merchants sold them all over Britain and beyond the sea. As trade moves two ways the merchants brought in good things from foreign parts: wines, sugar and conserves and little wizened oranges; books and music and fine cloths and all such ministers of delight without which culture cannot thrive, nor the hungry spirit know wonder. There was also a trade with the Baltic in which Aberdeen merchants prospered—for instance, Robert Gordon, the founder of Gordon's College, was a Danzig merchant. In all that earlier time Aberdeen's trade was wholly on the sea since the roads were impossible. Scotland may seldom have had a navy: it did have a mercantile marine.

As their markets grew, the merchants encouraged their clients in the countryside to produce more, by advancing money for improving the land or by themselves buying estates. That was a natural thing, because the merchants were often the younger sons of lairds. It was no shame in those days for the sons of country gentlemen to engage in trade; it was necessary for them then as it has become necessary for them now. The merchant had an intimate knowledge of, and contact with, the country, and was a powerful agent in improving it. And as it improved, so his trade increased. That brought a natural increase to the town of Aberdeen. Ships had to be built which started the Aberdeen shipwrights on a career which came to its glory with the building of the lovely clippers like *Thermopylæ*. The trade in salmon and less noble fishes made work for coopers. And so on. Mr William Kennedy, the Annalist of Aberdeen, says that the several corporations of Aberdeen tradesmen were originally the Litsters (dyers and weavers); the Smiths and Hammermen; the Tailors; Skinners and Furriers; the Cordwainers (Shoemakers); the Fleshers; the Barbers; the Wrights, Coopers and Masons; and the Bakers. There were other craftsmen in the town: for instance the Hammermen included blacksmiths, goldsmiths, cutlers, saddlers, clock and watch makers, copper and tin smiths, plumbers, armourers, pewterers and fish-hook makers. There is nothing in the list that could be called exotic—the exotic could hardly flourish in Aberdeen. The third town of the kingdom lived by cultivating its own backyard. It paid also some heed to the good life, for the Earl Marischal of Scotland, who had gotten the old Greyfriars Monastery, turned it into a college and endowed it as the University. As old Ronald, my master and my friend, said a long time after, the toun o Aberdeen wanted nothing but grace.

In the Aulton across the hill, grace abounded.

The origins of the Aulton may have been in the fisher village of

Seaton. As some believe, the Don used to enter the sea a little further south than it does now, and Seaton was on its bank. Seaton might have remained a humble place if it had not been for St Machar. The legend tells that Machar was sent by his master, Columba, north to find a plot of land where a river bent round like a bishop's staff, and there to build a church. Such a plot of land lay on high ground above the Don, and Machar built his church there. Some of the facts about those early days are obscure, but there must have been a church there long before the present building. The bishop of those parts in early times had his seat at Mortlach on the Spey, but in the twelfth century he translated himself to Aberdeen and made St Machar his cathedral.* In consequence the Aulton became a city, for a medieval cathedral entailed a large community living on the revenue of the diocese. The "chanonrie, in ancient times, comprehended within its precincts the cathedral and cemetery, the bishop's palace, the prebendaries' and chaplains' lodgings, gardens and glebes, also a hospital for twelve indigent men, the whole being surrounded by a stone wall." Outwith the wall there grew up a small secular community under the protection of the bishop, and for which the bishop obtained from the king all the privileges of a burgh.

In the first years of the sixteenth century the glory of the Aulton was further increased by the munificence of William Elphinstone, the bishop. That great and holy man, Chancellor to James the Fourth, obtained from Pope Alexander VI (Borgia) in 1495 a bull for the foundation of a college in his cathedral town. In the early years of the next century the buildings were erected and teaching began in the King's College or University of Old Aberdeen. The Aulton was now glorious with the things of the mind and the spirit and lived by ministering to the needs of the holy, the learned and the young. O happy little town, thus to make the best of two medieval worlds. But time was running out. In fifty years the Reformation came to Scotland and brought ruin to the Aulton. Parson Gordon of Rothiemay, writing after the Reformers had done their holy work, described the miserable state of the Aulton—most of the cathedral fallen, the bishop's palace entirely removed away, the canons' houses ruinous or passed into secular hands, the gold and silver and the priestly vestments, of a richness "scarcely credible if it were not attested by an ancient manu-

---

* Old Ronald knew about the translation from Mortlach: "Aye, the Cathedral was first biggit in anither place. But coorse [evil] men troublet the Bishop—he was the minister at that time—and, being a Pape, he workit a miracle. Aye: he made a road through aneath the hills and they took doun the stanes o their Cathedral and carried them aneath the grund till they came to Aulton, and there they biggit them up again and nae man ever saw naething. If ye daena believe me, look at the Cathedral. The stanes in't were never quarriet near Aberdeen." There is substance in what he said. The stones were not all quarried in Aberdeen. The present cathedral was begun by Bishop Kyninmunde in the fourteenth century.

script", all gone, all lost, all stolen. The library—we can imagine how richly Bishop Elphinstone endowed it in the noon of the Renaissance—lost, all gone, dispersed and blown about by the ravening winds of faction.* The same had happened to the Library of King's College—most of the volumes stolen away or lost by the negligence of the librarians. The Reformation had very different results in the twin but rival burghs. The canons had gone home to be country ministers and the revenues of the diocese were no longer spent in the Aulton. Without the University the little town must have quickly dwindled away. Once a burgh, always a burgh, of course: but the Aulton could have become like Old Sarum. Aberdeen in contrast went steadily on, for, as Professor Tawney says, the Reformation was good for trade. Surviving all the troubles caused by Kirk and Covenant, it acquired a university of its own; and, still the third town of Scotland, heard the wheels gather pace for the Industrial Revolution, heard with a ready ear and kept an eye open for all the chances.

There is for me a deep and enduring interest in the thought of Aberdeen at the end of the eighteenth century—the time when it began to break clean out of its ancient bounds. That of all past years is the time I would like to live in for a day or a year. I have no desire for the remote past, which was dark and troubled and stank of fish. But in the later half of the eighteenth century, when Aberdeen was drawing a new breath of the world's wonder, and industry had not become a burden—how I wish that for a little while I might be living then.

The contrast between the Aberdeen of 1758 and the present day is so great that it requires a considerable effort of imagination to call up any idea of what the town was like at that date, and indeed continued to be until the beginning of the last century . . . a small medieval town, for the most part built on three hills, the Gallow, Castle and St Katherine's hills.

"The chief streets were the Gallowgate, Broadgate and Castlegate. By the Gallowgate the town was entered from the north. . . . The Gallowgate Port, built in remote times, still stood at the northern entrance of the picturesque old street, which extended along the side of the Gallow Hill, the ground on the west side sloping down to the loch, then partially drained, and on the east rising to

* Old Ronald had two women he considered above all human kind. One was the Queen of Hell, that I will come to in "The Dark Side of the Moon". The other was the Laird of Stoneywood's wife. She was, he said, "a fair maisterful woman. Johnny, she made her pies in the skin o the Pape's back". Any parent will know what precise ideas and images that stirred up in the mind of a child of eight or nine. It was not until I read what Parson Gordon had to say about the dispersal of the cathedral parchments that I got a clue to the deed behind the fable. What wonders of old cathedral music may have made cases for the Lady Stoneywood's pies?

the ridge of the hill. The Gallowgate led into the Broadgate, which continued in a south-easterly direction, till brought to an abrupt conclusion by a large block of buildings facing its entrance, and leaving but a narrow exit, appropriately called the Narrow Wynd, giving access on the east to the Castlegate and on the west to the Shiprow.

"The Castlegate was more a handsome *place* than a street, in the centre of which stood the Cross surrounded by the 'Plainstanes', used both as a market stance and as a promenade by the citizens. The Castlehill was to the east of the Castlegate, and overlooked the harbour. In very early days, the kings of Scotland had a castle on this hill,* but it having, at one time, fallen into the hands of the English, who burned the town, the townsmen, when they retook it, razed it to the ground, to prevent it ever again being used against them, and in its place built a chapel to St Ninian. On the east side of this chapel there was, at this time, a night beacon attached, so that it served as a lighthouse for vessels entering · or leaving the harbour during the winter months.

"To the west of the Castlegate rose St Katherine's Hill, so called from the chapel to a saint of that name which at one time stood on the top of it. The base of this hill was for the most part fringed by houses, with gardens behind them, stretching to the top. . . . The narrow, steep lanes, for they can scarcely be called streets, which encircled St Katherine's Hill were, on the east and south sides, the Shiprow; on the west side, Putachie's Walk and Carnegie's Brae, which joined the Netherkirkgate at Wallace Neuk; while the Netherkirkgate ran along the north side and joined the Shiprow at the Round Table.

"Originally the town had not extended further west than the Upper and Nether Kirkgates; for the great church of St Nicholas stood outside the gates; but in time the gates were removed and some streets and lanes crept westward approaching the Denburn Valley. This, however, placed an effectual barrier to further extension. The descent on the east side to the pleasant green sward through which the Denburn, then a bright clear stream, wandered, was rather steep, but on the west the ground rose rapidly and much higher to the top of the Corby Heugh, along which Union Terrace is now built.

"This valley of the Denburn barred easy and convenient access to the town from south and west, making it most inconvenient. All roads coming from these directions converged into the Hardgate, and then plunged down the Windmill Brae, to reach the level

---

* The kings of Scotland had also a hunting forest at Stocket immediately outside and to the west of the medieval town. From the Castle of Aberdeen the Scottish kings pursued the hart by day and perhaps the hind by night.

of the stream, which was crossed by the Bow Bridge, or Brig, as it was called, and the town was entered by the 'Bow Brig' Street and the Green. The Green lay at the foot of St Katherine's Hill and to get to the upper part of the town, the Shiprow, steep, narrow and tortuous, was the easiest and most direct route. The citizen of today has only to read these facts to realise how much he owes to those who levelled part of St Katherine's Hill to lay out Union Street, and who spanned the Denburn by Telford's beautiful bridge . . . in 1803."*

The town was still confined within its natural bounds by the Denburn and the Loch and the country beyond was hardly inviting. For miles to the west it was still the remains of the Forest of Stocket, covered with the boulders that the glaciers had carried there, and overgrown with whins and shrubs. Dreadful roads led out through the farm touns and villages in the desolate country beyond. Public life also was confined, and perhaps cramped, by tradition. There was no nonsense of democracy or universal suffrage; but, instead, a proper high regard for privilege and a great care to make sure that privilege remained with those to whom by tradition it belonged. There were only two sorts of citizen that had any say in public affairs. First, and of small importance, the members of the incorporated trades— the Hammermen, Wrights and Coopers, Weavers, Bakers, Fleshers, Shoemakers and Tailors—skilled craftsmen, who had to pay big fines before they could be admitted brethren of their trades. Second, of great importance, the burgesses, who were the merchants and who often included country gentlemen among their number. The town council, which had the guiding of the town's affairs, was chosen from the burgesses, along with the representatives of the trades; and it was chosen by itself, which ensured the greatest continuity and the minimum of public interference. It was accountable to no one but itself, and it held the town in its pocket. Alas, the rich savour of privilege often bears a faint stink of corruption. The council managed the very extensive properties of the town, and transferred too many of them into the pockets of its members and friends, either by feuing them at small rents or selling them outright at a bargain. It was the custom of the time and there was no great shame in it. We may regret the properties, now immensely valuable, that were signed away so cheaply, but we can hardly denounce the old town council as fraudulent trustees for the common people, for I doubt if the burgesses thought they had any obligation to the common people in this matter. It is never very wise to judge the past by the standards of the present. In those days it was the possession of money and chattels that gave a man standing in the

* Margaret Knight and Mary Forbes in *Beattie and his Friends*, an excellent and valuable book about the eighteenth century in Aberdeen.

community and a say in its affairs; the baillies would have been scandalised by the idea that a man's only real property is in himself. On the contrary, they believed that a public body such as a town council, was not fit to manage property, or to develop it; and that the town lands would bring the greatest increase if conveyed over into private hands. They were probably quite sincere in that, for most beliefs contain a certain measure of self-interest.

Though Aberdeen was confined within its ancient limits and ruled by a close corporation, it may not have been a bad place to live in. There was a certain order and responsibility in public affairs. Local government was not creative, but it recognised a function to ensure fair-play. The incorporated trades set up standards and saw that they were observed. Before a man could be admitted a brother of his trade he had to produce a sample of his own work of a sufficient standard, and each trade elected overseers to ensure that no shoddy stuff was passed off to the people of Aberdeen or went furth the town to disgrace it. The town council were constantly making and revising regulations to restrain the natural wickedness of traders, who might corner supplies in a bad season or give short measure or otherwise show enterprise and initiative. After reading the rules of the trades and the decisions of the town council, you get the impression that all parts of business were very closely supervised for the common good. Regulations, controls, inspectors and general interference, which are supposed to be part of the sin of socialism and a product of the present day, may be nothing more than the rules of old discovered again, the rules that men must always make if they are to live in any comfort together.

I find something very attractive in the settled state of the town as it was then. There was the small body of merchant burgesses, some with country estates and others with valuable connections on the Continent. There were the master craftsmen, skilled and prosperous men. There were the professors in the University and the students, making yet another privileged corporation. And then there were the unprivileged common people. It may look like a division into two or several nations, but there was not yet an east end and a west end; everyone lived close—too close—together within the ancient bounds. That alone would have insured the common people against real degradation. There is no sign in the records that the poor had any great sense of injustice. They were undoubtedly poor, but they were certainly looked after—it was not till the glorious days of *laissez-faire* that the poor man was left to sink when he could no longer swim. Though the town council was not a democratic body, it could act very well when the need arose. In the eighteenth century the town of Aberdeen depended on the country for its food, and when the local harvest failed—which happened too often—the price of meal would have risen enormously, and there been great suffering in the town. At such times the magistrates tackled the situation like a Ministry of Food. They convened a meeting with the county gentlemen, and thereby discovered what stocks of meal would be available locally and what must be bought elsewhere. They then bought in a supply to carry the people on to harvest. At the same time they raised money by subscription to meet the differences between the prices at which they had to buy and the price their people could pay. Thus they prevented the making of undue profits by a few at the expense of the community. It was not charity: it was good government.

All government is an effort to catch up with affairs and bring them into some sort of order. Perhaps the reason why no government ever seems very efficient is that affairs are always a few moves ahead of it. In Aberdeen in the eighteenth century I think government may have been fairly adequate for the job in hand. The town was not perfect: it was defective in the matters of public health and plumbing; but a secondary thing like cleanliness does not become a religion till greater satisfactions have failed. There do seem to have been satisfactions— in handwork through long hours at a leisurely pace, in games, in gossip and in being really a part of a small and intimate community. Most of the people had no votes and probably had no desire for them; but then many of us take no heed of politics until our situation becomes intolerable and our spirits are profoundly troubled. I know: I'm like that myself; I've been a reluctant politician for the last twenty-five years.

It was Aberdeen's good fortune that the Industrial Revolution came to it gradually and in its least dreadful manifestations. There was neither coal nor iron by which venturers could defile the country with the spoil of mining and the smoke of manufacture, and leave ruin behind, once the wealth had been extracted. On the contrary, when Aberdeen's one mineral had been extracted, the land became more valuable. About 1764 Aberdeen stone was found very suitable for paving the streets of London. At first it was quarried at Torry, but that proved very expensive, so the contractors bargained with Aberdeen masons to buy dressed stones from them, the masons to find them where they could. The stone lay everywhere on the ground and under it. The owners of the land near the town got enough for the stone to pay a large part of the cost of bringing the land under the plough, and very soon were able to let for £5 an acre as market garden what had been useless waste. That was the beginning of the granite trade which attracted hundreds of poor country people to work in the quarries and which was to remain a great standby for the town for a hundred and fifty years. The Aberdeen stonemason became a highly skilled tradesman, unequalled at his trade. Fifty years ago it was quite common for Aberdeen masons to go to the United States in the spring, work there till the fall and then return to their families in the winter. No one would have suspected such a wonder in 1764; it was wonderful enough when stones had become money and the waste became market gardens.

The old Aberdeen trades of spinning and weaving began to develop. About 1749 a company of Aberdeen merchants, generally known as Leys, Masson and Company, started "on an extensive scale" the manufacture of linen threads and cloth. They found a good market for the thread in London, and so prospered that they built a spinning mill on the Don, where 240 spinning frames were driven by water power and the produce was 10,000 spindles of yarn weekly. By 1817 this firm gave constant employment to over one thousand families and continued to be an important part of the town's life till a black day in 1848 when the firm went bankrupt and the works closed down. The success of Leys, Masson attracted an English manufacturer called Maberly, who developed the works at Broadford, then outside the town. The Broadford Mills have continued in operation in the linen trade to this day, with varying fortunes, and Broadford mill girls are still regarded with a mixture of admiration and respect, or fear. Several other firms soon came into the trade, which grew to considerable size and value.

The woollen trade also expanded. There had been the long tradition of fine stocking knitting, and this was now developed on a mass-production scale by a firm called Alexander Hadden and Company, whose factory in the Green put out coarse stockings and cloth. In 1789 Mr Charles Baird, a silk dyer, brought two carding machines and four spinning jennies from England, and set up a factory on the banks of the Don at Stoneywood. His success encouraged others, especially in the county—for instance, Crombie Knowles and Company, who set up a mill at Cothal in Fintray about eight miles from the town. After Leys Masson failed, Crombie's took over the Grandholm Mills, where they have continued prosperous through the manufacture of tweed and been of great value to the town.

Cotton was introduced in 1779 by Gordon Barron and Company in a mill on the Don at Woodside. Twenty years later another concern, Forbes, Low and Company, opened a factory on the south side of the Denburn. By 1817 the cotton trade employed over four thousand workers, of whom fifteen hundred were children between nine and fifteen years old. Wages for skilled men seem to have been high, printers being able to make five shillings per day on piece work. Mr Kennedy, the Annalist, was a little worried by that, for high wages, by introducing habits of dissipation, might be a loss to the community.

The cotton trade has disappeared from Aberdeen, but paper-making, which began to develop at this time, has remained one of our chief industries. The first paperworks was established in 1696 or thereby at Gordon's Mills on the Don by Patrick Sandilands of Cotton, but probably did not long survive. In the 1760's Alexander Smith started a paperworks at Stoneywood on the Don, which was later carried on by his grandson, Alexander Pirie. The mill and the name remain famous in the paper trade. Papermaking caught on in Aberdeen, and the trade was developed at Mugiemoss, Donside, Port Elphinstone and Culter.

About the middle of the eighteenth century, as the shipping at the port increased, there was a demand for ropes, and soon four companies were making cordage, which gave work to 150 men and boys by 1817. About the end of the century shipbuilding, which must have been an immemorial craft at the seaside, began to develop along the lines of the shipbuilding yard. In 1817 Mr Kennedy reported that the *Castle Forbes*, a ship of 439 tons burthen, had been lately launched for the trade to India, the first ship built at Aberdeen for that purpose. *Castle Forbes* was the first of a lovely race that came to its finest flower in the glorious clipper *Thermopylæ*.

There were other works: several tanneries, one of which had been conducted on a considerable scale since the middle of the century; a nail works, and, especially in the new century, the manufacture of straw hats and pins, coaches, pianofortes and other musical instruments; several brickworks, foundries and a saw mill. Brewing had been a home industry, but in 1768 a large-scale brewery at Gilcolmston began its beneficent work, and it was joined in that work by the Devanha Brewery on the Dee, and the Aulton Brewery next door to King's College.

Besides all those manufactures, there was the fishing for salmon and for whales. The salmon fishing was very valuable—in 1798, a good season, the Dee gave 1,890 barrels of 4 cwt. each and the Don 1,667. The average was about 1,100 barrels from the Dee and 900 from the Don. The salmon were salted and sent to the Continent or pickled in vinegar and sent to London. But when sailings became frequent, and ice was available, most of the salmon went to London fresh. The salmon came up the river to the fishermen's doors; the whale was not so convenient in its habits. In 1753 a company with a capital of £8,000 was started to seek the leviathan where she sported. They sent two ships to Greenland in 1753, which returned with seven whales between them. That was enough to encourage a second venture, but it was not successful, for one ship was damaged by the ice and returned clean, while the other caught only two. The company was then dissolved, having lost much of its capital. In 1783 another company fitted out two ships, *Hercules* and *Latona* which had varying degrees of success, but the company did well enough in the end. By 1817 Aberdeen companies had 14 whalers that brought back

48 whales and 668 seals, yielding 688 tons of oil—besides an intolerable stink around the oil works.

Aberdeen did not forget its agricultural background. The state of the roads was an obstacle to trade, but if roads were bad, canals were fashionable. In 1785 a number of gentlemen in the town and the county got an Act of Parliament constituting them under the name of "The Company Proprietors of the Aberdeenshire Canal Navigation." Their canal from the harbour at Aberdeen to the Don at Inverurie took a long time in building and cost much more than had been estimated, but it was opened for navigation in 1807. The work, 18¼ miles long, rising to a summit of 168 feet in 5½ miles, with seventeen locks and a basin at each end, cost in all £43,000. It was a most valuable work, for it opened up some of the best parts of the county and brought others within far easier reach of the sea. It is not possible now by any exercise of the imagination to realise what a wonder that new, smooth transit was to people who had endured the unsprung wagons on the dreadful roads, or who had paid the carriers' charges from the sea. Things that had seemed an intolerable labour now became easy. Within ten years the canal had made a very great difference to the state of farming along its banks because of the ease with which the lime and manure that the land so hungered for could be brought up from the sea and the town, and the ease with which the corn and cheese could be sent down to the market in Aberdeen. Of course no blessing is ever unmixed, and there are always farmers who are carried away by a new thing. One writer in the Statistical Account of 1843 said the canal had made the getting of lime so easy that some farmers had applied too much of it—had, in fact, blown the guts out of their poor soil. A litttle harm was well paid for by much good. In another way the canal set the country people free from a heavy labour. Those that lived any distance from the coast had had to cast peats for firing, a tiresome job that came in summer when the hands would have been better employed in keeping down the weeds. Again and again in the Statistical Account of 1843 the writers say that, since the canal was opened, people used sea coal instead of peats; they were better employed keeping the turnips clean. The canal never made money of itself and the proprietors were glad to sell it as a permanent way when the railways came along; but it paid fine dividends indirectly to the landowners whose rents had benefited, and to the merchants of Aberdeen who had got so much trade by it.

That was how one old town began to grow at the impulse of the Industrial Revolution. The change in sixty years from 1758 to 1817 must have been very remarkable, and the figures of population, however unreliable, give some idea of the extent of it. Mr Kennedy gave the population in 1643 as 9,000. By 1707, he reckoned, it had fallen to 6,000, as a result of the religious troubles, and of the plague in in 1647 by which 1,700 people died. In 1755, Dr Webster estimated the population at 10,488. In 1801 it was put at 13,057 for the parish of St Nicholas, in which all the old town lay; but by then there were many houses going up outside the boundary. In 1811 the population of Aberdeen was 21,639, with another 3,570 in the new parts; in all 25,209. Mr Kennedy estimated that in 1817 the total must be 28,000. In the ten years between 1801 and 1811, it may have doubled. Such a sudden growth might have produced many strains and tensions in the life of the town, but there is not much evidence that it did so. The reason may be that the increase came from the country districts of the north-east. The Irish never ventured so far north, and Aberdeen was a little too cold for the West Highlander. The Aberdonians, though greatly multiplied, remained true to type. That has given the town and people a very distinctive character. But is it a blessing? I sometimes wonder if a strong infusion of the west would not have given us a little more imagination. But at other times I am not so sure. What exactly have the Celts and the Gaels, those so imaginative tribes, done with the old Scots city of Glasgow?

There was, however, another reason why the growth of population did not produce any great social strain or tension. When it became obvious that the town must break out of its old bounds, the development was done by the town council, under two excellent provosts, Alexander Hadden and Thomas Leys. The work was planned with imagination, and carried out in good order. To allow expansion two streets were to be driven west and north from the Castlegate. It was a big labour to be undertaken by what was still a small community. St Katherine's Hill had to be removed, two streets bridged over, the ground made up on the south side and finally a bold granite arch thrown across the Denburn before Union Street could extend into the level ground to the west. As a complement, King Street was opened for a short distance to the north. At that time, too, the town council, glorying in expansion, financed great works at the harbour, to build quays and a tidal basin with a lock. Unfortunately their vision was wider than their means. The expense at the harbour proved endless and, added to the money spent on the new streets, brought the council into serious difficulties. If Aberdeen was not quite bankrupt, at least its liabilities exceeded its assets; and the interest payable was more than the council's revenue at a time when the possibilities of putting a something extra on the rates was very dimly understood, and, when tried, very grimly resisted. The embarrassment was temporary: the town council had over-invested in some very sound securities.

Aberdeen was fortunate in having three men who could dignify the new streets with proper buildings. The native architects John Smith and Archibald Simpson discovered a style proper to granite, and John Gibb, of Rubislaw Quarry, supplied them with the beautifully dressed stone their designs required. Those three gave the town some fine streets and buildings and set a standard of building in granite from which most later work has been a sad and, in extreme cases, a comic decline.

Archibald Simpson was the son of a merchant and born in the Guestrow, a narrow street behind Broad Street, most of which has been cleared away as a slum. Even in 1790, when the Guestrow was a fashionable place, it must have been cramped, dark and insalubrious. Any architect born there might well have grown up to desire an ampler style. When Archibald was twenty he went to London, where he worked under Robert Lugar, then celebrated as the author of *Villa Architecture*. Archibald went on to Rome, where the study of the ancient buildings finally determined his style. He returned to Aberdeen when he was twenty-three and practised there for the rest of his life.

It was a fortunate thing that he had been influenced by the severe and noble Roman style, for no other could have better suited the stone he had to work with. Granite is hard and heavy and has a monumental quality. By its nature it is a very geometrical, not a malleable thing at all; and in building it demands severe lines and exactly proportioned masses. Decoration must be subtle and refined. It needs economy; it is no good for whimsies and extravagances; it is the native stone of Aberdeen.

Simpson had the style for the stone. The Music Hall in Union Street, which is usually considered his best work, shows a perfect proportion. It had harmony among its parts. It is in proportion to its surroundings and to the town itself. It is solid; yet it has lightness; and it has got a grace by the most economical means. There are many other examples of his public works—the old Infirmary in Woolmanhill, the older part of the Girls' High School, the Medico-Chirurgical building in King Street, the Post Office in Market Street, which show his sympathy with the stone and tact as to site and purpose. To my mind the most attractive of his work is the head office of the North of Scotland Bank in the Castlegate. He had there the problem of a corner site in the main square of the town, a great temptation for an architect to let himself go. But how modestly and rightly he did the job, with the plain, elegant frontages to the Castlegate and King Street and the rounded portice on four pillars in the corner, on a lower roof line than the rest of the building; the portico being surmounted by the figure of a woman sitting on a beast, the Spirit of Aberdeen resting on Deposit Receipts. There is nothing in the town to compare with it for strength and grace and tact. What a safe and charming place in which to keep an overdraft with sympathetic bankers. And how heavy the Municipal Buildings next door, baronial and repelling, as if designed to be a fortress in which public officials might immure themselves against public interference.

Simpson was a town planner at the end of a great age of planning —remember Bath and Nash's London and the New Town of Edinburgh. He left a complete and lovely example of domestic planning in Bon-Accord Square and Bon-Accord Crescent. The curve of the crescent on the top of a slope and facing the sun is intimate and completely satisfying. Other examples of this sort are Rubislaw Place and Victoria Street, and Marine Terrace in Ferryhill. Of single houses No. 28 Albyn Place is a little treasure. You can see how much the standard of taste declined after Simpson's time if you compare No. 28 with some of its neighbours, especially the one near Queen's Cross that looks like a granite hedgehog. Simpson built many country houses, some of which have been destroyed, but Park House, which can be seen across the river from the South Deeside Road, is an exquisitely proportioned thing, the outward expression of an inward grace. Examples of his public work out of town are the Gordon Schools at Huntly and Anderson's Institution and St Giles' Kirk in Elgin.

His works outside the classical style include St Andrew's Episcopal Church and the East Kirk of St Nicholas, which may have their points, but I have never been able to enjoy them. His group of churches opposite the Art Gallery is an interesting piece. When the Kirk of Scotland broke in two in 1843, buildings were required urgently and cheaply for the new congregations. Simpson produced something truly remarkable—the walls being rubble, the windows faced with brick, and the whole thing surmounted by a brick tower; in Aberdeen. The tower is a masterpiece, slender and aspiring.

For those who like to reflect on the mutations of taste, there is wonder in Marischal College. When Simpson was commissioned to build what is now the older part, it is said that he intended something in his classical manner, but his clients insisted on Tudor. He was too true an Aberdonian to quarrel with the customer, but he saw to it that Tudor granite was more granite than Tudor. In later days, when the east side of Broad Street had been removed, it was replaced by the present front of the College. This twentieth-century work cannot be described; it must be seen. Proud Aberdonians say it is the finest granite building in the world; it is certainly the most wonderful —the wonder being that such a hard and dignified stone could be so fretted and hacked about and twisted up into screws and pinnacles. I have often wondered what Simpson would say if he could see it. Now I think I know. There is a story that Simpson went to look at the Scott Monument in Edinburgh, a very spiky piece of Gothic. Asked what he thought about it, he said, "It minds me on a fun buss"; that is, a whin bush. He might see the same familiarity in the Marischal College.

There remains one more building, the New Market. On a difficult, sloping site he built a utilitarian building that, when looked at from the Green, has the mass and the proportion of a small Roman theatre. The market is divided into three parts—a basement for the sale of fish; a main hall for grocers and butchers; and a gallery all round for the fine arts. Only the shell is Simpsons, for the place was burned out, but it is a very adequate shell. Go into the basement on a summer day and notice how cool the fishmongery, as if a perpetual salty wind blew in from Fittie. Go into the hall among all the mortality of ducks and cockerels, sheep and prime black heifers, the cold jellied tripe and the mealy puddings, the icecream sundaes and the market candy— see them all on the verge of dissolution and notice how cool and inoffensive it is. Look down from the gallery and notice how the crowd, even on a busy day, move easily around, and their noise—even the shrill female voices, even the brisk and slapping sales talk, even the hacking and sawing and the smacking of pale hands upon paler fat— all those busy, gossiping, esurient noises, are subsumed to a pleasant murmur under the vast umbrella of the roof.

It seems to me that Simpson was not only a great Aberdonian— he was also a typical one. He was not an original artist. He did not invent anything. He did, however, most excellently use his means to produce the end he was paid for. He was a practical genius, and practical genius expresses itself in an economy of effort to achieve the result. It may be that economy—the nice adjustment of means to ends—is the very heart of loveliness. At any rate I wish some later architects in Aberdeen had practised it and spared us their granite contortions. We are beginning to realise that the inward economy of a classical style can go with an inward harmony; that a building economical to build may be lovely and economical to live in.

While Simpson was building terraces for the well-to-do there was not at this early time any building of workers' rows, of the kind that were slums before the roofs were on—no back-to-back and none of the other devices for housing the greatest possible numbers on the smallest extent of land. Indeed, there has been very little, if anything, of that sort in Aberdeen. Good houses were built on new streets over towards the loch, of which Berry Street remains an interesting example. Then, as the well-to-do moved to Golden Square, their substantial old houses in the Guestrow and the Gallowgate were taken over by the artisans. As those old houses became more and more crowded and decayed, they did slowly decline into slums, and by the beginning of this century Aberdeen had some choice ones. But it is only fair to remember that they had come down from some considerable dignity. Nearly all of them have been cleared away. Cumberland House in the Guestrow remained till recently in the full degradation that could overtake a fine house, but the tenants have now been placed elsewhere and the town council are restoring the house. So, while the sort of houses built for workers in Aberdeen was hardly perfect, a certain decency and order have always been observed.

BOOM AND BUST

Throughout the early part of the nineteenth century Aberdeen developed at a steady rate in spite of the booms, slumps and financial alarms that were the growing pains of capitalism or the first pangs of dissolution, according to your point of view. There was plenty of money about, and a spirit of optimism that sometimes led the citizens into rash speculation. No story of an industrial town would be complete without that imaginative artist the financier, an inescapable functionary of private enterprise who acted as the prophet of the future and as its midwife, hurrying on the birth by shock tactics that sometimes killed the patient. Aberdeen found one such in Alexander Anderson, but again, Aberdeen was fortunate, for Anderson had a practical genius and most of his schemes were essentially sound, and paid in the end, whatever troubles they met on the way. Some of them met plenty.

Anderson was a lawyer and partner in the firm of Adam and Anderson, a partnership that recalls Box and Cox and Howe and Hummell, though much more reputable than either. By 1830 this firm was building up a very valuable connection as factors and legal agents to the local gentry. Because the gentry were then drawing high rents from their improved estates the connection gave the firm an access to free capital in search of investment. Adam and Anderson were very willing to oblige. In 1836 they were promoting a fire and life insurance company, now the very successful Northern Assurance. In the same year the North of Scotland Bank, conceived in the same office, began business with Anderson as one of the directors. Anderson was showing himself a man with a boundless sense of possibilities, being perhaps one of those through whom progress forces itself upon a reluctant world. His office floated a £50,000 company to build the New Market. In 1844, displeased with Aberdeen's gaslight company, which rooked the public, and perhaps wishing to have the rookery in their own hands, they floated a rival at £50,000 and by relentless competition forced a merger, after the fashion of the young lady and the tiger. Those were appetisers for the great railway jamboree. Railway fever was late in coming to the north-east, but when it did come Adam and Anderson were ready. In 1844 they produced a scheme for a line between Aberdeen and Forfar to join the Arbroath and Forfar line already in operation. They floated the Aberdeen Railway Company at £900,000 on a high tide, which, by the end of the first year, carried the shares to double what the holders had paid for them. In 1845 Adam and Anderson issued a prospectus for a

Great North of Scotland Railway from Aberdeen to Inverness with several branches. The capital was £1,100,000 and the company floated on a real spring tide, the shares being subscribed for seven times over. In the same year they announced plans for lines from Dyce into Buchan, and from Inverurie to Macduff, for which they asked £700,000. That autumn they announced the Deeside Railway and the Alford Valley line, at £100,000 each. Still in that wonderful year, the yet more wonderful firm floated an exchange company at £500,000. But that was perhaps going a little too far. Exchange companies were fashionable at the time—a rival was founded in Aberdeen in the same year—and their function was purely speculative; the shareholders exchanged their cash for stock and the directors lent the money principally to gamble in railway shares. Speculative certainly; useless perhaps; but business all the time. There seemed no end to profit.

These were very, very large financial matters for what was still a small community in the far north, and although people may have subscribed for more shares than they could pay, knowing they would not be allocated all they subscribed for, the sums do indicate there had been a great growth of capital in fifty years. Not only in the town; much of the capital came from the country gentlemen and some from the prosperous new farmers.

But trouble was treading close on the financiers' tails. In 1847 there were serious failures among English companies; a cold wind blew north, and railway building was held up through a sudden scarcity of cash. The Great North of Scotland and the Aberdeen Railway were thus temporarily embarrassed. But children of the same father must help each other. The railways and the North Bank had both sprung from Anderson's engendering brain, so in a brotherly way the Bank loaned £73,350 to Adam and Anderson for the use of the railway. There was more to follow. Then, just as all affairs were in a delicate position, the fabric of such elegant improvisation collapsed in 1848. Suddenly and without warning, the two big textile firms of Leys Masson and Hadden and Company failed, throwing 3,000 persons out of work. That caught the directors of the North Bank in a very awkward position. When they counted up their losses they found that the textile companies had cost them £160,000. That might have been written off as fair wear and tear; but when they made a full examination of their estate, they found that their manager had borrowed £44,000, while advances, *listed as doubtful*, to other parties amounted to £69,000. In addition, £200,000 had been advanced to "a legal firm" and half of it was not only unsecured but presumably bad. The capital of the Bank was only £383,000. Greater enterprises have been sunk by a smaller loss and the directors of the North Bank might very reasonably have decided to close their doors.

Anderson's position must have been in great danger. The Exchange Company had disappeared with the railway boom. The Bank was in a precarious state. There was a certain breath of scandal. But he had a greatness in him. He had faith in his own schemes and he could give courage to his associates. Though he had to retire from his directorship of the Bank he armed the directors with resolution, so that they carried on and rebuilt their fortunes within a very few years. His firm repaid all the Bank had advanced them. In spite of the fact that his sins were never forgotten, he kept his position as the leader in affairs, for he had the imagination and the courage and the will to be a leader. Being firm in his own mind he did not worry about public opinion; he made it.

Although he had resigned from the Bank, he very quickly reasserted his dominant position in railway building. That pre-eminence was challenged by another Aberdeen lawyer called John Duncan, a challenge that led to a glorious free-for-all in which the whole of the north-east joined. Duncan proposed a railway from Aberdeen to Peterhead and Fraserburgh by the coast. Anderson at once revived his schemes for a Buchan Railway from Dyce, and the Alford Valley Railway, which he had been promoting in 1845. All railway schemes had to be sanctioned by Parliament, which remote senate was supposed to give effect to the will of the local majority. Duncan and Anderson stirred up the voices of democracy, so that they could be heard in London. They could certainly be heard in Aberdeenshire. It was like an election with Duncan and Anderson as candidates. Their supporters held meetings in the towns and villages at which they praised their own schemes and damned their opponents. They organised petitions, Duncan getting 11,000 signatures to Anderson's 9,000. Orators lashed up the lowest feelings of the mob and, carried sky-high on the head of that emotion, thundered slanders which, in yet more frenzied meetings, called out more slanderous replies. At last Duncan went too far and suggested in print that Anderson and his friends had their hands in the till of the North Bank, right up to the elbows. Anderson and his friends would have treated that as just one more shot in the battle—they had probably said as much, or worse, about Duncan. But the North Bank was outside the fight and refused to accept this handful of gratuitous dirt, being conscious of financial virtue since 1848. They initiated a legal action against Duncan, as did four officials of the railway company. When the four slandered gentlemen were awarded damages of £250 apiece, Duncan withdrew all his charges. Anderson's schemes then went through. The king was still secure on his throne; even the stirring up of old financial mud had not shaken his innate authority. In 1859 he was elected Provost of the town.

He must have been very much the man of the time and the place he lived in. He had the tireless energy and optimism of the Victorian business men who knew that the world was wide and that money waited everywhere for the clever man to pick it up. He did not invent anything new in financial rackets; and I cannot see that he was even a gambler. His ideas were good. His gaslight company, the New Market, the Assurance Company, the North Bank, the railways, all became useful things and paid their dividends.

Anderson had the mastery that comes from superb competence in practical things, plus a sure knowledge of the people he had to deal with. Once, while Provost, he thought himself dishonoured by some resolution that the council had made in his absence, so he immediately resigned from the chair and from the council. At the resulting election of a councillor, he stood as candidate, was re-elected to the council, and by the council to the chair again. The man who had created whole boards of directors could easily handle a mere town council. As a member of the council he carried through some large schemes of improvement—the bringing of an adequate supply of water from the Dee, the rebuilding of the Grammar School, and the building of the present Town House—though that last was perhaps hardly an improvement from the æsthetic point of view.

The tough native spirit carried Aberdeen through the bitter days of 1848—that and the sound bases of the town's economy. Already the industries were so diverse that the failure of one could not desolate the town. By the middle of the century the granite trade had graduated from paving stones into a far nobler business. An African traveller had brought back from Egypt specimens of polished granite found in the tombs of the kings. These inspired Alexander McDonald, an Aberdeen granite merchant, to try his hand on the local stone. After many trials and much hard labour he discovered a method and in 1832 he sent the first polished granite headstone to London. That stone—Aberdeen's Stone of Destiny—was erected in Kensal Green and no doubt it stands there today, for nothing could destroy a granite headstone, and no one would wish to steal it. McDonald's work may not have added much to the sum of beauty in the world, but it did bring wages and profits to Aberdeen. Not all of the polished granite went for headstones. It became fashionable as pillars and panels in official buildings, where it can look very handsome indeed. A few columns of Kemnay granite, dignified and cold, are just the thing to strike awe into a debtor and condition him to receive the bank manager's final blow. It was popular in clubs of the more magnificent kind, perhaps because the members could not strike matches or pencil rude rhymes on it. But it is not a domestic creature. For the high ceremonial—yes, indeed, in great spaces where one can get well away from it. But even there I feel that the polishing is a mistake, especially of the grey and silver granite. There is an artificiality about the polished stone; a dead alien surface over the austere but living face that removes the stone from contact. Polishing brings nothing out of the stone, but imprisons its virtue as behind a plate of glass.

The Aberdeen stonecutters got a wonderful proficiency in the dressing and carving of the unpolished stone, wonderful in the way that the façade of Marischal College is wonderful, in being just a little too much. There was no nonsense about finding a style to suit the medium. When the stonecutter set to make an angel for a deceased wife's tombstone he did not consider what angels would look like if they were by nature granite; not at all, he knew the customer expected a realistic angel like a deceased wife and he gave the customer just that. When the stonecutter got pneumatic tools capable of delivering many thousands of strokes a minute, he could make a reproduction of anything. He could: and he did. How many hundreds of memorials were raised after the 1914–18 war, topped by the figure of a soldier leaning on a rifle reversed and immured for ever in a granite kilt, exactly reproduced. The things that have been done to granite! But, finely squared, it's a noble thing and fit for noble purposes.

Towards the end of the century the town, which had been famous for salmon in medieval times, found a new source of great wealth on the blue water. It is curious that Aberdeen had not greatly cultivated the sea fishing before this. Whaling never came to any great importance, nor did herring fishing. For some reason it needed the trawler to inspire the Aberdonian. But as soon as the trawler had been tried out from the Tyne, Aberdeen took it up with great enthusiasm. Perhaps because the trawler is such a practical method of catching fish. Most methods of fishing are rather primitive: either you throw out a hook and hope the fish will try to swallow it; or, as in herring fishing, you hang out a long curtain of net and hope the herrings will catch their gills in it. In both cases too much depends on the unconscious and unpredictable co-operation of the fish. Now the trawl is very different. To put the matter very simply, the trawl is a bag with a wide, open mouth and a narrow, closed end. If you hang it over the blunt end of your boat, you can steam away for hours, sweeping the ocean, and any fish you meet or overtake is yours if it comes within the wide, mouth of the net, unless it is small enough to slip through the meshes, in which case it is not worth having anyway. The trawl seems the most efficient way man has invented of catching fish and the only improvement worth while is one once suggested to me by a gentleman in a public house, that the trawler should suck in the sea at the sharp end and pass it out again at the blunt end, retaining all the fish, wreckage and bottles with messages in them. Even when that idea is made perfect, the trawl will remain the second best thing.

About 1880 the trawl had been tried out from the Tyne and the

Wear, mostly from tugboats that were unemployed at the time because of the slump in fishing. In 1882 an Aberdeen syndicate bought an old tug called *Toiler* at Dublin for £1,550 and on March 23rd of that year she made her first paying trip across the bay, the catch being three boxes of haddocks, worth 37s. In the first month *Toiler* took over £200 and at the end of the first year the syndicate paid a dividend of 100 per cent. There must have been a lot of high dividends in trawling, but never another to equal the first. It was not long before the first real trawler came from an Aberdeen shipyard and the boom was on. Trawlers, always bigger and better found, went longer trips after the white fish—to the Faroes, to Iceland, to Greenland waters. They stayed out eight days; they stayed out three weeks. They brought back not three boxes of haddocks but a hundred tons of halibut, plaice, cod and all that sort. Trawling thus became something entirely different from herring catching. The herring drifter remained and still remains a share venture and there is no large-scale capital in the catching side. The trawler from the beginning attracted the joint stock company. Again, unlike the herring trade, the white-fishers made their big money in the fresh market—if any fish can be called fresh that was caught three weeks ago off Spitzbergen; but then the British public likes its fresh fish well matured, as connoisseurs like their game.

The trawling was another new draught of life to Aberdeen. The shipyards began to specialise in trawlers and took an immediate pre-eminence which they have never lost. There was a new demand for ice and bunker coal and all ship's stores. A fish market was required, big enough to be a mortuary for the northern seas. A million hundred-weights of fish had to be handled on shore—requiring porters and carters and ice and boxes for sending the fresh fish to market. That brought a lot of work to the box-makers. There was work too for curers, making the smoked white fish called finnan haddocks after the little village of Findon where the art was perfected long ago. And—although we are inclined to overlook them—there were also the trawler crews. These came originally from the off-shore fishermen of Fittie and Torry; but, as the Aberdeen trawler fleet grew rapidly, outsiders, some from the small fishing villages, were attracted into the town, and not only increased the population but strengthened its intimate contact and sympathy with the whole north-east. Within twenty years Aberdeen had become one of the three biggest white-fishing ports, the others being Grimsby and Hull; the air was subtly permeated with the smell of fish; and that smell was said to be strongest in Queen's Road and Rubislaw Den, where the richest people dwell.

No industry can work by itself alone; it requires auxiliaries to give it the tools; so engineering developed in Aberdeen, auxiliary to the textiles, shipbuilding, granite working and agriculture, until it became of the first importance. For instance, William McKinnon set up an engineering shop in the Windy Wynd in 1798 from which he supplied castings to manufacturers in the district. In the middle of the next century the firm began to make plantation machinery—for coffee, cocoa, sugar and rice—and now undertake to build machinery for any such process work, even shredding suet, making cement and washing diamonds. A consequent of mining granite is the production of mechanical handling gear by John M. Henderson and Company. The aerial cableway called the blondin, after the famous tight-rope walker, was first used in Kemnay Quarry for moving stone and has now been adapted for heavy handling on public works construction where there is a long carry, for excavating and for coal storage. Henderson's have also supplied tackle to goldfields in Klondike, phosphate beds in the Pacific, sugar estates in the West Indies and oilfields in the Near East. These are only two examples to show how a highly specialised engineering grew out of the industrial needs of the town.

By the early years of the present century the pattern of Aberdeen industry was well defined and has not changed in any material particular. It depends on a quite remarkable variety of trades. Though the Aberdonian is inclined to be a specialist, the community has not specialised in anything except skill of the hands and the good, clear organising brain. That proved a great blessing in the bad days to come. During the 'twenties and 'thirties there was unemployment and suffering in Aberdeen, but those incidents of capitalism bore less heavily on Aberdeen than on some larger and wealthier towns. Dundee, for instance, had put too much of its money on jute; and when jute became a bad trade through Indian competition, Dundee became almost a depressed area. Clydeside suffered at the same time because it had specialised too much on heavy engineering.

It was the variety of trades that saved Aberdeen. In those worst of times, the diet of the common people was fish and chips: Aberdeen trawlers brought in great masses of the fish and Aberdeen merchants handled a lot of the potatoes. Whatever the times people die, and in bad times they perhaps die more willingly; but good times or bad, their heirs think it a duty to raise some memorial: there was always some demand for granite headstones. There was always a demand for paper. There was, in fact, always some sort of demand for the things that were made in Aberdeen. Knitwear was becoming fashionable—and Aberdeen had knitwear firms. The diesel engine was coming in—an Aberdeen firm began to produce diesel motors. Mechanical handling was becoming very important—an Aberdeen firm had already a long experience in handling gear for the quarries. Agriculture was in a depressing state, but the agriculture of the north-east never lost heart and Aberdeen had always a great bulk of stuff to handle even though the margin of profit may have been very small. . . . . Aberdeen came through those bad years tolerably well and proved how wise it is to have small eggs in many small baskets rather than have all your capital in one egg, however great and golden.

Looking over the past and the present one may have a reasonable confidence that Aberdeen industries will survive for quite a long time to come. The thing which strikes one as most outstanding about them is just their power of survival. Two hundred years ago the town lived by fishing, textiles, papermaking and the usual crafts, and by acting as a market for the countryside. Nothing has changed very much, except in degree. There is still fishing; there are still textiles—though cotton and jute have come and gone, linen and woollens remain; the paper mills are larger and busier than ever. The granite trade, though reduced, maintains a place. The combworks, a very old-established business, has turned over, very successfully, to plastics. Out of these the engineering has developed in various specialised ways. And Aberdeen is still the market town for the countryside. That market is worth more to the town than a stranger might think. Aberdeenshire is by far the biggest arable county in Scotland: and by far the largest part of the produce is sold through Aberdeen. Even more important for the town is the bulk of stuff those thousands of farmers buy. There is work for Aberdeen in making fish meal, grinding cereals and compounding food for cattle, pigs and poultry. To supply thousands of tons of fertilisers, there is a sulphuric acid plant at Sandilands and several big mills where fertilisers are compounded and granulated, ready for the fields. The auction marts pass through some thousands of animals every week. There are a dozen firms or more supplying seeds and machines, including tractors. Curiously enough with such a big farming district, and one now so well mechanised, Aberdeen engineers have not taken as much advantage of that market as one might expect. Threshing mills made by Garvie and by Barclay, Ross and Hutchison have been known far outside for some time. Other firms had a reputation for ploughs and other horse-drawn implements. But Aberdeen firms have not been very prominent in the recent development of farm machinery: indeed more has been done by some country firms, such as Sellars of Huntly and Shearers of Turriff. However, Tullos, working in a handsome war-time factory, show promise of developing the kind of machines that make big business. Somebody should do it: Aberdeen craftsmen have the skill and north farmers have the will and the money to buy it.

Trawling is the one industry that seems to be in trouble. The Aberdeen trawling has depended on nearness to the North Sea fishing grounds and cheap transport to the south. Now those grounds have been over-fished and transport is no longer cheap. Trawlers must go on longer voyages to far distant grounds. In that Aberdeen should be no worse situated than its rivals, Hull and Grimsby, but, for once, the Aberdonians have slept in. Hull and Grimsby owners have put some of their profits into new and bigger boats, equipped with every device for better fishing and economical handling. Aberdeen owners have not. The Aberdeen fleet is now too old and the boats perhaps too small to compete on equal terms. It is a curious story—curious to find in Aberdeen where so many old trades have flourished for so long, partly because some of the profits were always put back. And it is interesting that the trawling was the one trade which expanded suddenly and produced enormous profits. Perhaps the profits came too easily. As to the future—all is obscure in the financial entanglements of the catching and the shore sides of industry. Fish salesmen, curers, chandlers, ice manufacturers, coal merchants may have shares in the catching side, and it is possible that there is still a lot of money in the industry, though it is not being used where it is most needed—in building new trawlers. The industry will not continue very long unless it is so directed.

There are other trades in Aberdeen—printing, paint-making, the compounding of patent medicines, canning of fish and vegetables. There may be others: there must be. Somewhere, unobtrusively, an engineer, or a business man with an idea, is developing in a modest way something that in fifty years may be known in many places, though not in Aberdeen. At least I hope so: that is the way it has been:

> The gains that we have won and kept
> Were not attained by advertising:
> While others vaulted we have stept
> By sound finance and early rising.

Nothing remains of the medieval Aberdeen except the ground plan of the older streets. That is not for surprise, because houses were built of wood and clay, with thatched roofs: and what fire did not destroy, weather decayed. Temporary houses are no new thing in Scottish towns. None of the public buildings remain. The Kirk of St Nicholas had to be rebuilt, the Greyfriars and the Blackfriars were removed, and the remote past has gone as if it had never been. There is not now much left from the sixteenth and seventeenth centuries, except empty spaces along the Shiprow, the Guestrow and the Gallowgate, and to the north of Castlehill whence in my own time the houses of the old merchants were swept away as slums. And what slums they were. Shuttle Lane and Peacock's Close were tremendous places forty years ago. Their names were names to conjure with, and conjure is the word, for some of the women who lived in them were as near like witches as latter-day mortals could be.

I remember well those fearful citizens. When I was five or six and thereabout my grandfather grew perhaps ten or fifteen acres of potatoes every year. Then, as now, potatoes were lifted by casual labour—and our casual workers were the dragons of Peacock's Close and Shuttle Lane. A dozen of them came out every morning in two taxis, driven furiously by men in fear of their honour, and even of their lives. They got, as I remember, danger money for the job. The women were of all ages, but they had some things in common—high, tearing voices; a vocabulary limited in everything except scolding, swearing and obscenity, but in these it would have been a lexicographer's manna from heaven; their clothes were old and various and stank, and they were very, very natural after their fashion. Every morning there was a tremendous row before they started work; a great screaming from them, a great swearing in a rude baritone from my uncle Charles; the whole thing working up to a climax in the rudest gestures of final contempt. Then some older and wiser woman said, "It's time I had ma mornin'," and produced a bottle of whisky from out of her petticoats, and others did the same and passed them round till everybody had had their mornin' and the work proceeded, and proceeded happily all day, with much conversation of the directer kind. As a little boy of five or six or seven I loved them all very much. Now and then at the break time, some woman would cry "Daena dae that" or "Daena say that in front o the bairn", but I couldn't see what the fuss was about, for everything they said and did was exciting, just as the burns were exciting when they were in spate. Sometimes an old harridan with whisky on her breath and the smell of immemorial filth on her clothes took me into her bosie and kissed me and told me about the chamber pots they emptied on the policemen's heads in Shuttle Lane, and that was as good as a fairy-tale from the shores of a resounding sea. One day the foreman, a gallus chield I hated, took some liberty with one of the women at the dinner hour and got his face harrowed with bloody weals.

Great ladies: they were my friends. I had in them confidence, and for them love. Perhaps love of human kind was the only decency left to them. They had that in plenty. And they had a something else that was perhaps truly of Aberdeen. Their week at the potatoes was more than a way of getting some extra money for whisky. They enjoyed it, even when the days were wet and the fields were glaury. They enjoyed being in the country. There was an elderly woman called Meggie, the one who was always first to bring out the cutter, a grey-haired creature, soaked and sodden in whisky, who used on fine, dry days to rub the mealy earth between her hands and say to me, "It's like new meal from the mill." I remember those hands yet, feeling the texture, the sap and the coolness of the earth. As I discovered a long time after, she came from a farm, had been seduced and left, had taken her shame to town where it throve and, as they would have said in those days, completely ruined her. When she could not get whisky she drank methylated spirit, which makes a dead furnace in the wame, but every autumn, drawn by a homing instinct, she came out from Shuttle Lane for a short contact with the sane and fruitful fields. I think that some others came for that reason, because the heart beat an echo of a country heritage, and the circling blood hungered for the country air, and the senses for the country sounds and smells. And perhaps even in Peacock's Close they remembered the harvest, and in their hearts remembered its ancient wonder, and, even in a time when the poor were nothing, knew their right in it. The potato-gatherers were well paid according to the ideas of the time, for my grandfather was always generous with what he never had; but over and above their pay the women demanded potatoes. Every night they took home bags and baskets with a stone or two. I would not say that the potatoes were more to them than the money, and no one would have dared to pay them entirely in kind, but it seems to me now that the potatoes had an occult value. To some at least the potato-gathering had an emotional value for the slum dwellers, reminding them of the country slums from which their people had come, and giving them for a little while that contact with nature without which the spirit must wholly die.

The old closes have gone: and the sort of people they produced have gone too. I am not to say that everyone in Aberdeen has become civilised within a generation, or that every house is fit to live in. But there is no longer the same weight of degradation. There may, indeed, be less of it than in most industrial towns.

From the later years of last century and the earlier years of the present one we have inherited that commonest feature of Aberdeen's architecture, the tenement. I think it is fair to the speculative builders to say that tenement was always rather above the general standard of the time—not difficult, perhaps, considering what that standard was. At first, the Aberdeen model was a two- or three-storey building, of which the top storey was an attic. There were two tenants on each floor, served by a common stair. A small drying green lay at the back, with a line of privies and wash-houses. About the end of the last century an improved type had a water closet at the turn of the stair between each floor, each closet being shared by two tenants—a sociable thing, or a cause of bitter strife, according to the users. There are thousands of those tenements in the city, easily distinguished by the closets projecting at the back. The half flats consist usually of two or three rooms: a kitchen with a bed recess and a sink in the window— a sink with a graceful goose-necked tap—and one or two other rooms; if two, one is likely to be a parlour full of furniture, as uncomfortable as Sunday clothes and much less often used. The tenement streets are a little grim in the relentless regularity of the granite, the houses are a little too like boxes to keep human beings in. The outer wood-work shows signs of hard wear and weather and one may speculate doubtfully about the state of the interior. But the squared granite retains a dour dignity which· a little redeems even the greyest street.

There is one thing more to notice—in a hundred years of building a certain order has always been maintained. At the end of the war in 1918 Aberdeen was a compact little city even though more than 150,000 people lived in it. Between the wars it was due to expand as the population increased and the old slums had to be removed. It did expand, but fortunately it was not allowed to sprawl. It has been Aberdeen's good fortune to find at need a man who has the right idea, and to set him in some authority. At this time Aberdeen found Henry Alexander, a man who had time, money and taste and an appetite for public affairs. As a member of the town council and as Provost he inspired a plan for the expansion of Aberdeen, one of the first effective schemes of town-planning in Britain in recent times. Thus the town grew in an orderly way south, and west and north—there was a small obstacle to the east. These new parts are examples of good planning in the matters of lay-out and of shops and schools. Unfortun-ately the planning did not cover the design of the individual houses, and some speculative builders filled out the new streets with angular boxes for middle-class people, each standing, rather assertively, in its little bit of garden. No doubt some of them are very comfortable to live in, and their owners are very proud of them, but they are not so good to look at. A good design might have cost no more, and been a whole lot better to see. Perhaps I am too fussy; but I think that our colonies of well-sited aluminium houses are far less offensive to the eye than some streets of bungalows put up between the wars. If only the plan had included design—you can see what a chance was neglected if you look at some of the new council houses on the west side of Anderson Drive, above Forresterhill. There the architect has found a style for granite that is modern and brings out the dignity of the stone, while bright colours have been used in the doors and windows with a stimulating effect. If we had had twenty years of such building between the wars, what a wonder the new parts would have been. Or some companions to the circular court of flats in Mount Street, like a miniature of Quarry Hill in Leeds, but much more intimate and domestic.

When all that has been said, even a native finds it difficult to believe that Aberdeen is really a big industrial town. The factories and work-shops do not intrude. One would think that the largest paper mills in Britain would be difficult to hide—yet Stoneywood Mill is hidden among the trees on the banks of the Don. So are Mugiemoss and Don-side mills—and the big weaving sheds at Grandholm. When I was a student and God was disillusioned with progress and T. S. Eliot was His prophet, we all knew the lines

> Down behind the gasworks . . .
> Thinking on the King, my father's death . . .

that bitterness of spirit in the waste land of an industrial age where the back of the gasworks was the only place in which one could be alone. Curiously the places where we went to study that work were the bowers and shades along the side of the Don between the paper mills, as lulled and quiet as if they had lain by the Old Vicarage, Grantchester, with the only difference that the hum of unseen wheels was heavier and deeper than the hum of bees, and the effluent dyes on the river were brighter than all the coloured counties of England. I have never seen another place where industrial buildings lived so unobtrusively, so happily, in their surroundings—so happily, at least to me, because even when I was a dweller of the waste land, I was also a son of the north-east and knew that work and wages were as essential to life as bread and wine, and breath.

The factories inside the town are not at all dominating; they do not browbeat the dwellings around them. The reason is that they are rather small in size and modest, even humble in appearance, and one may live with them for a long time without realising that they are famous in many and distant parts of the world. The exception to this amenity is the Broadford Mill which rears up a mass of red brick in the middle of the town, as a counterpoise to the granite mass of Marischal College. But Broadford is not offensive: the very fact of brick in a granite town makes it remarkable; and by some trick of association it has for a long time reminded me of Hampton Court.

There is, however, one part where the horrors of industrialism stand up naked and unashamed—though it may be that they are blushing behind their coat of soot. Aberdeen might have a fine sea front—for nature gave it a good start in the curving bay, edged with silver sand and backed by the links where the bent grass and the sharp thyme grow and the larks sing above the sheep and the golfers. Unfortunately, this is also backed at the south end by the gasworks and its offensive co-partner, a chemical factory. It is, of course, a little unfortunate, now that Aberdeen is becoming a great holiday place, especially with Glasgow people, though not so great a misfortune as it might be, since a factory or two in the midst of their pleasure gives Glasgow people a homely feeling. Something, no doubt, will be done about these twin offences in the interest of the holiday trade, although a gasworks is not the easiest establishment to shift, being like a great tree whose roots spread everywhere beneath the town. Meantime we old natives take comfort from the fact that the horse factory at the foot of School Road is now a memory. That was only a small building, but its offence was great. Its function was a good one—it converted diseased horses into fertiliser, driving off their evil in a stench that pervaded Old Aberdeen when the wind blew from the east and caused nausea to bathers when the wind blew from the west. That at least has gone. And if the town council would cause ivy to grow on the gasworks and the chemical factory Aberdeen might then be the industrial city without reproach.

That the fathers of the community should be worried by the fact that the gasworks spoil the sea front shows how very important the holiday trade has become to Aberdeen. It also proves again that Aberdeen lives by cultivating its own garden. In this case, however, our fathers did not realise that sand and sea air would ever be a commercial asset. Having always a little too much fresh air off the sea, as soon as they could afford they built out west, leaving the sea winds to those who could afford nothing gentler. They turned their backs upon a treasure which Glasgow people in due course discovered. People came up from the steamy basin of the Clyde to Aberdeen whence their ancestors had gone, and there for a week they recovered the ancestral gust and potence. When I was a little boy the Glasgow Fair brought a return of the exiles whose fathers or grandfathers had left the north to better themselves on the railways round Glasgow. Fifteen years later when I had become a man Aberdeen had become a sort of Rothesay on the east. Catering for the Fair was a sort of industry and Aberdeen had become a resort. There are not many industrial towns of which that can be said.

THE AULTON

While Aberdeen was growing rich, what was happening on the other side of the Spital Brae? Nothing very much, as in any place that has missed the tide of time and rides out eternity on a still water. The Aulton began as a cloister and it has retained a cloistral air that is likely to endure. When the reformers sent the canons unwillingly home to their country parishes, the Chanonry fell into ruins, and the Aulton might have fallen too, become as dry as Old Sarum, but for Bishop Elphinstone's college. The cathedral city became a university town and the college not only kept the town alive but refreshed it with draughts of young life. After the residential system in the college broke down, the guidwives of the Aulton boarded the students and for a small pay gave them a mother's love and more than a mother's wisdom. The little town had no other source of income, except the pottery, the brewery and the change houses where the farmers got the first dram on the road in to market and the last on the road home.

The university and the little burgh maintained their individuality against their neighbours across the hill. But everything was against them. It was rather absurd that a poor corner of Scotland should have two universities, so proposals for union were made; and, after a debate that lasted through several generations, the two were united. One marriage is said to lead to another, and it seemed reasonable that Aberdeen should absorb the Aulton. The town council fought it off nobly, but they were fighting the inevitable. The Aulton lost something by the union. No provost, no baillies. The Town House, the prim eighteenth-century town house, declined into a police station with a reading-room on the first floor; girls read magazines where baillies had once drunk claret at the Common Good's expense. In exchange the Aulton got sewers and those other services which are a part of civilisation and are so easily mistaken for the whole of it. The Aulton may have lost more than it gained; yet perhaps not, for it never lost its greatest treasure—its individuality.

There is not much of the Aulton—the narrow street called College Bounds that becomes the High Street up to the Town House where it divides, the Chanonry leading to the Cathedral and Don Street leading to the Brig of Balgownie. It is little more than a street's length with, at the north end, the extent of the old cathedral precinct. It is only a street's breadth, but in the old Scots style, with many of the houses set gable end to the roadway; and small, rather private, lanes and closes, leading back by cottages to the green fields beyond. So the line of the street is broken and yet has a complete propriety. The college stands a little back from the street on the green lawn, a range of buildings not in themselves remarkably beautiful, yet beauti-fully suited in that place. The manses of the professors are side by side with the cottages of labouring people; trees hang out their branches over garden walls; small children play in the gutter; old men stand patiently by the Town House, perhaps waiting for the day when somebody will invite them into the St Machar Bar; the bell of the Cathedral replies to the bell of the College, both a little casual now in beating out the hours they have beaten out so long. Dead men lie in the Cathedral Yard within hearing of the river that might have carried their years away. There are not many towns that have so happily missed the tide of time.

Of course it is not quite what it used to be; some variety has gone in the last thirty years; the Aulton is less the little burgh remote in spirit from its neighbour across the hill. There were more green fields round it and more of the country in the streets when I was a boy. The town dairies still survived and the Aulton had at least one and may have had more. In behind the Town House and at the top of School Road there were many more houses than there are now, and somewhere in the huddle I remember the urban cow. The dairyman kept perhaps a dozen of her in the back street. He bought turnips and straw from the farmers out about. The town cow did not get a deal of pasture, but she did have an exercising ground beyond Cluny's Port, to which she was driven twice a day in summer. It was a fair treat to see the dozen sociable, inquisitive beasts come round the front of the Town House, with their udders swinging and their tails scourging the summer flies, all so innocent and exuberant. It was best when the procession got mixed up with the stately progress of the Chanonry gentlemen going home to their lunches. They had a curious effect on the cows, filling them with whimsies and obstructiveness. The cows pretended terror and surprise; put down their heads and up their tails; voided themselves like torrents and volcanoes while the gentlemen waved their ineffectual umbrellas and muttered "outrageous". Then to show that they had made a gross mistake in not knowing old friends, instead of going quietly to their fields the cows insisted on following the gentlemen along the Chanonry, with their nostrils blowing great snorts of breath and a slaver trickling on the pavement, amorously, as you might have said. It was delicious, for there are great powers of embarrassment in a cow. And she knows it. But not in the Chanonry; not there no longer.

The Aulton is—but I cannot describe the place, for my emotions are not sufficiently disengaged. Far otherwise; say Aulton to me, and all our past comes clamouring in. My people lived there for a long time. My great-grandfather was a potter there before he became a farmer more than a hundred years ago. A great-uncle who lost the half of his nose in the slaughterhouse helped to repair the roof of the Cathedral. Another uncle never made any great mark but, as his brother told me, helped away with a deal of drink. We appear in the records of the kirk session for grave sins—when I remember those things, I feel that all the ages of the Aulton are mine. It is difficult for me to distinguish now between the living and the dead, for some that lie, out of all reach of sin, by the Cathedral wall, seem more alive to me than a few I could name that utter vain words upon the pavements. They were wholly alive in their time and they live in us, their latest descendants. I feel very rich when I walk down the Chanonry.

I have a relation—she is dead long time but I have her still—who was in her own day the residuary legatee of Kininmonth and Elphinstone and all who ever lived in the Aulton. When I knew her she lived in the Chanonry, in Mitchell's Hospital, a charity for the daughters of burgesses. She had no property except in herself and she was a very humble woman, but the Aulton belonged to her, for she had the long memory that goes further back than title deeds. I have sat with her on the wooden form beside the sundial on summer afternoons when the Cathedral bell chimed three and she has talked to me about the people she had known. She was a great reporter—a moral person, and yet not a preacher, telling the story as she had seen it. She was more than a reporter—she was the voice of the Aulton. The stories I heard from her, on the hard seat between the sundial and the antirrhinums. Stories of the gifted boys who came to college with a sack of oatmeal and two guineas in gold and starved on the lower slopes of Helicon. Stories of professors who tunnelled so deep into the dust of a dying culture that they suddenly threw the roast out of the window and danced along the garden path in their small clothes. Stories of the beadle who distilled illicit spirits in a vault and hiccupped the minister into the pulpit. Stories of the great and good, their state and possession withdrawn to show the essential man and woman. Equally some obscure but exciting accounts of our own relations, of the joiner who had ideas about carving wood after the style the old carvers had used for King's College Chapel, and he would have done it that way, but there was always the drink. Of the foreman fisher at Balgownie who used to waken out of a deep sleep at any hour of the day and night and say "They're runnin' " and call out the fishers and catch a mighty draught of salmon. Of Bishop Elphinstone, that he was a Catholic but a good man, for they didn't know any better with their papes and pre-lacies, but he would have got on very well with great-grandfather— the good one—who, on a notable Sunday morning when the minister had died at breakfast, got into the pulpit, announced the event, put up a prayer, gave out the psalm and dismissed the congregation—"Go home, my friends, wi' a humble hert; for wha kens wha the next will be." Of these she used to tell me, and of so much else while the golden hand of the Cathedral clock crept round the minutes and the bell tolled for all humanity.

She was a woman all compact of charity, for the things she liked to tell were the good things; and when they were not, she found some cause to excuse them. In that she was not quite the voice of the Aulton. But there were in the hospital some other old ladies, virtuous daughters of burgesses, who may have been gay and lovely in their youth, but Time had made them grim and gruntulous. One or two of them, drawn by their mission to destroy anything that seemed good and beautiful, would hobble out and join in the conversation. Then the Aulton was ripped open from the chaps to the navel, and every scandal made plain. It distressed my old friend, but it didn't distress me. The tales of evasions, treacheries, the carnal appetites that lurk beneath a transcendental philosophy, the whisky that supports an academic reputation, the shifts a man must make in order to live in the world— those particular instances only confirmed what I had begun to suspect, that my elders were no better than the worst of people. I know they destroyed my old relation's pleasure in speaking about old things, which was their purpose, but they did me a service they had never intended. They displayed the last most deeply hidden secrets of the

Aulton. Like faithless attorneys doing good by accident, they helped me into the fullness of my inheritance.

You may understand it is not easy to disengage emotion from such memories. Indeed memory is not the word to use, if memory is just the faculty of recalling things that can be forgotten. There are some or many experiences one can never forget; they are relived over and over again and each time with an immediate effect so that the emotions spring as strongly as at the first time of feeling; so strongly that the original incident cannot rightly be said to live in any past. Certainly in the Aulton, when I walk there now, I walk in the historic present; I am there today but I am there thirty years ago, perhaps I am there long before I was born. I am certainly there twenty years ago when I was a student.

However one may deplore the official part of education, designed to be training and a test of reason and mechanical memory, and from which few people survive with their reason unimpaired, to spend four years at a university may be the best gift that can be given to the young. I know now that it was very wonderful to have been given leisure and intellectual space in which to grow between the years of eighteen and twenty-two and to have got that in a place both old and beautiful. Something of the wonder of that time and place still runs along my nerves; it is in my ears and eyes; the smell of the sea and the lash of the autumn rain can stir it.

What I remember about the Aulton in those years are moments and hours which could have been enjoyed without attendance at a university. The ring of feet and voices in the quiet street at midnight as we convoyed each other home with discourses fantastic and profane. The way the branches hung across the lamps in Chanonry and threw shadows that made the quiet place grow vast and secret. The incredible northern midsummer nights when the last of sunset passed into a high green light in the north that endured there like a remote and tideless ocean till sunrise. Summer afternoons under the old trees, reading anything except the prescribed books; summer evenings at the Brig of Balgownie, when I added a few more lines to the epic, or to the narrative poem in rhyming pentameters. Such things can be enjoyed without attendance at a university, but they can be perhaps more fully enjoyed if the mind and the senses are not troubled by the insistent need to earn a daily wage, even though that need cannot be long ignored. And always they need the right climate of the mind.

It was my good fortune to spend those years in the Aulton and at King's College where the spirit of humane learning still strongly persisted through the wrack of dead ideas, as a silver birch springs up through the brushwood of a ruined forest. There was perhaps not very much to enlarge the mind or the spirit in the classrooms, but I begin to see now that our teachers were more humane than I sometimes thought them. They led us to the prescribed pastures but did not worry us to eat there. If we did not eat, we would be the lean sheep at shearing day. Perhaps they knew that, while they piped, some were listening to other and far different music from the further slopes of Helicon. Having brought us into the fields they left us alone to find the foods our various natures hungered for. I see now they may have been wise men as well as good; for, as a young man or woman of eighteen years wants to have a key and the freedom of the streets, we wished also to have the freedom of all knowledge and all experience; and that is what we were offered in the Aulton; and we took and used that freedom in great measure or less, each of us in our private fashion.

I was, perhaps, doubly fortunate because I was a native of the Aulton, or at least a neighbour, so the College was doubly wonderful to me. I know what it must have been to many a boy and girl from the dubby farmyards of Buchan who found in King's not only the last enchantment of the Middle Ages but enlargement into so many things so very different from home. It was the symbol of everything they wished to get away from; and that is wonderful enough. Now it was that for me too, but I found it at home. For the College was never something apart from, and above, the Aulton. It had always been our college. My grandmother had said, from the time I was seven or eight, that I would go there if she had the money and I had the brains. It was not anything far and high and almost out of reach. It was all a part of our inheritance. How very wonderful, then, to discover there such freedom, as if I had opened a door in my own house and walked straight out into celestial fields.

And to find in the celestial fields so many well-known characters. What a wonderful little society was contained in the Aulton twenty or thirty years ago. The prim, the old and ageless ladies who had conversed with the Grand Turk and seen the dawn rise through the cigar smoke in Janina; ladies who had been chained to pillars; ladies who had said dreadful things to masters of colleges; ladies who had made Oxford turn in its grave; ladies who wore hats. The hats—ah, it's the hats I remember; those black hats with white wings, real wings nicely dissected from the bodies of white birds, wings deloused, disinfected and embalmed, wings stuck on hats for the daughters of classical professors to give them a classical look, as if Mercury were their uncle. Hats long out of date; hats sadly out of fashion; hats so completely right; for the ladies had grown superior to time and fashion; right out of fear of human kind into the large air where one lives by oneself alone. The hats—they are and will be to me for ever the symbols of the Aulton. They cover the men as well as the women. They cover a society in which only the great and the ruthless could live. A society in which individuality had become an august tradition.

A rich and imposing society—not rich in money but imposing in a sense of its own value. It would have been easy to have thought them a little above all human weakness. But—I remembered the old ladies in Mitchell's Hospital, and my old friend Betsy, those, the voices of the Aulton. The Sunday roast thrown out of the window. The small clothes. To remember those also may be the beginning of wisdom.

That is why I am in two minds about the present state and the future of the Aulton. Our burgh is rapidly becoming a university precinct. In the last twenty years or so the University has bought up nearly all the houses that have come into the market and is now restoring those houses for the teaching staff. One half of my mind says that is a good thing. The restoration is very well done; the native character of the houses is never spoilt and in some cases, as in Cluny's Port, the present state is far better than the original. One cannot be too grateful for the work that is being done. This modest, and in its way perfect, piece of antiquity should now be safe from destruction by the irresponsibility of private persons in search of profit or gratification. As to what the University may do yet, no man may guess. The intention is to transfer to the Aulton those departments at present in Marischal College, which will lay a great burden of stone, or steel and concrete, on the few open spaces that are left, the one-time grazings of the urban cow. We know that the old Aulton will survive; we can only hope it will not be overlaid by the new.

As a native I do welcome this change, but there is one thing I fear. The University might possess all the Aulton. There would be none left in it but the professors and lecturers and a few shopkeepers. I can't help thinking it would be a loss when the professor no longer lived next door to the scavenger; when the voices of the common people were still; when there was no place for me and mine; and there was nothing left in the Aulton but accents veneered over by Oxford and Cambridge. We should have lost something then.

We are not in immediate danger. The Principal has said that, while he hopes more of the University staff will live in the Aulton, the University will preserve a balance, for it is not good that university people should live by themselves, outside the community. We can stay assured, in his time, for he is a man of his word. If any that come after him have a different idea, I can only say this—we old aboriginals will not be easily dispossessed.

Children that love their parents dearly have been known to criticise them. Some of us have been guilty of that unfilial conduct towards our mother town—even I that wish to stand well with everybody have been accused of saying things about Aberdeen that should not be said, when I suggested that not every house in Aberdeen was beautiful, not every Aberdonian a master of the King's English. Between ourselves I have seen and still see very much that is deplorable in our town. When I was twenty-two I left it gladly, thinking never to return. Twenty years after, I was walking along Union Terrace with a friend, an older man and one who had made himself far more unpopular with the loyal citizens that I would ever dare. He too had left Aberdeen, and he too had come back again. We walked along Union Terrace at the red end of an autumn day, about six o'clock when the last of the citizens were going home to supper and the first of the evening crowds were coming in to the pictures. As we walked from Union Terrace to Schoolhill, through the smoke and the mist of the evening, a keen but not unkindly wind blew in from the sea, and suddenly Aberdeen shone out in a clean and living air under the last red light of the sky. In a second the red had gone and the sky enfolded deep and blue above us. We saw the Library where both of us in our own day had pursued knowledge through deserts of the printed word; the theatre where we had stormed up to the gods; the Art Gallery and Gordon's College, the spire of St Nicholas; and with the remembering eye we saw so many other things that were hidden or gone. I said, "You know, Aberdeen's not a bad place to live in." And Joe said, judicially, "You know, it's not, after all, and never has been."

In many ways it is a very good place. It is about the right size and shape for a town. By the right size I mean that it is big enough that one may be a little anonymous and have a life of one's own without being eternally spied on by somebody that knew one's granny; yet not so big that the individual is lost in it. By the right shape I mean that a town should be compact, so that if one is invited to supper at the other side of it, the best part of the evening is not wasted in getting there. Aberdeen comes well out of those tests. It is big, yet not too big to be a community, and it is wonderfully compact without being overcrowded. Ten minutes in a tram and a five minutes' walk will take you from the centre into the country—the deep country where farmers go about their curious intromissions with nature.

The town has at least some of the things considered necessary for a civilised life. A senior football club, for instance, whose team draws crowds of twenty, thirty and forty thousand to Pittodrie for rites that seem almost religious in the exultations and agonies they produce. The club recently won a competition among the senior Scottish teams, whereby they immediately became a sad disappointment to their worshippers; since everything they did thereafter, however excellent, was in some way anticlimax.

The town has a theatre where you may see fashionable successes from the London stage and sure favourites like Gilbert and Sullivan and *Snow White*—weeks when no sure-fire pieces are available being filled in with cinema shows. Considering the mortality among provincial theatres, one must be grateful that the Aberdeen one is still a legitimate house, even though its programmes give the impression that Coward and Dodie Smith are the best brains working in the theatre today. There is also a theatre of varieties where the best variety artistes appear and the young men of the town are introduced to ideas of pulchritude at a safe distance. And, of course, there are many cinemas.

There is a little music. The Scottish Orchestra performs once a month in winter and the virtuosi include us in their tours. Besides these, there are many amateur societies willing to crucify the Messiah once again. The Choral Society, however, has a high standard, and performs along with the Scottish Orchestra. The Music Department of the University is growing in scope and in performance

There is a good art school; and an art gallery which the curator is trying to make an inspiration and a delight, a little handicapped by the pictures too generously gifted by local benefactors. In painting, as in other things, people from the North-east can be very competent craftsmen. George Jameson was one of the earliest Scottish painters now known by name and there have been many since who became successful by portraits.

When all that has been said there may seem to be rather little, but there are at least the makings, and that is a lot to be thankful for in a world where there are so many total deserts.

It is not a bad place to live in. It is probably a better place to live in than most big towns. It is unique. In spite of its university and its manufactures, it remains the market town of the north-east. It is the only big town I know where, instinctively and without surprise, a gentleman will step off the pavement to make way for a cow, as he would do for any lady. At a time when big towns seem an infliction on the country round them, Aberdeen remains a necessary condition of our lives. Take away Aberdeen and the north-east would be a poor dismembered thing. It is the sum of our best qualities; it is our capital. And that is the answer to the question I began with. How can a town of nearly two hundred thousand people live so far north? Because it is completely revelant to the country it lives in. In that it is perhaps unique.

CHAPTER IV

THE FISHING COMMUNITIES

No man, as Dr Donne said, is an island; but the fisher communities of the north are near to near about it. They are at least peninsulæ surrounded on nine sides by water. The fishermen are so different from the country folk that it may help to think of them as wholly people of the sea who of necessity make their homes on shore but so mistrust the land that they build on the very edge of the waves and shun intercourse with the land dwellers.

There are two types of the fishing village. Some—of which Inverallochy and St Combs are examples—stand on the edge of sandy or chingly beaches. Anyone who has been brought up in the shelter of even a single bourtree bush might wonder why people ever built their houses on such a flat and windy foreshore. The reason is that the earlier fishermen used small boats and looked for a beach where those boats could be easily drawn up. Then they built their cottages near to the boats, each with its shoulder against the prevailing wind. Since they had a bent towards religion they reared up a kirk with a spire: and since they were also schismatic, they reared up other kirks and meeting-houses. Thus they put the distinguishing marks on their settlements. Under the infinite rolling sky and in an air so clear you might see beyond the Pole, the villages lie low at the margin where the waves of the earth meet the waves of the sea, each with its spires, like a grey barque grounded. You may get nearer their true inwardness on a dark day in February, when the heavy clouds bear down on the land and the wild seas fling themselves on the beaches driven by a south-easterly gale: the horizon is contracted to a little space, the wind howls, the sea ravens and thunders, tormented spray flies round the houses; then the village is a barque awash, seemingly doomed but always miraculously preserved from destruction.

The second type of village is found in those parts where the land ends in cliffs along the shore. Sometimes the cliff wall has been broken down either by streams eating their way to the sea or by the eroding of the waves, and the result is a wide bay or perhaps only a narrow anchorage where the fishers have made their homes. There are many such between Montrose and Wick that have a similar setting—the bay with long arms of dangerous black rock at its extremities, a small harbour where the boats are grounded at low tide, a narrow pier-head poorly paved or badly rutted; then the houses, some within reach of the spray and the others, huddled together as for shelter, up the slope; and, somewhere, the kirk spire pointing in trust to heaven. Pennan, the most remarkable of them, lies deep down under the cliffs, out of the sun and almost you might think out of the world, at the end of a precipitous road through wild country. Could there be a greyer or a harder life than must be lived on that narrow foothold between the cliffs and the sea?

Those are the homes of the herring fishermen, but there are few boats in the little harbours or drawn up on the foreshore, for the men now fish from the bigger ports—Peterhead, Fraserburgh, Lossiemouth, Buckie and Wick. They do not lose any of their native character thereby. Though Peterhead and Fraserburgh have important industries besides the fishing and Lossiemouth is a popular holiday place of the quieter and more expensive sort, they are still unmistakably fisher towns. They have in their older parts a certain grey dignity in the sober lines of traditional cottage building, a plain proportion lacking grace but blessed with a sense of fitness. The view of Peterhead across the bay on a quiet afternoon, with the decent houses standing along and above the still water, has the composed quality of an eighteenth-century print in which everything lives at peace with its neighbours; and though the other towns have nothing quite as good as this, their older parts do have an architectural decency which comes from buildings in a good plain style decently set down together. Peterhead, of course, has an advantage, for it was a resort of fashion in the eighteenth century when the local gentry and distinguished persons like Dr James Beattie ("The Minstrel") went there for the bathing, and the sober elegance of that time can be traced in the shape of some of the houses.

For a complete contrast one may look at Buckie. By some unfortunate accident Buckie looks like a Victorian piece of work. It leaves the impression of one very long, very wide street and many side streets, of angular dressed-stone houses, all shapes and sizes, with churches, hotels and whatnot built arbitrarily along the pavement's edge. The other fishing towns and villages have little ground plan but organic unity: Buckie has enjoyed too much planning, and not enough. The streets seem to have been laid out with a ruler, then none bothered about the shapes of the buildings put up along them. It is a mixture of predestination and freewill, with the confusion that might be expected. How strange to find something that looks like the main street of some small graceless industrial town thus affronting the Moray Firth. As if that were not enough, the railway that runs along the foreshore has been allowed to proliferate into a large goods-yard. A stranger who comes from the main street and gets an eyeful of smoke from the shunting engines below looks instinctively for the mills, the foundries or the pithead gear. It is a sudden surprise to see

Dunnottar Castle

Country town: Stonehaven

Balmoral

Auchindoun Castle

Glen Rinnes

Elgin

Elgin Cathedral

The noble Spey

Lochindorb: The Wolf's Lair

Culbin sands

Inverness on the waters

Cullodden, Inverness and the Black Isle

The fantastic West

The far West: Loch Broom

Crofting community, Sutherlandshire

Strathpeffer

County town: Dingwall

Township in Strath Halladale

A laird's house: Meldrum

Cornlands: Aberdeenshire

Farmland along the Conon

Well-laboured uplands: Moray–Banff

Corn and timber: Glenlivet

Marginal land: the Cabrach

Where the tide turned back

St Machar's Cathedral

Brig o Balgownie, Aberdeen

Quayside, Aberdeen

King's College, Aberdeen

Fishing village: Gourdoun

Herring port, Peterhead

Fishing village: Gardenstown

Fishing village, Helmdale

Fishing port: Wick

Dunnet Head, Caithness

Drum Castle

Braemar Castle

Cawdor Castle

Ancient monument: Huntly Castle

Caithness: north from the Ord

Heavy event

The Glen of the Dee

Invercauld on Deeside

Cairngorms from Rothiemurchus

A Caithness moor

Dornoch: cathedral and castle

Near Invershin

On the Berriedale river

. . . but their work remains

the harbour and the blue-grey firth and beyond that, far away, the transpontine hills.

The fishermen of the north are mostly herring catchers, and the largest part of the British herring fleet belongs to the ports from Wick to Peterhead. In order to understand the fishing communities one must know something of the trade they follow and of the fish on which that trade depends.

Unfortunately no one knows very much about the herring, a creature of so far unpredictable habits. This, however, is known: the herring live off our shores in great congregations of many millions, vaster and more savoury Londons of the sea. The shoals live by plankton, a form of marine life, and move about the waters by some sort of mass instinct. It used to be said that they appeared around the Orkney and Shetland Islands in the spring of the year and moved slowly southward till about midsummer they were off Peterhead and Fraserburgh and by autumn were off East Anglia. That is what I was taught at school, but it is now disfavoured—one more of the things that make me distrust all schools and all instructors. The most the experts will say now is that the herring are likely to appear off Peterhead in early summer and off East Anglia in autumn. They decline to say if these have moved down from the north or up from the south, or are the results of spontaneous generation *in situ*. The important thing is that herring catching is a seasonal trade in any one area, and if it is to be pursued further the fisher must follow the herring.

In the older days, when the fisher communities were founded, the boats were small and could not go far from shore with safety. We can guess that the catchers followed the herring when they were in their area and at the other seasons they followed the inshore fishing for white fish. Those small boats were family concerns, owned and worked by a father and his sons, or by a family of brothers, or on a similar sharing principle by village neighbours. When the men brought in the fish, the women carried them in wicker creels on their backs far into the countryside, exchanging them for money if there was money and, if not, for eggs and butter, chickens and oatmeal and cheese. It had been so from time immemorial. The Mucklebackits in Sir Walter Scott's *The Antiquary*, though they do not belong to the north, are magnificent prototypes of the modern fisher folk.

In the early part of the nineteenth century the market for herrings began to open up like a cabbage rose, though less fragrantly. Sir John Sinclair of Thurso, a man who had ideas for developing everything he turned his mind to, brought over Dutchmen to teach the Scots how to cure herrings. The lesson was quickly learned: all the more quickly because there was a market for the herrings. The Industrial Revolution was in full blast in Britain: a vast and hungry populace was in receipt of wages, even if the wages were small; Britain was become a hungry market for food. That was one market; but there was another, and a greater, preparing. After Waterloo there was peace in Central Europe, a real and enduring peace for the first time since 1618, however unholy the alliance that maintained it, a peace that lasted without serious break for a hundred years. In North Germany, Poland and Eastern Russia there was a new industrial population and an old peasant population raising cereals, both hungry for cheap protein and able to pay for it. Throughout the century they were the faithful customers of the herring and the prosperity of the northern fishings depended on them. That Central European market defined the pattern of the herring trade. Wherever the herring appeared the catchers appeared too, from Lerwick in the Shetlands to Lowestoft in East Anglia, so that a Buckie boat might be fishing from Lerwick at one season and Lowestoft at another. That made a change in the technique of catching. The small boats had been limited to a small radius from the shore and the catches were small. With a bigger market to sell in there was incentive to seek the herring wherever they might be, and that required bigger boats. The new boats could not be hauled up on the foreshore, they needed a better harbourage, and so, for instance, the fishermen of Inverallochy and St Combs began to use Fraserburgh as their port. The old fishing village became a dormitory while the landings were concentrated into a few big ports.

There are three ways in which a herring can be sent to market—fresh, kippered or salted. In the first case the herring is packed in ice as soon as it leaves the boat and is sent off by express train or motor lorry. The distance of the market, the speed of the transport, the efficiency of the fishmonger—these determine its quality when it gets at last to the kitchen. The kipper is a fresh herring that is gutted as soon as landed and then cured by hanging in the smoke of oak chips. No other herring, however cured or artfully dyed, is a kipper—but only a decaying fish with a hectic flush on it. The true kipper is a lordly fish. The salted herring was the standby of the trade for more than fifty years. When the boats came in the curers bought their fish at the cheapest price and then proceeded to make them into food for the poor. Along the quayside they had long troughs, attended by girls and women called gutters. The herrings were emptied into the troughs; the gutters gutted them, placed them in the barrels, showered salt on them row on row till each barrel was full. Then the coopers closed the barrels, which were piled up ready for a ship to come in. Half a million barrels might go from one port in a single season; and it was on those salt herrings that Peterhead, Fraserburgh, Buckie and Wick grew into towns. That trade remained good till 1918.

Though the fishing had grown into an industry supplying a big foreign market, the catching side kept the old village pattern and no large-scale capital came into it. Boats were built larger, steam took the place of sail and the diesel engine is replacing steam, but even now the money for a new boat is found within the family or the village. If a group of fishermen decide to have a new drifter, each puts down what money he can afford. If the total is not enough, some local merchant or other capitalist may join in the venture. Each then has a share according to what he has put down, but whatever outside money there may be, the effective control remains with the fishermen. The boats are worked on a share system: that is, the fishermen divide the profits, if any, and except in a very few cases do not live by wages. The driver and the fireman, however, are always hired men and paid a weekly wage. Now the shares in the profit are divided in an old and rather interesting way. Of the profit, one-third goes to the boat, one-third to the nets and one-third to the fishermen. The boat's share is portioned out among the owners, according to their investment. The nets' share is portioned among the owners of the nets: and this is something peculiar to herring catching. A drifter has seven fishermen including the skipper, and there are ten nets a man. Usually each fisherman owns his own nets, but sometimes not, through youth or ill-luck or improvidence. In that case another fisherman may have two sets, or someone on shore may provide them. Whoever owns nets takes their share in the profit. Then each fisherman has a share, as a fisherman, unless he happens to be a hired man working for a wage. Thus a fisherman's earnings for the season may come to him under three heads. He may have a half share in the drifter, which will give him a sixth of the profit. He may own two sets of nets, which will give him two forty-seconds. And he will have a twenty-first as a member of the crew. His son, who owns his nets and is a member of the crew, will get two twenty-firsts. And Jeanie's Jock, his nephew, who has no nets, a twenty-first. The skipper gets nothing extra for his position and responsibility and may draw less than some other members of the crew. It is an old-fashioned organisation, which is not necessarily anything against it. But it is perhaps not very well fitted for the conditions in which the industry must now live. Even in better times it may have been a disadvantage by encouraging individualism and thus making the fishermen more easily exploited by those whom they consider their natural enemies—the curers and exporters.

Those merchants were the dominating figures in the great days of the industry. They were of two types. Some were of the native fisher stock but had seen where the big money was to be made. Others were Germans and Russians brought up in the distributing side of the trade. Between them they controlled the whole export. Sometimes they made enormous profits and sometimes enormous losses. They lived in a larger world than anything the ordinary fishermen could understand

and because of that they were usually the masters. When catches were light the freshers and kipperers, having daily bargains to fulfil, competed for what was on offer and made a good price, but the curers stood aside. When catches were heavy the freshers and kipperers had no need to bid so high, and the curers could hang back till the price suited them, because they alone could clear the market at the end of the day. It was a constant grievance among the fishermen that the curers always thus took advantage of heavy landings and the perishable nature of fish to force a price that was unfairly low. The curers may have done so: it is probable that they did: it would have been very strange if they had done otherwise, for they were working in a very individualistic trade—and there were no more confirmed individualists than the fishermen themselves.

The fishermen suffered from the paradox with which farmers everywhere were very familiar—too good a harvest might be a misfortune. All primary producers know about that and the fishermen may have suffered no more than others have done. But there were circumstances in their trade which gave them a feeling of greater injustice. As the herring is a creature of unpredictable habits the fleet might go out for weeks and make no more than working expenses. Suddenly they found the shoals and drifter after drifter come in with a sixty- or a hundred-cran shot. Where there had been nothing there was now far too much and the curers could take the enormous surplus at their own price. It did not always work out too badly, but there were times at the end of a successful fishing season, as far as catches were concerned, when drifter fishermen had to borrow the coal to get them home. Sometimes it was not even that they had caught too much in the season but that they had all made their big catches at the same time; and, herring being so perishable, each day's landings must be cleared that day. The fishermen were inclined to think that fate was against them. They knew they could do nothing to control the herring, whose movements were directed by God. They also thought they could do nothing about the curers, whom they suspected to be the spawn of the Devil. As to the nativity of the curers they may have been right; when they thought nothing could be done about them they were probably wrong. It was a pity they did not try. When catches were heavy and the curers were depressing the price the fishermen might have agreed among themselves to limit catches unless the curers agreed to a fair minimum. But any suggestion of that sort made by the more responsible fishermen never got as far as action. There were always those who would not combine because of principle, and those who would not because of fear, and the "lucky" ones who were always doing well enough anyway. Perhaps the fishermen could not have brought the curers to order; that they did not try shows up their character and their weakness in making a bargain. They were too individualistic; too suspicious; too selfish. It was every boat against every other boat: and where everyone plays his own hand, there can be no common and effective plan. So the curers and exporters got the best of it.

The war of 1914–18 and the peace that followed it made a havoc in the export market. Those who had debts owing from the subjects of the Czar could not collect them from the Soviets. That was a heavy loss which might have been got over. Unfortunately the Soviets not only denounced the old bargains but were very unwilling to make new ones. So the eastern export market became an uneasy ghost that troubled the industry with vain hope for many years. At times the Russians bought some salt herrings and at other times seemed about to buy on the old scale: but little came of it. The eastern market has grown still smaller and there seems little chance that the salt herring trade can ever again be what it was unless some entirely new market can be found in Asia or Africa.

The home market cannot—or, so far, will not—make up the loss. People in this country have lost the taste for salt herrings. I myself am not altogether surprised at that. When I was a boy there was always a seven-course rotation of dinners: on Sunday hot roast; on Monday cold roast; on Tuesday stoved tatties with the orrals of the beef. On Friday there was always a milk dinner—milk broth followed by rice pudding; on Saturday, fish brought from town on the previous day. Wednesday and Thursday were problem days and on one or other we usually had salt herrings. My grandmother bought them by the barrel and for years kept the barrel in the back scullery, till everyone complained so bitterly about the smell that they were put out to the workshop among the blunt saws and rusty chisels. As the saws grew blunter and the chisels more rusty my grandfather maintained it was the herrings that did it. They were certainly very strong fish. Now the method of preparing them for the table was this. On a Tuesday afternoon my grandmother took enough to make a dinner and enclosed them in a wire cage that had once been a mouse-trap. Then we took them to the nearest stream and anchored the cage at the bottom of a little pool and left it there for a day, or two. We then brought home the fish, which were first boiled and then baked and served with potatoes and a thick coating of mustard sauce. They tasted, to me, like old dishcloths full of bones and impregnated with salt: I am sure of it, for I can taste them yet, after so many years. One of the first things I really understood in the history books was that skirmish in the Low Country called the Battle of the Herrings. I could understand the salt herrings being used as lethal weapons and soldiers dying, salted, as you might say, to death.

As the home market could not take up the herrings, there were hard times in the fishing communities between the wars. Many of the boats were old and deteriorated rapidly, until their owners, faced with big bills for repairs and no money to pay them, took the boats to the nearest beach and abandoned them. Those who had the money built new boats and fitted diesel engines and managed to keep going. But to increase catching capacity while the market was shrinking was no way out of the troubles. Some fishermen did well even in the worst times, for there are always some that have a sort of mastery, part luck and part skill. That may have been unfortunate for the industry as a whole, because the successful ones were always indifferent, if not opposed, to any idea of combining to regulate the market. During the war of 1939–45 the drifters were on Government service and since then they have done well enough. The Herring Industry Board has brought some order into the trade with fixed prices for freshing, curing and manufacturing into meal. Assistance has been given for buying boats and gear. Running costs are very high, but the fishermen are not now at the mercy of the buyers. They may, however, have still one enemy—themselves. Until quite recently a man from one village would not have dared marry a girl from another; and although that is no longer true, the communities have still a tribal suspicion of each other. If Peterhead and Fraserburgh agree on a course of action, Buckie is likely to stand out against it. But it is hard to get agreement even in any one port. Individualism is too strong. Every crew wish to make their own bargain because they do not trust their neighbours, and to keep their independence for some hypothetical advantage in the future, however real the cost of that independence in the present. That made the herring fishermen meat for mammon in the past and will deliver them as a willing sacrifice again if ever Government control stops and the fishermen are left alone to deal with the distributing end of the trade.

The catching industry is on an unsure foundation; the more intelligent know it but the great majority, through their peculiar and selfish cast of mind, have shown themselves incapable of making a common plan and sticking to it. That is a great pity, for their industry is in need of a deal of thought. Too many of the boats are far too old —so old as to be dangerous. But an even more difficult problem is the public's taste for herring—or lack of it.

It is my own private opinion as a sympathetic neighbour that the herring is the fundamental and the greatest difficulty. Not to catch him, but to sell him. Now the herring is a most excellent fish, far superior to any of the flat fish and almost equal to the trout and the salmon. It has great food value; when really fresh it has a rich, inspiriting taste—but it is rather a devil in the kitchen: unless the cook is careful with her pans everything soon tastes of herring. It can be a nuisance to eat, especially to the people who like all their food to be slob that they can shovel down without chewing. A nuisance in the kitchen and a trouble to eat—these are two big handicaps for the herring, and they are shared by the kipper. What people like as fish is a slab of stuff like well-soaked cotton wool that can be fried with chips and causes no trouble, except perhaps in digestion. But even the faithful who think herrings worth the trouble are too often discouraged. I like fresh herrings. I have gone down to the pier—and gotten a fry off a boat newly come in and hurried home and cleaned them, while they were so firm they leaped out of my fingers, and coated them with oatmeal and fried them and eaten half a dozen, and my mouth waters whenever I think about it. Those were fresh herrings. But too many herrings in the fish-shops are not fresh. They are tired and flaccid; if you squeeze them they keep the marks of your fingers. Offered that kind, I say, "No thank you. I know the taste of death and decay." I often have the same difficulty with the kipper. Now I have got kippers straight from the kiln in Peterhead, warm from the smoke and oily with their own fat, and have feasted on them—there is no other word large enough. But too often when I have asked for kippers in a shop I have been offered flat, flabby things richly tinted with synthetic dyes. That sort of thing brings the herring into disrepute. As a consumer I would say there is only one way in which the herring can hold the market and that is by being fresh, really fresh, when offered in the shop, and kippers must be fresh herrings, properly, honestly cured in wood smoke. Even then a difficulty may remain—will women buy herrings if they can get something easier to cook and to eat, without the bones and the smell? That is the real problem that the fishermen have got to face and are unwilling to face: for that will determine the future of their trade. They are perhaps inclined to think that we have a duty to eat fish and that the Government has a duty to make fishing profitable; but a sense of duty is not a very good foundation for a trade. The fishermen would do better to persuade us that the herring is a real delicacy and to offer us the herring in the most attractive way. Something is being done about it. A lot of herrings are now tinned, and they are excellent if you have the patience to remove the tomato sauce in which they are usually soused. There are hopes of making a trade with North America in kippers done up in tartan packages. But there is a wide space of difference between selling carefully selected kippers in cellophane and a million barrels of herrings salted as they come. Perhaps the future of the herring trade is in quality, not quantity. If so, there will be a consequence which the fishermen are very unwilling to think about: fewer fish will be required and fewer boats to catch them. But that is happening now. The fleet is shrinking and will shrink still further as old men retire and old boats are broken up. There will always be a market for herrings, either as human food or as a source of oils and cattle food, but it is reasonable to guess that the fleet will gradually be reduced to a small number of new and efficient boats. This is a matter easy enough to discuss on paper but not so easy to discuss in one of the herring ports. The older fishermen are inclined to look on the troubles of their industry as some perverse interference with divine order—all except the few, the very few, whose warnings have been unheeded. Most of them feel that the herring fishing is in the nature of things eternal and that what has been must always be. In a way they are right; their forefathers probably fished for herring as soon as they made boats fit for the sea. But the large-scale herring fishing on which Peterhead and Fraserburgh were built up is a modern thing, based on an export trade. Fishing may be eternal but export markets are subject to change, and those who look to the home market to eat the herrings which once nourished Central Europe are probably looking in vain. But there is always a temptation to say what has been in my time must have been always and always must be, whoever pays for it. One must be a little sorry for the older herring catchers—all except the prescient and unpopular few. They are a little too inveterately old-fashioned for the world they live in. They are the sort that are always sending to ask for whom the bell tolls, refusing to know it tolls for all alike.

Can science help? Science does. Asdic, the electrical sounding device which tells the depth of the sea by echoes from the seabed, can help to find a shoal of herring, for the shoal also returns an echo. If from a part of the sea where you know the depth is three hundred fathoms you get an echo at thirty, there is a reasonable presumption of herring. Radio also is used to tell the fleet where the shoals are when they have been found. But there is no real problem in catching fish, and bigger catches are not going to help the industry in its present position— what it needs is the big-paying trade. Science helps after the herrings are landed. Cold storages are being built where today's surplus can be held against next week's scarcity. Science can help to get the fish to the consumer in better order. Out of a large number of small things there can come a great advantage, but the scientists are not yet within sight of doing enough. If only they could get rid of the bones and the smell of herring. That seems a lot to ask for, but the scientists may do it yet. They have been able to get the character out of many things. Look at milk, now so disinfected it might have come from a sanitary inspector, not a cow.

It is interesting to regard the present state of the herring industry as another end-product of the Industrial Revolution. It has certain marks typical of that economic movement. For instance it was so very much an export trade into socially backward areas such as Poland and Baltic Russia. Also it was an exercise in specialisation: the herring fisherman followed the herring and nothing else; unlike his fore-fathers who caught herring in the local season and white fish at other times. Looked at in this way, the specialised herring catching is perhaps only a thing of an age, something encouraged and made important by a certain set of circumstances and something that must change when those circumstances change. In this it resembles some other Scottish industries—cotton, linen, jute and heavy engineering. Suppose the herring becomes less popular and the home market declines, what will happen to the fisher communities? The fish may be taken in always larger quantities for manufacture into feeding stuffs and fertilisers. But that is not likely to be a very paying trade. What else is there? The communities can go back to the more general fishing they once lived by. Some have already done so. Lossiemouth, for instance, has changed over to white fishing with the seine net and the line. There is a movement the same way in Fraserburgh and Peterhead. Caithness ports that were started as herring stations now live entirely by the white fish. There is a good living to be made in that business. As they go only a few miles out, those fishermen land their catches sea-fresh, which gives them an advantage over the trawlers that go to the distant fishing grounds. The trawlers that work as far out as the Barents Sea, which some of the big new English ones do, have refrigerating chambers and land their catches technically fresh after the fish have been dead a month—fresh enough for fish and chips but hardly fresh enough for anyone who has ever tasted fish new come out of the sea. Slowly as the dream of herrings by the million barrels fades away, the herring may again take a modest place in the economy of the fisher communities, a seasonal holiday from the haddocks, the soles and the whitings, or be left to a small number of drifters equipped with every technical resource. This is not to say that the herring fishing should be neglected or that it will not remain valuable—that would be a loss of good living; but no tears or time should be wasted over vanished glories. While the British people are being educated into a taste for herrings, full advantage can be made of their undoubted liking for white fish. There is a home market for those who can suit it.

The fisher communities are unlike any others in Scotland, though the miners a generation ago might have had a near resemblance. There is that isolation I have mentioned already which has cut them off from the country people round them. This is not a new thing. The minister of Cullen wrote of them a hundred years ago: "The almost invariable habit which prevails of intermarrying with those of their own craft, and the no less general practice which obtains of every fisherman's son following his father's occupation, prove serious drawbacks to the progress of this order of the community in the march of improvement, having the effect of rendering them a distinct class of society, with sentiments, sympathies and habits peculiar to themselves. Until some amalgamation shall take place between them and their brethren of terra firma, their advancement in the improvements of civilised life must necessarily be slow and partial." That is rather a mouthful but the fact remains today, although the fishermen may be well off without some improvements of civilised life. It would be interesting if some good reason could be found to explain an isolation so old as to seem inherent. Is it perhaps racial? I don't know; but that it still exists is certain.

There has been intensive inbreeding in the villages for many generations. Now inbreeding is a good thing if the stock is good, and it seems to have done no harm in this case, physically; though mental inbreeding has produced a certain narrowness. It has had one result that is rather confusing to a stranger—in one village there be only a few surnames. Where everybody is a West or a Buchan or a May and there is no enterprise in choosing Christian names, there are bound to be many John Wests and Thomas Buchans. So there has grown up a system of tee-names. Let us suppose there was a man of Portallochy called Thomas Buchan. He would be called Tam. Now suppose he had a son John and daughters Jean and Annie. Contemporary with those children there would be others with the same surname and Christian names. So those three might be called Tam's Jock, Tam's Jeanie and Tam's Annie. Their children would require to be further distinguished. If Tam's Jock had a daughter Jean she might become Tam's Jock's Jeanie. And there might be Tam's Jeanie's Willickie and Tam's Annie's Mary. It is really most logical and gives a pedigree along with the name. There is a common tee-name "Pow" pronounced "Poo". A father may be called John Buchan "pow". His son may be Pow's Sandy or Pow's Tam. He might be Willie Pow, and his son if he too were William by the use of one of our many diminutives might become Willockie Pow. Sometimes the fisherman gets the name of his boat—Seahorse or Heatherbell. There is no end to the combination of unlikely words. Even the house address may be used. One old man, the wisest of the fishermen, who has always been thinking a generation ahead of his time, is known from Wick to Lowestoft as Seven-and-a-half.

The result of this sequestered tribal life is that the fishermen live in a very narrow, very rigid family society, with a strict and narrow code of morals, offset by great heights and depths of emotion. Their religion is deeply felt and hardly at all a matter of intellectual persuasion. That is quite natural; as an observer who had lived a long time beside them once told me, "When you are accustomed to have nothing but the thickness of a plank between you and a watery grave, you do want to feel that the Almighty's hand is strong to save." Or, considering the age of some drifters—both hands. That may be a way in to the heart of the matter—the natural piety of the fishermen and the superstitious fear or caution with which they move among the dangers of the world.

They are superstitious, more than most people. If a fisherman meets a black cat on the way to his boat it troubles him. Pigs also are of evil omen. Recently while writing a radio script to illustrate how trawlermen send messages to their wives over the short-wave, and wishing to use a message that would interest children, for whom the programme was intended, I put down that the trawler skipper would say among other things, "Tell the bairns to be sure to feed the guinea-pigs." But the fishery expert to whom the script was referred said the guinea-pigs must come out, for no fisherman would speak the name of pig on his boat. The fishers used to be much concerned about the evil eye and persons liable to bring bad luck. There were in some of the villages women thought to be—if not witches, at least of evil omen. If one of them stepped across a fisherman's lines she would bring bad luck. Ministers of religion too, though sacred, had no place on the quay. Among the many stories of superstition there is none to beat that about the new minister of religion who did not understand the primitive beliefs of his parishioners. McPherson says:

"Two or three years ago a minister was newly inducted to a church in the same town [Moray Firth]. Soon after, taking a walk along the shore, someone told him that A.B.'s boat was about to set out for the English fishing. Thinking he would greet his parishioner before his departure, he made for the harbour and hailed the skipper but found him surly, uncommunicative and lacking in ordinary courtesy. A.B. did not dare ask the new minister 'Throw us good luck', in order to counteract the evil influence of his presence. The skipper was disturbed but not dismayed. At once he took the necessary steps to avert disaster. He ordered the loosening of the mooring ropes and followed this up with 'Full steam ahead,' as he grasped the steering wheel. Out into the bay the vessel sped. When about half a mile out it began to turn in a huge circle. Seven times round the bay went the vessel, always following the way of the sun. A.B. himself held the wheel, and during the whole performance had his hand on the cord of the siren which he kept blowing continuously. The townsfolk were somewhat alarmed at his behaviour, thinking that a man had fallen overboard, and that he was circling round the spot where the man had disappeared. They looked on the blasts of the siren as calls for assistance from shore. But no boat put out to sea. Those who went down to the sea in ships knew the cause. To the landsmen they explained, 'Oh, A.B. had the minister seeing him off. Somebody might tell the minister to bide at hame; it wad save a hantle o trouble.' My informant saw and heard this effort to outwit the powers of darkness."

One must not deduce from the story that fishermen have no respect for kirk religion. But as McPherson has suggested somewhere, there are also the powers of the sea which must not be annoyed even though the Almighty is on your side. Sir James Frazer in *The Golden Bough* wrote:

"We should deceive ourselves if we imagined that the belief in witchcraft is even now dead in the mass of the people. On the contrary there is ample evidence to show that it only hibernates under the chilling influences of rationalism. The truth would seem to be that to this day the peasant remains a pagan at heart—and that it would start into active life if that influence were ever seriously relaxed."

If we add the old natural religion to witchcraft and the fisherman to the peasant, the quotation may describe the matter in hand very well. Except that many of the fishermen have been spared that chilling hand of rationalism.

The fishermen do value religion of a more orthodox kind. They like the kirk services and join with great spirit in the singing. It is perhaps unfortunate from a purely musical point of style that the proof of power is the ability to sing higher than anybody else, so that a few competitive soprani assault the very courts of heaven; but, if the purpose of psalm-singing is to call attention to one's faith and hope, that style may serve very well. They have an old-fashioned taste for sermons and an old-fashioned ability to concentrate on a lengthy discourse, divided under three heads and argued out to a conclusion about sin and punishment. Some of them have a gift of extempore prayer and an enjoyment in using it. Better even than a closely reasoned discourse, they love declamation. A political speech full of fire and fury and pointed with Biblical texts is as good as an orgy to them and far more worth than any reasoned arguments. There are also in the fishing communities at least two sorts of Brethren and a varying number of the even more esoteric and evangelical sects. Some of those carry still further the isolation of fisher society. For instance, they take no part in public affairs: they do not vote in elections or offer themselves as any sorts of candidate. They confine themselves rigidly to their devotions in public and private, sparing just enough time to make a living, at which they are said to be rather successful.

The fishers used to be subject to intermittent bouts of revivalism. Now and then some evangelical spell-binder would run a campaign and work up an audience till all their inhibitions were relaxed in halle-lujahs. People leaped up and confessed their sins; the light-witted got into a frenetical state, and the fever worked up to a bonfire of vanities. "Bring out your gauds. Bring out your trinkets. Throw your cigarettes and your pipes on the flames. Your mirrors and your powder puffs. Your song sheets and your musical instruments." As the fire blazed up, the preacher thus called on the sinful and the sinful responded. It was at least a fine scavenging of rubbish and no doubt it did the participants good; having some virtues of a good blind without the physical nausea of the morning after. Those orgies in the name of the Lord are in the past; and that there have not been any these last twenty-five years may be a sign that the tensions of life have been relaxed. Whether that is good or bad I am not called on to decide.

Having written so much about the fishermen I realise I have missed perhaps the most important thing. Among the best of them there is a simplicity and a dignified way of living and a complete integrity that is seldom found anywhere else. The wisest of them are very simple people who have come to an understanding of essential things; and, having broken out of the rigid confinements of the tribe, voyage through strange seas of thought alone, keeping an even course. They stand very square among all the confusions of the world and they have a power of greatness in them.

CHAPTER V

BALLADS: ANCIENT AND MODERN

THE literature of the north is extensive and popular. There have been few poets who tried to comprehend all heaven and earth and rive the last secrets from eternity, no great territorial lords of the spirit; or if there were such their writings never won out of the asylums where they were confined; but, as might be expected from such a countryside, there have been many who did smaller things in a very competent way—people that might be called literary smallholders and honest tradesmen. Their talents come out best in drawing a simple character or telling a story of action in prose or verse. Their work is best when it is objective; and, when suffused with tender emotion, it is sappier than a rotten pear. In that, of course, they may be no different from more sophisticated writers, except that as the sophisticated ones use more difficult language the sappiness is not so immediately seen.

In the traditional style there were many songs, ballads and tales that were sung and told at the firesides on the long dark nights. Those that have survived through being written down have the qualities found in all the old strouds—they tell the story of some notable event in a simple metre, with terror and pity and wonder at the mischances of life. "The Fire of Frendraught" celebrates an event that happened in 1630. Crichton of Frendraught and Gordon of Rothiemay had fallen out, as neighbouring lairds so often did. Lord Huntly, the head of the Gordons, made peace between them; and, in earnest of the new goodwill, sent his own son, John Gordon, and the laird of Rothiemay to convoy Frendraught home. They were welcomed by Mistress Crichton—

> false Frendraught
> Inviting them to bide.

> Said, "Stay this night until we sup,
>   The morn until we dine;
> 'Twill be a token of good agreement
>   'Twixt your good lord and mine."

> When mass was sung and bells were rung
>   And all men bound for bed,
> Then good Lord John and Rothiemay
>   In one chamber were laid.

They had not long cast off their cloaths,
    And were but now asleep,
When the weary smoke began to rise,
    Likewise the scorching heat.

"O waken waken, Rothiemay!
    O waken, brother dear!
And turn you to your Saviour,
    There is strong treason here."

When they were dressed in their cloaths
    And ready for the boun
The doors and windows was all secured
    The rooftree burning doun.

The young men, trapped in the flames, tore at the iron stanchions of the windows and cried "Mercy, mercy" to Lady Frendraught who stood on the green below—

O then out spake her, lady Frendraught,
    And loudly did she cry,
"It were great pity for good Lord John,
    But none for Rothiemay.

The keys are casten in the deep draw-well,
    Ye canna get away."

And so they were burned.

"The Battle of Harlaw" tells of the encounter in 1411 between a highland host under Macdonald of the Isles and the lowlanders of the north-east, in which the citizens of Aberdeen took a valiant part:

As I came doun by Dunnideer,
    And doun by Netherha,
There were fifty thousand Hielandmen
    A-marching to Harlaw,
Wi a dree-dree-dradie-drumtie-dree.

As I came on and further on
    And doun and by Harlaw,
They fell fu close on ilka side
    Sic fun ye never saw.

They fell fu close on ilka side,
    Sic fun ye never saw,
For hieland swords gied clash for clash
    At the battle o Harlaw.

· · · · · · · ·

163

Macdonnell he was young and stout,
    Had on his coat o mail,
And he has gane out through them aa
    To try his hand himsel.

The first ae stroke that Forbes strack,
    He garrt Macdonnell reel,
And the neist ae stroke that Forbes strack,
    The great Macdonnell fell.

And siccan a lierachie
    I'm sure ye never saw,
As was amang the Hielandmen
    When they saw Macdonnell fa.

. . . .

On Monanday at mornin
    The battle it began,
At Saturday at gloamin
    Ye'd scarce ken wha had wan;

And sic a weary buryin
    I'm sure ye never saw
As was the Sunday after that
    On the muirs aneath Harlaw.

Some of the ballads deal with that enduring substance of tales—love—especially when it is unfortunately placed. The laird who loved the shepherd's daughter, the poor youth who loved the high-born lady—those had to dree their weird even in the north. The most romantic ballad of this sort tells of Andrew Lammie, trumpeter to the laird of Fyvie, who loved and was loved by Annie, the miller of Tifty's daughter:

But Tifty winna gie's consent
    His dochter me to marry,
Because she has five thousand merks
    And I have not a penny.

The laird of Fyvie interceded on behalf of his trumpeter, but Tifty was obdurate:

"I'll never never gie consent
    To the trumpeter o Fyvie."

When Fyvie looked the letter on
    He was baith sad and sorry,
Says the bonniest lass o the countryside
    Has died for Andrew Lammie.

O Andrew's gaen to the house top
O the bonnie house o Fyvie,
And he's blawn his horn baith loud and shill
Oer the lowlands leas o Fyvie.

"Mony's a time hae I walked aa nicht
And never yet was weary;
And now I may walk wae my lane
For I'll never see my dearie.

"Love pines away, love dwines away,
Love, love decays the body;
For the love o thee now I maun dee,
I come, my bonnie Annie."

I cannot see Andrew as a typical north-easter; for, although love does sometimes decay the body in these parts, it is seldom the unrequited sort.

The Baron o Leys was more in the native style. He seems to have been one of those careless and gallant young men who are celebrated in all folk tales because they never let their morality come between them and their senses. His ballad tells how the "rantin laddie" went to Edinburgh without his wife and there colleagued with a well-fared lass. When the issue promised to be only too fruitful, the lass, no village maiden but a metropolitan lady, said:

"Gin your name be Alexander Burnett,
Alas that ever I saw ye!
For ye hae a wife and bairns at hame
And alas for lyin sae near ye.

"But Ise gar ye be headed or hangt
Or marry me the morn,
Or else pay doun ten thousand crouns
For giein tae me the scorn."

Word has gaen tae the Lady o Leys
That the laird he had a bairn.
The worst word she said tae that was—
"I wish I had it in my arms.

"For I will sell my jointure lands,
I am broken and I'm sorry;
And I'll sell aa, to my silk gouns,
And get hame my rantin laddie."

There is quite a stir of life in that ballad, and of northern life at that. Especially in Lady Leys' worst word, which shows a strong regard for life however begotten, which is one of the kindlier qualities of the north. It recalls an incident of a much later day. A country doctor was called in by a small farmer because his only daughter had gone to bed with some mysterious trouble. After a very short examination the doctor suggested to the girl that she was going to have a child, which did not greatly surprise the girl. It did upset the mother, who seemed overcome at the shame that must follow. As the doctor left the bedroom he saw the father, an elderly man, waiting for him in a state of deep anxiety. The doctor wondered how he could ever tell the man the news and what effect it would have on him. The father said, "Doctor. Doctor. What's wrang—what's wrang wi the lassie?" The doctor told him, "Well, I'm afraid she's going to have a child." The father drew a deep breath, and his face cleared and he said, "A bairn. Och, doctor, that's something that'll come away o itsel. I was terrified it was something that would hae tae be cut out."

There is one more ballad I would like to quote because it has a quality of fantastic humour, fantastic and matter of fact at the same time, which is indigenous in the north:

> There lives a man in Rhynie's land,
>   Anither in Auchindore,
> The bravest man among them aa
>   Was lang Johnny More.

> Young Johnny was an airy blade,
>   Fu sturdy, stout and strang;
> The sword that hung by Johnny's side
>   Was just full ten feet lang.

> Young Johnny was a clever youth
>   Fu sturdy strong and wight,
> Just full three yards around the waist
>   And fourteen feet in height.

> But if aa be true they tell me now,
>   And if aa be true I hear,
> Young Johnny's on tae London gaen
>   The kings banner to bear.

> He hadna been in fair London
>   But twelvemonths two or three,
> Till the fairest lady in aa London
>   Fell in love wi young Johnny.

> This news did soun through London toun
>   Till it came to the king
> That the muckle Scot had fallen in love
>   Wi his daughter Lady Jean.

Whan the king got word o that
    A solemn oath swore he
The weighty Scot sall straight a rope
    And hanged he sall be.

When Johnny heard the sentence passed
    A light laugh then gied he—
"While I hae strength tae wield my blade
    Ye darena aa hang me."

The English rogues were cunning dogs,
    About him they did creep
And gied him drops o lodomy
    That laid him fast asleep.

When Johnny wakened frae his sleep
    A sorry heart had he;
His jaws and hands in iron bands,
    His feet in fetters three.

"O whar will I get a little wee boy
    Will work for meat and fee
That will rin on to my uncle
    At the foot o Bennachie?"

"Here am I a little wee boy
    Will work for meat and fee,
That will rin on to your uncle
    At the foot o Bennachie."

"Whan ye come whaur grass grows green,
    Slacken your shune and rin,
And whan ye come whaur water's strong
    Ye'll bend your bow and swim.

"And whan ye come tae Bennachie
    Ye'll neith chap nor caa,
Sae well's ye'll ken auld Johnny there,
    Three feet abune them aa.

"Ye'll gie to him this braid letter,
    Sealed wi my faith and troth,
And ye'll bid him bring alang wi him
    The body Jock o Noth."

Whan he cam whaur grass grew green
    He slackt his shune and ran;
And whan he cam whaur water's strong
    He bent his bow and swam.

And whan he cam to Bennachie
    Did neither chap nor caa,
Sae well's he kent auld Johnny there,
    Three feet abune them aa.

"What news, what news, my little wee boy?
    Ye never were here afore."
"Nae news. Nae news, but a letter here
    Frae your nephew Johnny More.

"Ye'll take here this braid letter
    Sealed wi his faith and troth,
And ye're bidden bring alang wi ye,
    The body Jock o Noth."

Bennachie lyes very low,
    The Tap o Noth lies high,
For aa the distance thats atween
    He heard auld Johnny cry.

When on the plain thae champions met,
    Two grisly ghosts tae see,
There were three feet atween their brows,
    Their shoulders were yards three.

Thae men they ran ower hills and dales
    And ower mountains high,
Till they cam on to London toun
    At the dawn o the third day.

And whan they cam to London toun
    The yetts were lockt wi bands,
And wha was there but a trumpeter
    Wi a trumpet in his hands.

"What is the matter, ye keepers aa,
    Or what's the matter within,
That bells do beat and bells do ring
    And make sic dolefu din?"

"There's naething the matter," the keeper said,
    "There's naething the matter to ye,
But a weighty Scot to straight the rope,
    And the morn he maun dee."

"O open the yetts ye proud keepers,
    Ye'll open without delay,
Or here is a body at my back,
    Frae Scotland has brought the key.

"O open the yetts, ye proud keepers,
　　Ye'll open without delay."
The trembling keeper, smiling said,
　　"O I hae not the key."

"Ye'll open the yetts," says John o Noth,
　　"Ye'll open them at my call."
Then wi his foot he has drave in
　　Three yards braid o the wall.

Sae they gaed in by Drury Lane
　　And doun by the toun's hall
And there they saw young Johnny More
　　Stand on the English wall.

"Ye're welcome here, my uncle dear,
　　Ye're welcome unto me;
Ye'll loose the knot and slack the rope
　　And set me frae the tree."

"Is it for murder, or for theft,
　　Or is it for robberie?
If it is for heinous crime
　　There's nae remeid for ye."

"It's nae for murder nor for theft,
　　Nor yet for robberie;
Aa is for the loving a gay lady
　　They're gaun tae gar me dee."

"O whaur's thy sword?" says Jock o Noth,
　　"Ye brocht frae Scotland wi ye?
I never saw a Scotsman yet
　　But could wield a sword or tree."

"A curse upon their lodomy
　　On me had sic a sway,
Four o their men, the bravest four,
　　They bore my blade away."

"Bring back his blade," says Jock o Noth,
　　"And freely tae him it gie,
Or I hae sworn a black Scots oath
　　I'll gar five million dee."

"Now whaur's the lady?" says Jock o Noth,
　　"Sae fain I would her see."
"She's locked up in her ain chamber,
　　The king he keeps the key."

So they hae gaen afore the king
  Wi courage bauld and free;
Their armour bricht cast sic a licht
  That aamost dimmed his ee.

"O whaur's the lady?" says Jock o Noth,
  "Sae fain as I would her see,
For we are come to her wedding
  Frae the foot o Bennachie."

"O take the lady," says the king,
  "Ye welcome are for me;
I never thought tae see sic men
  Frae the foot o Bennachie."

"If I had kend," said Jock o Noth,
  "Ye'd wondered sae muckle at me,
I would hae brought ane larger far
  By sizes three times three.

"Likewise if I had thought I'd been
  Sic a great fright to ye,
I'd brought Sir John o Erskine Park,
  He's thritty feet and three."

"Wae to the little boy," said the king,
  "Brought tidings unto ye;
Let all England say what they will,
  High hanged sall he be."

"O if ye hang the little wee boy
  Brought tidings unto me,
We sall attend his burial
  And rewarded ye sall be."

"O take the lady," said the king,
  "And the boy sall be free."
"A priest, a priest," then Johnny cried,
  "To join my love and me."

"A clerk, a clerk," the king replied,
  "To seal her tocher wi ye."
But out then spoke auld Johnny More –
  Thae words pronounced he—

"He want nae lands or rents at hame,
  He'll seek nae gowd frae ye;
I am possessed o riches great
  Hae fifty ploughs in lea.
He will fall heir tae my estate
  At the foot o Bennachie.

"Hae ye ony masons in this place
    Or ony at your call.
That we may now send some o them
    Tae mend your broken wall?"

"Yes, there are masons in this place,
    And plenty at my call,
But ye may gang frae whence ye came
    Never mind my broken wall."

They've taen the lady by the hand
    And set her prison-free.
Wi drums beating and fifes playing,
    They spent the night wi glee.

Now auld Johnny More and young Johnny More
    And Jock o Noth aa three,
The English lady and the little wee boy
    Went aa to Bennachie.

The north has a rich inheritance of songs about the labouring life. Not, curiously, the songs that are sung in time to the work of the hands and feet, to lighten and speed the labour, a sort of instinctive time and motion exercise, of which there are so many examples in the Highlands. The lowland songs are in praise of some trade, or in complaint about it. Most of them are ploughmen's songs and therefore are called bothy ballads, after the bothy in which the unmarried ploughmen lived, or cornkisters after the corn kist in the stable where they often sat when singing. The tunes are popular, perhaps traditional, and can be found in other parts of the country, in variation: the words have been fitted to them to suit some local purpose and celebrate some local condition, such as the meanness of particular farmers, a favourite subject:

As I cam in by Netherdale
    At Turra market for tae fee,
I fell in wi a farmer chield
    Frae the Barnyards o Delgaty.

He promised me the ae best pair
    I ever set my eyen upon;
But when I gaed hame tae the Barnyards
    There was naething there but skin and bone.

The auld black horse sat on his rump
    The auld white mare lay on her wame,
And aa that I could "hup" and crack,
    They wouldna rise at yokin time.

The farmer of Drumdelgie (they are real names) was a hard driver:

> The farmer o yon muckle toun
> He is baith hard and sair,
> And the cauldest day that ever blaws
> His servants get their share.

> At five o'clock we quickly rise
> And hurry doun the stair,
> Its there to corn our horses
> Likewise to straik their hair.

> Syne after working half an hour
> Each to the kitchen goes,
> Its there to get our breakfast
> Which generally is brose.

> We've scarcely gotten our brose well supt
> And gien our pints a tie
> When the foreman cries "Hello, my lads,
> The hour is drawing nigh."

> At six o'clock the mill's put on
> To gie us a straight wark,
> It taks four o's to make to her
> Till ye could wring our sark.

> And when the water is put off
> We hurry doun the stair
> To get some quarters through the fan
> Till daylight does appear.

> When daylight does begin to peep
> And the sky begins to clear,
> The foreman he cries out, "My lads,
> Ye'll bide nae langer here.

> "There's six o ye'll gang tae the ploo
> And twa will drive the neeps,
> The owsen they'll be after ye
> Wi strae raips round their queets."

There is no end to the infamies of farmers, but horses are different:

> We will sing our horses' praise
> Though they be young and sma,
> They far outshine the Broadlands anes
> That gang sae full and braw.

When the six months' engagement is ended, the ploughman is ready to move on:

My candle now it is burnt out,
    The snotter's fairly on the wane;
Sae fare ye well ye Barnyards,
    Ye'll never catch me here again.

The parting gesture can be like the crack of a whip:

Sae fare ye well, Drumdelgie,
    For I maun gang awa.
Sae fare ye well, Drumdelgie,
    Your weety weather and aa.
Sae fare ye well, Drumdelgie,
    I bid ye aa adieu,
And leave as I found ye—
    A maist onceevil crew.

Two songs, the best remembered of this sort, are "The Bonnie Lass o Fyvie" and "Mormond Braes". The first is in the simple ballad style:

Green grow the birks on sweet Ythanside
    And low lies the bonnie Lewes o Fyvie;
In Fyvie there's bonnie, in Fyvie there's braw,
    In Fyvie there's bonnie lasses mony.

There cam a troop o Irish dragoons
    And they were quartered in Fyvie.
And their captain's fallen in love wi very pretty maid
    That was by aa caaed pretty Peggy.

"Come doun the stair, pretty Peggy," he said,
    "Come doun the stair, pretty Peggy;
Come doun the stair and comb back your yellow hair,
    Tak farewell o your mammie and your daddie.

"I'll gie ye ribbons for your bonnie yellow hair,
    And I'll gie ye beads o the amber;
I'll gie ye silken petticoats wi flounces to the knee
    If ye'll convoy me to my chamber."

"I hae got ribbons for my bonnie yellow hair,
    And I hae got beads o the amber;
And I hae got petticoats befitting my degree
    And I'd scorn to be seen in your chamber."

Even though he raised the bid as high as marriage—

"I've gien ye my answer, kind sir," she said,
    "And ye needna ask me any further;
I do not intend to go to a foreign land,
    And I'd scorn to follow a sodger."

Early next morning they aa marched awaa,
    And O but the captain was sorry;
But the drums they did beat by the bonnie Bog o Gight,
    And the band played "The bonnie Lewes o Fyvie."

Lang lang ere they won to Auld Meldrum toun
    They got their captain to carry;
And lang ere they won to bonnie Aberdeen,
    They got their captain to bury.

He was caaed Captain Ward and he died on the guard,
    He died for the love o pretty Peggy,
And he said, "When I'm gone, ye'll let it be known,
    That I died for the bonnie lass o Fyvie."

A touching but rather anonymous piece—take away the place names
and it could have happened anywhere. Not so "Mormond Braes":

As I gaed doun by Strichen toun
    I heard a fair maid mourning,
And she was making sair complaint
    For her true love neer returning.
"Its Mormond Braes where heather grows,
    Where aft-times I've been cheery,
O Mormond Braes where heather grows,
    Its there I lost my dearie.

"Sae fare ye well ye Mormond Braes
    Where aft-times I've been cheery;
Fare ye weel, ye Mormond Braes,
    For its there I lost my dearie.

"O, I'll put on my goun o green,
    Its a forsaken token,
And that will let the young men ken
    That the bands o love are broken.
There's monys a horse has snappert and faaen
    And risen and gaen fu rarely,
There's mony a lass has lost her lad
    And gotten another right early.

(Chorus)

"There's as guid fish intae the sea
    As ever yet was taken;
I'll cast my line and try again,
    I'm only ance forsaken.

> Sae I'll gang doun tae Strichen toun
> Where I was bred and born,
> And there I'll get another sweetheart
> Will marry me the morn."

That comes right from the heart and the head of the north. If there were ever such things as native wood notes wild, surely these are they. There may be others as good or better, forgotten but not perhaps lost, for Gavin Grieg, a schoolmaster in New Deer, spent the leisure of many years in collecting old songs and fragments of songs from the people who still sang them. The results of his labour are now in King's College Library in Aberdeen: ninety manuscript volumes of them.

There is a bite in those old pieces, a sure-footedness and independence, the dry wit of the east wind. It is there in Auld Johnnie More's offer to repair the broken wall of London, a very nice example of the off-taking humour so strong in the north which can reduce every pretension, even kingliness, and frost the bloom of every impulse, even Christian charity. It is there in Mormond Braes:

> I'll bait my hook and cast my line:
> I'm only ance forsaken.

Which has the same sure spirit as the great modern hymn of the whole heart:

> Why should a woman that is healthy and strong
> Blubber like a baby cause her man's gone away?
> A-weepin and a-wailin that he's done her wrong—
> Thats one thing you'll never hear me say.

Only the Scots one has more bite and a higher voltage than the American. The heart is no less but the head is stronger. I must resist any temptation to suggest that it might be poetry, for obviously it satisfies no academic canons—you couldn't imagine it set as a question in Eng. Lit., or discussed in the places where poetry is taken seriously. It is obviously not literature, yet it communicates. It has content and that content is no less than a human being competent to deal with life, or at least to have a damned good try. There are only a few simple images and plain words, but then these have often been enough for poets who lived in happier times and knew what they wanted to say.

> Kissed ystreen and kissed ystreen,
> Up the Gallowgate, doun the Green:
> I've wooed wi lords and wooed wi lairds,
> I've mooled wi carles amd melled wi cairds,
> I've kissed wi priests—'twas dune in the dark
> Twice in my goun and thrice in my sark—
> But priest nor lord nor loon can gie
> Sic kindly kisses as he gied me.

These are the works of Anon., but there have been some writers in the north whose names are known and whose writings remembered. John Skinner, the episcopalian minister of Linshart near Longside in Aberdeenshire at the end of the eighteenth century, wrote "Tullochgorum", which John Buchan described as "that most rollicking and dance compelling of measures", a sort of eightsome reel in verse. James Beattie, a poor boy from Laurencekirk, made his way to Aberdeen University, became professor of philosophy there, captured the polite literary taste with his long poem "The Minstrel" and got a pension from that acute literary critic George III. He may not have been a great poet, but he was certainly a portent in the north, perhaps the first and certainly the most successful of those who learned to soar out of their provincial background and cultivate the literary fashion of their day. He did very well for himself, as can be seen in his *London Diary* and his *Daybook*, both edited by Mr Ralph Walker of the University of Aberdeen. A quarto volume of his essays on æsthetics brought him 400 guineas at a time when a guinea was solid gold; but his works, like the guinea, have passed out of currency. The same fate has overtaken the poems of William Thom, who may have been a better poet though a far less successful man. Thom was born in Aberdeen in the last years of the century and left fatherless at a very early age. He was apprenticed a weaver when he was ten in a shop which he afterwards described as a "prime nursery of vice and sorrow". He followed his trade in Aberdeen and the south till 1837, when he came north again and settled at Inverurie. Meanwhile he had separated from his wife and was living with Jean "of the deep dark eye" and their children. When he had turned forty Jean died. Out of his distress he wrote "The Blind Boy's Pranks", some sets of verses on the adventures of Love in the north. They were not the sort of adventures the old ballad-makers had celebrated. They have fancy and humour and the dialect is well handled, but one gets the feeling that Thom had read too many "Keepsakes" and "Young Lady's Garlands". The effect is just a trifle coy at times, but that may be inevitable, for even the strongest are a little corrupted by the times they live in.

> Men grew sae cauld, maids sae unkind,
>   Love kentna whaur to stay;
> Wi fient an arrow, bow or string—
> Wi droopin heart and drizzled wing
>   He fought his lanely way.

> "Is there nae mair, in Garioch fair,
>   Ae spotless hame for me?
> Hae politics, an corn an kye
> Ilk bosom stappit? Fie o fie!
>   I'll swithe me o'er the sea."

While floating down the Ury on a jessamine leaf, Love spied

a weelfaured deem
Wha listless gazed on the bonnie stream
As it flirted and played wi a sunny beam
That flickered its bosom upon.

Love glowered when he saw her bonnie dark ee
An swore by Heaven's grace
He ne'er had seen, nor thought to see,
Since eer he left the Paphian lea,
Sae lovely a dwallin place!

Syne, first of aa, in her blythesome breast
He built a bower, I ween;
An what did the weafu develick neist
But kindled a gleam like the rosy east
That sparkled frae baith her eyen.

An then beneath ilk high ee bree
He placed a quiver there;
His bow? What but her shinin brow;
And o sic deadly strings he drew
Frae out her silken hair.

Guid be our guard! Sic deeds were deen
Roun aa our countrie then;
An monie a hangin lug was seen
Mang farmers fat and lawyers lean
An herds o common men.

A curious mixture of literary fancy and native wit. When the verses were published in the *Aberdeen Journal* they attracted a deal of attention locally. Thom was taken up by the fanciers, who carried him off to the London drawing-rooms, where he became the talk of the town. There is nothing more destructive of a small talent than that sort of success. The literary fanciers drove Thom to drink, as they have driven many people of sensibility before and since. And that was the end of him. He was a true poet: his verses have feeling and they do communicate. "The Overgate Orphan", which he was moved to write by an account of a widow woman being found dead of cold and hunger in a hovel at Dundee with her seven-year-old child sleeping at her side, has the chill of experience in it, as when the dying woman speaks to her child:

"O wauken nae, wauken nae, my dowie dear,
My dead look would wither your wee heart wi fear;
Sleep on till yon cauld moon is set in the sea,
Gin morning how cauld will your waukenin be."

That comes from the dark side of the industrial bonanza, the side which Thom knew so very well. He was a gentle and lyrical spirit born into an evil state of society. His *Recollections* show how hard he worked to make a life:

"During my apprenticeship I had picked up a little reading and writing. Afterwards set about studying Latin—went so far, but was fairly defeated through want of time, etc., having the while to support my mother who was getting frail. However, I continued to gather something of music and arithmetic, both of which I had mastered so far as to render further progress easy did I see it requisite. I play the German flute, tolerably, in general subjects, but in my native melodies, lively or pathetic, to few will I lay it down. I have every Scotch song that is worth singing, and though my vocal capability is somewhat limited, I can convey a pretty fair idea of what a Scotch song ought to be.

"Employed seven or eight months yearly in customary weaving —that is, a country weaver who wants a journeyman sends for me. During that time I earn from 10s. to 12s. a week, pay the master generally 4s. for my keep, and remit the rest to my family. I eke out the blank portions of the season by going into a factory. Here the young and vigorous only can exceed 6s. weekly. I don't drink; as little, at any rate, as possible. I have been vain enough to set some value on my mind, and it being all that I possess now, and the only thing likely to put me in possession of aught afterwards, I would not willingly drown it.

"My books? I have few of my own—pick up a loan where it can be had, so of course my reading is without choice or system."

Poverty is considered a great begetter of virtues by those who are well-off, but it is not a good state to be born into; and if it bears hardly and for too long, it destroys a talent. Thom was too gentle a spirit for such a savage time, a man all love and friendliness—too much so, for he was quite without that touch of ultimate and inviolable selfishness which is so often necessary if a talent is to win to its full expression. Thom was probably exhausted before he got that ease in which his talent would have flowered most kindly.

This is not a full or an academic account of the literature of the north but only a personal excursion, and if some are not mentioned or are passed lightly over, that is nothing at all against them but due to a want of sensibility or interest on my part. For instance, I have never been able to make any contact with the novels and poems of George Macdonald, who had a considerable success towards the end of the nineteenth century—but his works remain to be enjoyed by those who can put up with a deal of theology for the sake of some excellent Scots characters and speech. I have no difficulty at all with

William Alexander, whose novel *Johnny Gibb o Gushetneuk* is what they call a minor classic. It describes farm life in the north and in a spirit of love and knowledge. Some parts of it are tiresome now, for they deal with the disruption of the Church of Scotland and the long legal disputes of that ten years' conflict. When these have been skipped over much remains, a true and quiet-toned picture of rural life a hundred years ago. The characters are lovingly done; a little too lovingly perhaps—they are all just a little too respectable, but Alexander was writing in a respectable time, when it had become the fashion to pretend that people had no vagrant impulses. Nothing goes on inside the characters, not even digestion: they are figures in a landscape. As a landscape it is delightful and as a piece of social history written in love it will have an enduring value. To me, however, it just does not have the stir of life.

I feel the same lack in the verses of Charles Murray. These made a great popular success early in this century. They were read by people who seldom read verses and who called their bungalows "Hamewith" after one of the collections. Murray spent most of his working life in South Africa and from that distance looked back on life in the north. His love for that life was expressed in verses that have technical skill and an exact feeling for the dialect; as in the piece about the whistle the herd boy made from a rowan twig:

He wheeplt on't at mornin and he tweetlt on't at nicht
He pufft his frecklt cheeks until his nose sank oot o sicht.
The kye were late for milkin when he piped them up the close,
The kitlins got his supper syne and he was bedded boss;
But he cared nae doit nor docken what they did or thocht or said,
There was comfort in the whistle that the wee herd made.

Nobody has ever more justly expressed what a toy can be to a child; and that is something. But it is observed rather than felt and that, it seems to me, is the case with most of Murray's verses. He makes no statement out of something passionately felt and believed in, except in the splendid piece "Gin I were God".

A master of the dialect for comic purposes was George Bruce Thomson. He was a lad o pairts, studied medicine for a time, gave it up and went to sea, then returned to the Aberdeen countryside. He got a local fame by his comic songs, which exactly expressed and delighted the humour of the North-east. They have the native sense of the fantastic and ridiculous, as in "M'Ginty's Meal and Ale," which tells what happened when the pig went on the spree. Then there is Macfarlane—

the grimmest chiel
For forty miles aroun;
Folk buy his photograph tae scare
The rottans (rats) frae their toun.

Boasting about the wonders of his farm,

> He said he had an ostrich
> Frae the wilds o Timbuktu
> He kept for scrattin up his neeps
> So he hadna them tae pu.

Thomson's name is little remembered but his songs have passed into common usage.

Looking back over a hundred years one feels the literary landscape was rather depopulated in the north. Times have changed and the north has been fair ringing with typewriters. Rachel Annand Taylor, Agnes Mure Mackenzie, Nan Shepherd, Catherine Gavin, Lesley Storm, Gordon Daviot, Neil Gunn, Eric Linklater, G. S. Fraser, Agnes Carnegie and Neil Paterson are all from these parts and most of them have passed through Aberdeen University. They are alive and can speak for themselves and defend themselves so I will pass on to two that are dead and need no advocate.

Ian Macpherson's people came from Speyside, but the family lived for a while at Drumtochty in the Mearns and Ian went to the Mackie Academy in Stonehaven. In 1922 we came together at Aberdeen University to study Eng. Lit. Anyone looking for the stir of life could always find it where he was around. He was the most wholly and intensely alive person I have ever known. He was not big but he was physically strong and even more so tough; and, if the muscles ever tired, the will carried on. He was fair-haired and had a curiously innocent face, made all the more so by spectacles, for he was short-sighted, but the eyes behind the spectacles were hardly innocent: they were very seeing and very very penetrating, or the mind was that looked out through them. He used to walk a little round-shouldered, with his head thrust forward, and if he happened to be in high spirits or in a tearing humour against some foolishness, he was a force of nature no one could stand against. He had rare wit and a power of language that was always vivid, completely expressive and seldom polite; and he was in himself the spirit of the north. He was contrasuggestive to the highest degree. Whatever statement was made he would contradict it and bring such a wealth of argument and scurrility against it, in ever more outrageous heights of fantasy, that he ended by denouncing himself. No one was ever more truly of the north or loved it better or damned it more justly. For although he could make a deal of noise and was never one of those who move softly about their secret occasions, he had a great power of sweetness and gentleness in him. He could pass quickly from being a destructive force of nature among the pretentious to standing modestly, a little shyly, on one foot with people that he liked. He made for himself the sort of affection from which time and mischance can never take anything away.

Intellectually he was outstanding. Although he was not the academic good little boy, he won all the prizes and could have gone on to the usual academic career of the lad o pairts. But then he hadn't that sort of pairts. After lecturing in the university for two years he found that kind of life intolerable. He got married, hawked fruit along Speyside, ran a shooting gallery, taxied navvies from the hydro-electric works to the pubs and back again. In those days of the hungry 'thirties he lived in a cottage above Laggan and made a little spending money as local correspondent for daily papers. When news was scarce he invented it; and, through the Scottish edition of an English daily, provided Speyside with a whole new body of folk-lore, history and weather wisdom. Towards the end of the 'thirties he took a farm on the edge of Dava Moor, of the sort they call marginal, and proceeded to show just what could be made of such land. All that sort of thing was deplored by many good people as a dreadful waste of a first-class honours degree; for, if you have the sort of mind that knows what Shelley meant, you must make a living by telling people what Shelley meant for the rest of your life. Still they kept on hoping that he would come to his senses, because they hoped so much of him. In 1944 he was killed in a motor-cycling accident. It was a profoundly shocking thing, and unbelievable, that one so alive could be so quickly and so utterly dead.

His novels—*Shepherd's Calendar, Pride in the Valley, Land of our Fathers* and *Wild Harbour*—have fallen out of regard, as usually follows an author's death. They are bound and are due to return, for they are alive. The scene is farm life on Speyside; the theme is the business of living; and the people live. They live, not as the usual peasants of fiction; for, although they use ordinary words about everyday things and never speak out of character, there are implications beyond turnips and sheep-dip and straw and bedding in the broom; and the things implied but not said are the measure of good writing—otherwise writing is just a public health report or a valuator's inventory. *Wild Harbour*, written under threat of the war which officially began in 1939, is the sort of thing that must always be described by reference to Defoe and Robinson Crusoe. A man and woman determine to save themselves from destruction by taking to a cave in the mountains. They do so and live beyond and above the conflict, until the war comes to their door, when they find that, being human, they are part of all humanity and cannot remain aside. With that knowledge they lose fear even of the death that comes to them so inevitably and so soon. The moral, of course, is seldom the most important thing, though it does make an end. The force of *Wild Harbour* is in the detail of living—the making of a home out of the cave, the finding of food, the make-do when people are forced back on their own resources, the eternal fascination of the desert island where people discover the infinite and so delicately balanced provision of nature and, finally, themselves. *Wild Harbour* is magnificently done, with the background of war so lightly stated, so ominously implied. For he knew—not only what Shelley meant but the instinctive movement of stags on the hill and how you could shoot a black cock from your bedroom window when suffering a hang-over, three things not as disparate as some people think. When they were published the novels seemed a little old-fashioned . . . they told a story, the images were clear, and immediate in their effect; the thing described could be seen at once without any labouring words or the mist of the writer's emotions interposed; and that was out of fashion when everyone was thinking up alibis against the wrath to come. The novels do not seem old-fashioned now: there is too much life in them; perhaps they have moved into that timeless state where all good work abides.

There are many books published every year and a large number of them are masterpieces. At least, people who should know, and are paid for knowing, describe them as masterpieces, and so they must be. People even write at some length describing the subtle differences between those works and between their authors. That sort of writing is called criticism and is very clever writing indeed, because those masterpieces are as alike as packages of any sound, safe breakfast food and just as exciting—guaranteed to please all tastes and keep the customers happy and regular.

Now and then a book appears that is not immediately recognisable as a masterpiece, that is not safe and does not please all the customers all the time. The characters are not characters that have been met ten thousand times before. The language in which they are described is not the same old syrup that drips so goldenly in time with the background music of the radio. Such books are dangerous, and tired readers should keep away from them. They are written by people in a passion about something and are liable to make the world seem real and dangerous. *Sunset Song* by Lewis Grassic Gibbon, which was published in 1932, is a book of that sort; so were *Cloud Howe*, 1933, and *Grey Granite*, 1934. Together they make *A Scots Quair*—a book that is not likely to be soon forgotten—nor, by some people, forgiven.

The three parts tell the story of a girl, Chris Guthrie, first as a daughter and then as a wife on a small farm in the Mearns; next as the minister's wife in a small manufacturing town also in the Mearns; and finally as a widow and mother of a son growing into manhood in a city recognisable as Aberdeen. The time is the last years of the last century and the first thirty years of the present. But it is a great deal more than just another of those long chronicles of family life. There is an intense feeling for the countryside of the north: it is, I think, a classical feeling, by which I mean that the emphasis is all on the community between man and what is usually called nature. There is a strong feeling for the past, due to Grassic Gibbon's belief that men were once primitive, innocent and happy until they were corrupted by property and power. For him the men who built the standing stones on the hillsides were at the peak of civilisation and all that have come after have been travelling at an always more furious and fatal pace down wrong roads that lead to disaster. He could be right; indoor plumbing and faster transport have not brought a corresponding increase in peace of mind. The standing stones on the braesides were powerful symbols to him and in *A Scots Quair* there is a constant return to them. They are a background of time and the spirit, in front of which unhappy people are driven to the meannesses of a degenerate age. There is also the quality of love, which is rarer than one might think, considering the number of times that word occurs in popular fiction. Mostly it is used to describe a sort of bedroom furniture— the consummation of the fumed oak; or a substitute for conversation among the inarticulate. At other times it is a wash of mild goodwill for the pleasure of elderly ladies and gentlemen who like to pretend that everything in the garden is lovely for their own comfort. There is, however, another sort which springs from a profound faith that man is really a good thing, however misguided; it is an instinct to understand people and put up with them and so make some pleasure in what is rather a short and harried life. That sort of love is full of generous feeling and quick to anger at injustice. There is a lot of it in *A Scots Quair*.

This writer's real name was James Leslie Mitchell, and he was born in 1901 at Seggat of Auchterless in Aberdeenshire. When he was eight, the family moved to a farm near Drumlithie in the Mearns. There he attended the local school, and then had a year at the Mackie Academy in Stonehaven, which he left when he was sixteen. He worked for some time as a reporter on the *Aberdeen Journal* and later on the *Scottish Farmer*. In his spare time he studied widely, particularly languages, and probably drove himself too hard, for he took ill and went home to the farm to rest. But he was not the kind that can rest and probably not the kind that can stay at home. He listed in the army and served there and in the R.A.F. for eight years as a clerk. Part of his service was spent in the Middle East, where, as Ivor Brown has written, "he could survey the greater relics of antiquity and muse upon the origins of society and the martyrdom of man". He was not the ideal serviceman, but those years may not have been lost. The long monotonies of service life in peacetime, the freedom from responsibility and the freedom from the interference by silly well-intentioned people that can be so harmful to a young writer—these may have been far more favourable conditions for the growth of a literary talent than the harried life of a junior reporter. In 1928 he left the service and began to live by writing. In the next seven years he wrote sixteen books and a great number of short pieces. In 1935 he died. Most of his work was published under his given name. In it he made use of his archæological studies and his experience of foreign countries. It has energy, ideas and individual character and is far superior to the ordinary bricks that writers turn out to keep the wolf away. In his last years his mind and spirit turned to the lands of his youth, and there they were powerfully refreshed, for he was possessed by something greater than himself or he had uncovered the deepest springs of inspiration. *Sunset Song* was written in six weeks, and it flows as if it had come from the heart of the living rock.

The style of the writing is individual, unique; more like the spoken than the written word. It has the real ring of the north: not that he reproduced the actual speech of the people—there are few vernacular words and none of those decayed English terms that pass for dialect with a scatter of apostrophes, like something the moths have been at. The effect is produced by long loose rhythmical sentences that have the cadences of speech and the dry bite of northern wit. If there is a likeness to anything it is to the old ballads—not only in the manner. There is also the stir of life. Much of it is not very edifying. Most of the characters torment each other and themselves, as people do in this our daily life, but there is always implicit a certain human dignity, even if it is only something from which the characters have been distorted away; even when they are spiritually dead they are the ghosts of men and women born to live. The moving forces in the book are love and pity. These alone do not ensure great literature but they are at the heart of it; and we have been too long without them. Perhaps the dark side of the Industrial Revolution is really passing away and our humanity winning free again.

CHAPTER VI

THE DARK SIDE OF THE MOON

IF it is right to say that the north of Scotland was in a rather primitive state until the early eighteenth century, and that changes came slowly even then, there need be no surprise that primitive beliefs remained strong in people's minds until fairly recent times. Even a century's preoccupation with turnips and straw was not quite enough to make everyone forget there might be a dark side to the moon.

When I was a boy more than thirty years ago on a farm in Aberdeenshire, I was fortunate to live with and listen to some for whom those primitive beliefs were just a little more than curious echoes of antiquity. My grandfather employed three workers, single men who slept outside in the chaumer but ate in the kitchen, and by custom sat at the kitchen fire if they so pleased till nine o'clock. It was there I got a great deal of my early education, in a school with such power over my imagination that my emotions are still deeply engaged by it. The kitchen, to me, was large and high—cool and shady in the full noon of summer and by night invested with shadows at all seasons. There were dark entries to the scullery and the milkhouse; black shadows in the peathouse under the stair; and the black night sighing at the window panes. The hung lamp cast a ring of brightness on the floor and the long scrubbed table; but, as it wore a round shade, it cast more shadows on the roof, shadows that swithered uncannily when a sudden draught made the lamp swing and the light flicker on the wick. Beset with darkness and uncertain light, we had one thing constant—the fire on the low, wide open hearth. When that fire was made up it took a big apronful of logs and peats; and, if scientifically built, soon blazed in a great dome of heat where the ardent wood was contained by the glowing peat. It was more than a fire: upon its step there was sanctuary against the powers of darkness. We gathered round this fire on most winter nights, the ploughmen, the kitchenmaid and myself. Now and then a ploughman from a neighbouring farm would join us, to speak to the men or cast a prospecting eye on the girl. Sometimes my grandfather stayed with us for a few minutes during his occasional journeys to the close. And, but far too seldom, we had Old Ronald.

He was a very old man, to me, with a long white beard which made him look like Time's elder brother, as indeed he may have been. He had worked on the farms in our part of the country when he was a young man, but had been gone elsewhere for a long time, and now in his old age liked to come back again. He came for a day or two and slept in the bothy and helped my grandfather to pass the time. In the evenings he sat with us at the kitchen fire and talked about the things he had known. That was our school. Three or four young men sitting on wooden chairs round the fire; the maid on the cheekstone at one side; I on the cheekstone at the other; the old man seated in the middle, leaning forward to light a spill for his black clay pipe. Then, with the spill flickering halfway to his whiskers, he would stop and look down at me gravely and say, "Aye, Johnny man, strange things have happened in this countryside. D'ye ken there are caves in the hills o Dyce?" The young men laughed, but not I; for an old man can speak direct to a small boy. "Caves," I said. "No, I didna ken." But I knew at once he was right. The hills of Dyce were innocent and familiar all day and when the sun went down behind them they invested themselves with a blue that darkened and swallowed up field and farm in a premature night while the western sky was still in blaze of sunset; but at the very moment when the last colour had gone, they suddenly stepped forward out of the cold green west, awful, imminent and alive. As soon as Old Ronald said the word I knew there were caves. I had known it always.

There were dwarves in the caves, he said, and they were bodies of a mischievous temper. Folk had found the caves and gone into them and had never come out again. Never. Never. Never seen again by man or woman. Folk that see the doors of caves should hurry by.

"But, mind ye, the dwarves could repay a kindly act with a kindlier. There was a crofter man by the hills of Dyce who found that somebody was stealing his potatoes from the drill. One night he spied on them and saw three dwarves, each one with a fork no bigger than ye'd carve a turkey with, digging up the fine new tatties. What did the crofter mannie do? He creepit home to his bed, like a wee mouse from a coven o cats, and saw there was aye a tattie left handy till the summer came. Now the next harvest that crofter mannie was stricken wi the shakin ague. When he got better the weather turned bad and the never a scythe could he lay to his corn. On the one good day in October he had to run for the howdie to his wife and his daughter both, so he lost that fine day too. But on the first of November when he looked out on another rainy day, he saw his corn was cut and stooked and led home and built into seven o the finest big ricks ever seen atween Dyce and Bennachie. Aye and each ane finished off with the likeness of a stem o tatties."

The old man stopped. The young men laughed. The old man shook his head at them. Then, as he leaned forward to light the spill again, he looked at me very seriously and said, "The dwarves have their kindly turns, but, laddie, never trust them."

From dwarves he went sooner or later to witches. He had never known any woman to be a proven witch, though there were plenty of them in his father's time around Lumphanan. But even in his own day strange, mischievous things had happened. At Burnside, for instance.

One of the young men would nod and say "Aye", because this was a more serious affair than dwarves. The others too were less ready to laugh, or the laugh had a touch of bravado in it.

The farm of Burnside was an unchancy place. People going to the house at night, up the narrow road between the broombushes, were liable to be flung over the dyke, suddenly, headfirst into a whinbush. Suddenly—just like that. They heard no step; they felt no hands on them; they were abruptly lifted and thrown down. The road led past the mill dam, in which many ploughmen and farmers too had landed after a swift transit through the air. In the close there were constant mechanters. Plough socks, lying at the stable door, rose up and rapped you on the shins. Yokes and swingletrees lundered you across the shoulders. One night a young man came to court the farmer's daughter, and in no marrying mind. As he slipped along to her bedroom window past the peat stacks, the peats came flying down on him, all forty load of them. Had he not been gie on edge already, he'd have been smoored among them, but he got clear with a long leap and scudded for home with a hail of peats about his lugs.

"Ye see," Old Ronald said, "the auld wife was a witch."

One of the young men said, "She was the Queen o Hell."

Then there was competition about who should tell of her greatest art; but Old Ronald always won.

"She was a woman of the maist wonderfu power. There was one night the farm lads had been all away out-about on some ploy among the quaens. It was late when they came up atween the broombushes and over the rise where you can see the farm below you. Aathing was quiet and still atween the broom: not a single clod flew at them; but, when the foreman looked over the rise, he cried out, 'Guid God, the barn's on fire.' The other lands looked and, man, it was a sight—a great blaze of light in the barn where everything should have been darkness. The lads ran down, ding-dang, through the close and up to the barn: but it was no fire. They stood up, halted at the door, the breath stopped in their throats and the hair risen on their heads. For the mill was on. The wheels ran round; the timbers shook and shivered; the drum boomed high and low. The corn sheaves came in through the sheaf door; the bands flew apart, the drum pulled in the corn and threshed it. The grain came from the head of the mill into the sacks that held open their mouths and tied themselves when full and carried themeslves up the corn loft stair. The straw came from the tail of the mill and trailed itself away through to the little cow byre.

Even the chaff packed itself into a muckle bag. All went on at a terrible speed without a hand put to it and under the blaze of light, though not a single lamp hung upon the crook."

Old Ronald stopped at the climax when we were all leaning forward—looking in through that barn door. The voice stopped, but I'd swear we saw the blaze of the lampless light and heard, still louder in the silent kitchen, the drum boom high and low. I, looking up from the cheekstone at the shadows on the roof, felt darkness and mystery crowding in upon our ring of light; and the others may have heard the drum of ancient mysteries and felt the catch in their breath at the fears which had beset the many generations of our ancestors.

The foreman pulled himself out of the spell and said to the girl, "For God's sake gie us a cup o tea to drown this nonsense." The girl cried out on him, as the girls always did; but pushed the kettle on the fire and then insisted he go with her to the dark scullery for the tea cups and the caddy. That time, all she wished for was protection.

There was one part of the old ritual magic that still had force in young men's minds—the horseman's word. It certainly did have great force in the minds of those of us who were boys then at the beginning of the century. Whenever we were allowed to lead the horses to water or ride them home from the plough, the men said we would not be any use till we'd gotten the horseman's word. If we showed a fondness for a servant girl who gave us jelly pieces, the men teased us and said we must get the horseman's word before we tried our hand. But when we asked what the Word was, we ran against an impenetrable secret. The men looked at each other and winked and laughed at us in a way that made the secret all the more real. More real, and most desirable, for the Word gave its possessor a power over horses and women and was the proof that he had become a man. We longed for the day when we would get the Word.

Old Ronald would never tell me anything about the Word although he was so ready to speak about other old things; perhaps because he believed so profoundly in it. But from others who held it more lightly I did get the outlines of what must have been a very important event in a young ploughman's life. When the youth was at the age to be a man, he was told he must appear for initiation. The place was the barn. The time eleven on a dark night. He must take with him a candle, a loaf and a bottle of whisky. At the barn door he was blindfolded and led before the secret court. This consisted of a few older ploughmen, presided over by a master of ceremonies at an altar made by inverting a bushel measure over a sack of corn, that strong symbol of fertility. The youth was then put through a long questioning and made to repeat certain forms of words. In later days, at least, he had to suffer many indignities, some of them sexual, according to the humour of the court. As the climax of initiation, he got a shake of the Devil's hand—usually a stick covered by a hairy skin. Then he was given the horseman's word. Then at last the bread and whisky, sacramental elements of universal significance, were passed round; and the youth had become a ploughman. Usually, in later days, several youths were admitted at a time, since the more initiates the more whisky for the court. But the Word—what was it? McPherson, in his book on our primitive beliefs, says it was "Both in one", meaning there would be complete harmony between the man and his beasts, whereby he would have power over them. He could reist them—that is, make them stand still so that no other person could get them to move; or he could make them come to him though he were miles away. He got a similar power over women: he had only to touch a girl and she would do his will—and as to that I do know that some young men had a strong magic.

Even in the early days of this century the horseman's word was the token of a sort of freemasonry among ploughmen. A young horseman who had not been initiated almost certainly had great trouble with his horses. When he went to put on the collar in the stable he might find that the horse drew back, with great restiveness, and refused to accept it. Or when he yoked the beast and the load went on the collar, the beast lashed out and perhaps became quite unmanageable. The older ploughmen said it was because he had not got the horseman's word. Very soon if he was simple enough, he was begging to be initiated and in due course was ordered to attend with the loaf and the bottle of whisky. After that he had no trouble and thus had proof of the power of the word. It may have been a long time before he discovered that the horse had refused the collar because one of the older ploughmen had tainted it with pig dung, a thing most offensive to a horse; or that the sudden distress in the plough was caused by a pinpoint or a small tack bedded in the collar.

It is difficult to convey what the horseman's word meant then because so much of it was in the atmosphere of the stable and the company of young unmarried men. There was the freemasonry; for those who had the word were bound to help each other on receiving the sign: and young men very taken up in the pursuit of women may have got some extra confidence, valuable in a sport where the will to succeed is so important and rewarding. Even when the ritual of initiation was no longer observed, there was something in being of an age to pretend it; as if by talking about the horseman's word you got something of its power. To Old Ronald, however, I am sure the word was very real. He had felt the power within himself.

Many of the old customs were more than customs to him. In those days we still celebrated the meal and ale on the day when the last of the harvest was brought in. By which I mean we had an extra good supper that night and everyone got beer or a glass of whisky, and there was sometimes the dancing of a reel or two in the kitchen. Old Ronald enjoyed it, such as it was, but next day he always told me about the meal and ale as it had once been. At the cutting of the corn, he said, the last sheaf was taken by the youngest person in the field; it was bound in the shape of a woman and called the clyack sheaf, or the maiden. That sheaf was carried home with honour and hung above the hearth. When the corn had all been led, they held the meal and ale. That was a supper at which the chief dish was composed of meal and whisky, with a ring in it. Everyone took a spoon and supped out of the one dish, hoping to get the ring which brought luck with it. Then there was dancing and the man who led off the dance had to carry the clyack sheaf, the maiden. That, Old Ronald said, was how it used to be done; and I knew he thought, in his own private mind, that was how it should always be.

The old man's head was full of rituals. For instance, washing the bridegroom's feet on the night before his marriage, a practice that is still common today. The bridegroom's friends catch him and, in pretence of washing his feet, cover him with blacking, fill him with whisky and make sure he will feel a total wreck in the morning. The custom is now regarded as rather a nuisance, especially by bridegrooms. They often do everything possible to avoid the indignity by avoiding their friends, who of course search them out and take them by force. One who had eluded the pursuit for a week was finally taken, converted into a scarecrow and tied to the market cross at three on a summer morning while his friends rang the kirk bell to call out the villagers. Old Ronald would not have approved of that sort of thing. An orgy after a feet-washing—that was all right; but that the bridegroom should try to escape it—never. The bridegroom was glad to see his friends and gave them whisky. They washed his feet in a tub of clean cold water from the well and sometimes emptied the tubful over him for a bit of extra luck. Then they took soot from the chimney and rubbed it into his legs. The ritual performed, he was safe to get married; without it he would not have dared the dangers of the marriage bed.

When the bride arrived at her new home, a married woman, there were certain things to be done before she could go in. A hen must be thrown in at the door; and a burning peat; and she must be carried over the step else there would be no luck for her. A quarter of oatcakes had to be broken over her head and the unmarried women took pieces to dream up a husband on. "Aye," the old man said, "I hear folk are sendin out wee bit knobbles o baker's cake in silvery boxies nowadays; but what power can there be in that? It should be cakes and whisky whan a bride gangs hame."

I remember the two of us sitting on the warm side of a dyke on a harvest day while the men were cutting barley and the heat brought out the sharp smell of the sap and the whirr of the grasshoppers under the whinbush. The old man stretched his long legs to the sun, folded his hands over his waistcoat and puffed out blue and grey smoke that smelled like a bonfire of deadly nightshade. I said to him, "Tell me another story about how things used to be." He said, "I mind there was a well that had a power o nature in't for married women." As always, having given out the theme, he went through the motions of lighting his pipe while he decided on the development. Then, "There's a thing that happens, though you are not o a family to understand it, but married men hae sometimes a difficulty o putting their wives wi a bairn. Now there are ways in siccan a mechanter. Sometimes it's the man that's no on his mettle and a diet o good green kale can kittle him. The Minister o Marnoch had kale in his yard that folk came twenty mile for in their needcessity, and it kept up the baptisings at a steady trade: aye, it did that. At other times the man was past aa remeid for he had spent his powder afore the battle began. Some folk tried prayer and some tried purging and some were just thankful for what they thought might be a god's mercy. But for them that were desperate, there was nothing better than that the wife should go to a well that had a power o nature.

"There was siccan a well on Willie's Muir when I was a laddie," he said. "Aye there was a hollow at the head of the muir and a spring of clean cauld water that came out atween the stones in the middle o a lythe place wi auld whin bushes round it. The barren wives used to gang there in the midsummer's week; three or four o them that were tired of waiting, and some auld wife went with them. As to what happened there I can tell ye the order o't, for I once hided in the whins and saw it whan I was a laddie. There were four of them, the three barren women and the auld auld wife and they came into the hollow wi many's a look over their shoulders in case they'd been seen. The auld wife went doun on her knees on the flat stone at the side of the spring and directed the women. First they took off their boots; and syne they took off their hose; and syne they rolled up their skirts and their petticoats till their wames were bare. The auld wife gave them the sign to step round her and away they went, the one after the other, wi the sun, round the spring, each one holding up her coats like she was holding herself to the sun. As each one came anent her, the auld wife took up the water in her hands and threw it on their wames. Never a one cried out at the cold of the water and never a word was spoken. Three times round they went. The auld wife made a sign to them. They dropped their coats to their feet again, syne they opened their dress frae the neck and slipped it off their shoulders so that their paps sprang out. The auld wife gave them another sign. They doun on their knees afore her, across the spring; and she took up the water in her hands again, skirpit on their paps, three times the

the three. Then the auld wife rose and the three barren women rose. They put on their claes again and drew their shawls about their faces and left the hollow without a word spoken and scattered across the muir for hame."

He stopped and looked at his pipe.

I asked, "Did it work?"

He said, "Capital: ye see, the well had a power o nature."

How it comes back to me: the hot sun on the barley field, the pair of chestnut mares in the clattering binder, the three men raising a line of stooks, the shimmer of heat, the scent of hay and harvest from the straw and the undersown grasses, the old man and the boy together at the side of the dyke; and within all that, the picture so clear in the boy's mind of the three barren women and the auld auld wife at the spring in the hollow, and the harmony there was then between the things that were seen and the things imagined, so that the sprinkling with water seemed as natural as the barley harvest.

Old Ronald certainly believed in those mysteries that remained from the old natural religion of the countryside. It was of course a religion without a gospel, but it would seem to have had two essentials of any religion—it allowed for certain human satisfactions and it tried to deal with the problem of evil.

It was certainly a religion of life: its greatest concern being the constant renewal of life by fertility and the need to protect it from mischance. It must have been a religion of true, not induced, humility, based on a right appreciation of man's place among the forces of nature. Man had no thought that he might control those forces: he must live under and, if possible, by them, for if he ran counter to them they might destroy him. Therefore he must try to run with them. Most of the primitive beliefs seem to have been inspired by the need to keep in step with nature. There is something like an empirical, a scientific attitude. The forces of nature are neither friendly nor hostile: impersonal forces—not a pantheon of temperamental gods; but they have the laws of their being and unless men take heed of those laws, disaster will come.

Our ancestors had a great regard for the power of fire, not surprising in a people who nested among windy shores and bleak hillsides. They celebrated the great fire festivals—Beltane around May-day; Halloween at the end of October; Midsummer at the solstice; and Yule in the darkest days at the turn of the year. Those were occasions of intense ceremonial. Sometimes all the fires in the community were put out and new, virgin, fire made by the friction of two pieces of hardwood. The ritual fire thus kindled, the people danced round it in the way of the sun; and some danced through it, thereby acquiring virtue; then torches or burning peats were taken away to light each hearth with a new fire. Sometimes the torches were carried round the fields to bless them. In Burghead in Moray there exists to this day the ritual fire at Yule, called the burning of the Clavie. McPherson says:

"On Hogmanay afternoon a band of young men, seamen and coopers, get busy building the Clavie. A tar barrel is secured, the gift of one of the merchants. . . . A herring cask and other materials are also provided. The tar barrel is sawn in two: the smaller part forms the groundwork of the clavie which is fixed upon a salmon fisherman's stake, some six feet in length, called the spoke. No hammer is used in driving the connecting nail, which is specially made and sent home by a smooth stone. The staves of the herring barrel are nailed at intervals of about two inches all round the lower part of the clavie, while the other ends of the spokes staves are firmly fixed to the spoke, an aperture being left sufficiently large to admit the head of the bearer. Then comes the filling of the clavie with pieces of wood and tar, a place being reserved for a burning peat. As twilight descends a youth is despatched for the live peat. The master-builder, 'the clavie king', receives it and places it in the opening awaiting it, where, revived by a blast from his lungs, it quickly bursts into flames. Loud cheers were raised and then the clavie bearer, popping his head between the staves, sets out with his blazing burden, and marches through the principal streets of the old town. Halts are made at appointed places where pieces of the burning faggots are thrown inside open house doors. Should the bearer stumble, it augurs ill for himself and the community, fore-telling disaster to the place and certain death to the ill-fated mortal. The circuit of the town being completed, the clavie is borne along the main street to a small hill near the northern extremity of the promontory, called 'the Doorie'. On the summit a freestone pillar has been built for its reception, the spoke fitting into a socket in the centre. There is nothing ancient or sacred about this pillar, which has only been the Doorie since 1809. Previous to this, a circular heap of stones used to be hastily piled up, in the centre of which the Clavie was fixed, still burning. Fresh fuel is now heaped on the Clavie, which burns more fiercely, surrounded by the cheering crowd. It used to be allowed to remain on the Doorie all night, but at the present time after burning about half an hour, it is hacked at and amidst great excitement, the blazing mass is scattered down the side of the hill. A general scramble ensures for the burned embers, the possession of which is regarded as a token of good fortune. The crowd now disperses with their lucky charms. These are eagerly sought after, and carefully preserved as a sure protection against witches and evil spirits."

They had great regard for the virtues of living water, as Old Ronald convinced me long ago, and something of that regard remains. When I took the whooping cough and could not get rid of the cough long after the trouble had gone, everybody said I'd be no better till I'd been taken across water. I was indeed taken across water—the River Don— and I did lose the cough in due course as all sufferers do, and there is proof for you. I heard only the other day a grandmother say her grandson would not lose his cough till he had been taken across water.

The larger pieces of water such as lochs, rivers and the ocean were not actively evil but they were certainly dangerous. The kelpie lived in the river and appeared to human eyes as a horse. He was a beast with a primitive sense of humour, for he often appeared to a foot traveller faced by a river in spate. While the poor man was wondering how he would get across, he suddenly noticed a good strong horse grazing beside him. Without considering to whom the horse might belong, he caught the beast, mounted him and rode him into the flood. Halfway across, the beast faded from between his legs and the river drowned him. That may be proof of the temper of rivers, or a parable against borrowing horses, but it is there and like all old beliefs susceptible to each man's interpretation. The sea, of course, was a very difficult power, as we still admit. The Vikings were so anxious to propitiate the ocean that they made human sacrifice at a launching. Later, in Aberdeen, when a boat left the slips, the shipwrights used to throw the apprentices after her and would not let them land till they had been thoroughly soaked. Our modern custom of having the ship christened by a good woman with a bottle of bad champagne, or *vice versa*, seems a survival of the ancient sacrifice rather than any Christian form of baptism.

Trees, stones and caves had their power. In a countryside as bare as ours was two hundred years ago, any tree must have seemed instinct with a tremendous power of nature. The rowan, which is hardly a tree and grows where few others will, was considered a talisman against evil. So was the elder, or, as we call it, the bourtree bush. If you see a farmhouse with one single tree in the garden—as you may see hundreds of them, you may bet your money the bush is a rowan or a bourtree. Stones had often very strong magic. That is reasonable, for they are so very withstanding. But that does not explain Clach-na-bhan, a rock in Glenavon. McPherson says, "By natural action a hollow had been scooped out of the rock, forming what looked like an armchair. Women about to be mothers climbed the hill and seated themselves in the hollow, believing this . . . ensured them an easy delivery." As late as 1836 a writer reported, he saw the chairing of as many as "twelve full-bodied women who had that morning come from Speyside, over twenty miles, to undergo the operation." The rock was also said to have the power of bringing husbands to single women. Among the stones of power there was the needle in the Dee at Dinnet, a fine upstanding stone with a hole in it, about eighteen inches in diameter, like the eye of a needle. If a childless wife passed through the eye, she would become a mother in due season, and many women proved its power. But there is a ritual in all these things which, if not properly observed, inhibits the power. "A noble lady essayed the ordeal, but her desire was not realised. She had gone through the aperture against the stream, whereas it was necessary to go in the direction of the river. A second attempt was made and she was successful." It is a fine old country story, but no psychologist could be trusted with it. What would he not make of childless marriages and rowing against the stream? And yet. And yet . . .

It seems to me that if our pre-Christian ancestors lived in a difficult world, it was not an evil one. It was certainly one in which men lived on sufferance and from which they might be suddenly irretrievably removed. But, by a very careful observance of certain rules, one might pass along to a good old age, tolerated if not revered by one's children. It is often argued that those older societies were dominated by fear, but people constantly in fear do not greatly desire children nor invent so many rites to induce human fertility. Perhaps those early times were not so bad after all. It may be that each generation breeds its devils as it goes along.

And that brings us to the Devil himself. Now the Devil is the principle of evil. He is evil, not incarnate perhaps, but certainly in spirit. But that may be a recent sophistication. He may have begun life as the symbol of mischance. There is evidence that the Devil in the older Scotland was not a beast ravening up and down after his prey. To the Celtic people he was Black Donald. In Danish tradition he is Old Eric. In the north-east he was often Auld Sandy. McPherson says, "There was something of familiarity, if not indeed of affection, in the way the Devil was regarded." But men can make a Devil after their own image, as we shall see hereafter.

Out of this old natural religion there developed the practice of witchcraft, common all over the world and, in the north, for a time an important rural industry. We can only guess at what witchcraft was in the natural religion and its full significance in prehistoric times. Certainly we cannot argue back from the written evidence which exists today, for that evidence belongs to the last days of the craft. But that evidence is fascinating for all it reveals of the old customs and of human hysterias that are perennial.

There are two pre-eminent sources of information about those rites in the north. The first set are the commission from James VI to try certain suspected witches and the dittays at their trials in Aberdeen in 1596–7. The second are the confessions in 1662 by Issobell Gowdie and Janet Breadheid of their devilish practices at Auldearn in Moray.

It is the custom to throw epithets of contempt at James VI, and fool is the kindest of them. That he was a fool is unlikely, considering how long and successfully he reigned. But he was certainly a curious fellow. He was neurotic: he may have been hysterical. None need be surprised at that. Considering the circumstances of his earliest years—the murder of his father, the abduction of his mother, the general insecurity of the country intensified a hundred times round the infant prince—it is surprising that he had enough balance to walk so delicately on the high wire of kingship. The case against King James must be reheard with a reputable psychologist—if there is one—as assessor to the court. He would be found guilty of neurosis and his worst actions would be seen to have proceeded therefrom. His excessive anxiety would have fed on the terror of witchcraft, as a danger to his own person. That, along with considerations of public order, led or drove him to extreme measures against the cult. One of those was the commission of 1596 to the provost and bailies of Aberdeen to deal with persons suspected of witchcraft. The dittays, preserved in the burgh records, have been published by the Spalding Club and make a fascinating piece of social history.

The first witch was Johnnet Wischert, spous of Johnne Leyis, accused of witchecrafte, socerie and murthouris. She, when Alexander Thomsoun, mariner, came furth of Aberdeen to his ship, ran as swift as an arrow between him and the sun and cast her cantryps in his way. At that moment, immediately, the said Alexander took an extreme fear and trembling and returned to his house where he lay, the space of a month, fast bedsick, one half of the day roasting in his body with an extreme burning drought; the other half of the day melting away his body with an extraordinar cold sweat. And the said Alexander Thomsoun, knowing she had cast a kind of witchcraft on him, said he would have her burnt and sent his wife to tell her so; whereupon she gave the said wife certain drugs and the said Alexander, having drunk them, duly mended and returned again to his wonted state of health. At Bartilday, seven years before, Andrew Ardes, webster, having offended Johnnet in his pastime, she spoke threatening words at him. Incontinently, Andrew took to bed, lay about the space of eight days, the one half day roasted in his whole body as in a furnace and the other half day with a vehement sweat melting away; so that by her cruel murder and witchecrafte the said Andrew died within eight days, and his wife within the month. Nine years previous to that Bartilday she had visited the same alternating rossen heat and cold congealing sweat on Malcolm Karris' wife with whom she had fallen at variance and discord. A servant, with the happy name of James Alehouse, having left her service, she cursed him and he too fell ill of the hot and cold, wherefor he was compelled to send to Bervie for another witch to take the witchcraft from him. For twenty years by-past the said Johnnet, when her husband and servant had gone to bed, put on a great fire all night and sat there at her witchcraft, contrarius to the nature of well-living persons. That that was the truth was testified by her domestic servants. And on many others, as witnesses testified, she cast the spells of sickness and misfortune. Fearful things were done. Johnne Leyis, lying one night in his bed, a cat came up to him and cried "Wallawa" and worried one of her own kittens, while his wife was sitting putting on her clothes. And the said Johnne then slew the cat and immediately thereafter his horse ran mad and his dog.

In the Tolbooth of Aberdeen, February 17th, 1596, the whole assize convicted Johnnet Wischert in eighteen points of the dittay of witchcraft, and the said Justice ordained her to be burnt to the deid.

The dittay against Thomas Leyis, son of Johnnet, alleged, imprimis, that on the Halloween last by-past, he, accompanied by Johnnet Wischert, Issobell Cockie and others named, sorcerers and witches, came to the market cross and fish cross of Aberdeen under the conduct and guiding of the Divell present with them, all in company, playing before them on his kinds of instruments. There they danced about the crosses and the mealmarket, in which Divell's dance Thomas Leyis was foremost and led the ring.

The dittay further bore that he had gone to his woman Elspet Reid and told her she was with child—which she knew not—and that the bairn would be a lass, and that she would be born on a Christsunday so many weeks after Martimas; which particulars came truly to pass. The revelation of these things he had of his master the Divell, since God has not given nor granted to true Christians sic secret and hid mysteries to know, but are reserved to his heavenly providence. Many other acts were cast against Thomas Leyis. The whole assize (of twenty-one) all but three found him guilty of leading the Halloween dances and on three other points of being a notorious witch by open voice and common fame.

It is not possible to make here even the most inadequate summary of the Aberdeen dittays. Let us pass on to the country practitioners; such as Isobel Coky, wife to a farmer in Kintore.

Imprimis: on her wedding day, she went to the house of Thomas Small in Kintore to have her head busked by his wife. The wife opened her butter kist and showed Isobel the store of butter she had made, and seven kebbacks of cheese; whereupon Isobel cast her witchcraft on the dairy whereby the cows gave from their paps thick strings of milk, like venom. Item: consequent on a quarrel about the above bewitching, she cast a witchcraft on Thomas Small whereby he was smitten with the roasting heat and the cold congealing sweat—half the day melting away as a burning white candle. Item: having met the master of the English School in Kintore as he was riding home on his young brown nag, of five years old, she put her hand on the shoulder of the horse, whereby it fell down dead and furthermore never rose again. Item: In anno 1594, Cristane Leslie, reader (of the Gospel) in Kintore, going out early from her bed found in the midden a little clew of wool of all colours; and the said Cristane, fearing it to be witchcraft, took it and threw it on the fire, where it gave such a great crack, that folk thought the house would have fallen down and smoored them. The said Cristane took to her bed immediately after and within twenty days died, by witchcraft. Item: two years ago she went to Andro Baxter's house and laid her hand on his cow, which thereafter gave no kind of milk, but sometimes water and sometimes blood. In consideration of those and many other dittays, the assize, in one voice, found Isobel Coky guilty in twelve points of witchcraft and a common witch by open voice and common fame.

A word for Andro Man, of Rathven in Banffshire, who, if justice had been done, should have got a ballad as well as a burning. Accused as a notorious witch, he had to answer first that when he was a boy in his mother's house, bringing in water from the well, the Divell appeared to him in the shape of the Queen of Elphen, and in that house the Queen was delivered of a child. Moreover, the Queen of Elphen promised him he should know everything and cure all ills except death. And moreover that several children had been born to the Queen of Elphen and himself. Item: that he had cured sundry people of witchcrafts laid upon them. Item: that he confessed that the Divell his master, whom he called Christsondy, and supposed to be an angel and God's godson . . . was raised by the speaking of the word "Benedicite" and by taking a dog under the left oxter in the right hand . . . and speaking the word "Maikpeblis." And that Christsondy beat a mark in the third finger of his right hand which he had there to show. Also he had affirmed that the Queen of Elphen had a grip of all the witches' craft but Christsondy is the gudeman (head of the house) and has all power under God and that the said Andro Man knew sundry dead men in their company and that the king that died in Flodden and Thomas Rymour was there. Item: on the day of the Holy Rood which fell on a Wednesday, he said he saw Christsondy come out of the snow in the likeness of a stallion, and the Queen of Elphen was there and others with her, riding on white hackneys, and they came to the Binhill (of Cullen?), where all made unspeakable abasement to Christsondy and the Queen of Elphen. Item: that he agreed the elves would make him appear to be in a fair chamber, yet he would find himself in a moss at dawn; and that they would appear to have candles and light, and swords which would be nothing else but dead grass and straws. Yet among them he was not afraid to go, as he had frequently all his days used their company and society. He was found guilty.

There were others tried in Aberdeen in 1596–7, including Helen

Fraser, who, to sustain herself and her bairns, pretended knowledge that she had not and undertook things she could not perform. That did not prevent her being found a rank witch.

There are one or two things common to all the dittays against those unhappy people. Many of their witchcrafts would now have a natural explanation—the roasting fevers and cold sweats are symptomatic of agues and influenzas; the stringy milk shows a streptococcal infection, the dairyman's nightmare, mastitis. And so on. We may suspect that the witches were guilty of being disliked by their neighbours, and of little else; and that the neighbours took advantage of the King's Commission to get rid of them, by fire. It is only in the case of Andro Man that we find a trace of the higher lunacy, and possession, shown so terribly in the confessions of the Auldearn witches sixty-five years later. There is one other point worth noticing about these trials of 1596–7. In one year twenty-three women and one man were burned at Aberdeen for their part in these rites. Now the burgh records have been well preserved from 1397, but there is no notice of any trials for witchcraft until 1596. In a very few years the spirit of enquiry or persecution seems to have exhausted itself. Perhaps the fever in Aberdeen was one of those outbreaks of popular hysteria which are quickly whipped up and as quickly disappear. Certainly there is little in the Aberdeen dittays that cannot be explained by reference to the old natural religion however debased, or to common spite and neighbourliness.

Pitcairn in his *Criminal Trials*, that noble museum of iniquities, reports that on April 13th, 1662, before "Master Harie Forbes, Minister of the Gospell at Aulderne; William Dallas of Cantrey, sherriff-deput of the sherriffdom of Nairne" and nine men of substance in the district, there appeared one Issobell Gowdie, confessing to the haynous sinnes of witchcraft. Issobell made her statement "without ony compulsitouris"—that is, voluntarily, requiring no torture to expedite the truth.

She was, she said, Issobell Gowdie, spous to John Gilbert, farmer in Lochloy. On a certain, and morally fatal, occasion while between Drumdevin and the Headis, she met the Devil and promised to meet him again, at night, in the Kirk of Aulderne, which she did. The first thing she did there that night, she put one hand to the crown of her head and the other to the sole of her foot and renounced all between them to the Devil. Meanwhile the Devil stood at the reader's desk with a black book in his hand. Margaret Brodie in Aulderne held Issobell up to the Devil to be baptised by him. The order of baptism was thus: the Devil marked her in the shoulder, and sucked out her blood at that mark, and spowted it in his hand and sprinkled it on her head and said, *I baptise the Janet in my awin name.* The next time she met with him was in the New Wardis of Inshoch where he haid carnall cowpulation and dealling with her. He was, she said, a meikle blak roch man, werie cold. Sometimes he had boots and sometimes shoes on his feet but always his feet were forked or cloven. At times he went to them in the shape of a deer or a roe.

Appearing for a second time on May 3rd, Issobell described, again without compulsitouris, the organisation of witches in a coven. There were, she said, thirteen persons in a coven, and each had a spirit to wait on him or her at will. When they were at meat, or in any other place whatever, the youngest witch, called the Maiden, sat next the Divell and served him and enjoyed his most intimate and fearful attentions. A man called the Officer was head over all the men in the coven. There was great respect shown to the Divell but sometimes among themselves they would be calling him Black Johne or the like, and he would know it, and beat and buffet them very for it. Alexander Elder in Earlseat, would be beaten often, and grat and cried under the scourging. But Margaret Wilson in Aulderne would defend herself finely: and Bessie Wilson would speak crustie with her tongue and would be belling again to him stoutly. He would be beating and scourging them all up and down with cords and other sharp scourges like naked ghosts, and they would be crying *Pittie, Pittie, Mercie, Mercie, Owr Lord.* But he would have neither pittie nor mercie. He would girn at them like a dog as if he would swallow them up and the scourges flew faster till the coven grew frenetical in the lowest ecstasies of sexual abasement.

In her third appearance, before a considerably larger gathering of gentlemen, Issobell told of the power given to witches of going abroad in the shape of beasts. The Divell, she said, would send her on errands in the shape of a hare. Sometimes the dogs would come after them, but though they might worry yet could not kill them. When they turned back into their own shape again, they had the bites and rives and scratches on their own bodies. When they were in the shape of cats they did nothing but cry and cauterwaul and worry one another and when they came to their own shapes again they found the rives and scratches on their skins. When going abroad the female witches put besoms in bed to delude their husbands until they returned. For conveyance to the coven Issobell had a little horse and would say *Horse and hattock in the Divell's name* and they would fly away wherever they would, even as straws fly on the highway. Wild straws and cornstraws were horses to them; they put them between their feet and said *Horse and hattock in the Divell's name.* And when any saw those straws in a whirlwind and did not sanctify themselves, the witches shot them dead at their pleasure. Any that were shot their souls would go to Heaven but their bodies remained with the witches, to fly as horses for them, as small as straws. They had no bow to shoot but spang elf arrowheads from the nails of their thumbs. As for the elf arrowheads, the Divell shaped them with his own hand and then gave them to elf-boys who trimmed them with a sharp tool like a packing needle. She saw those elf boys when she was in the elfes house; they were little ones, bent and boss-backed. When the Divell gave the elf arrows to the witches he said:

> Shoot these in my name
> And they sall not goe heall hame.

She confessed that the first voyage she ever went with the coven was to Ploughlands and there they shot a man between the plough stilts and he presently fell to the ground upon his nose and his mouth; and then the Divell gave her an arrow and caused her shoot a woman in that field, which she did and the woman fell doun deid. She admitted the murder of four persons, two men and two women; and having been at the death of others.

Issobell described the rituals through which they exercised the Divell's arts. It was their custom to steal away the fruits of a man's fields by a peculiar husbandry. Before Candlemass, she said, they went by-east Kinloss and there yoked a plough of puddocks (frogs). The Divell held the plough and Johne Young, their Officer, did drive the puddocks. The puddocks drew the plough, like oxen: quick grass served for traces, the horn of a riglen ram was the coulter, and a piece of a riglen's horn was the sock. They drew a furrow two several times about the field and the whole coven went up and doun with the plough, praying to the Divell for the fruit of the land—whereby the land might grow but straw and empty heads and the real corn be carried to the witches' barns in due season.

It was the custom of the witches, at the command of their master, to conspire against the health of the lieges. Issobell related that they made a picture of clay to destroy the Laird of Park's male children. Johne Taylor brought home the clay in the corner of his plaid: his wife broke it very small like meal and sifted it with a sieve and poured in water amongst it in the Divell's name and made of it a picture of the Laird's son. The words they spoke when they made the picture were:

IN THE DIVELL'S NAME—
We pour in this water among this meall
For lang dwining and ill heall.
We put it into the fire
That it may burn baith stick and stowre.
It sall be brunt with our will
As any stikle upon a kiln.

The Divell taught them the words. When they had learned them, they all fell doun upon their bare knees, and their hair about their eyes, and their hands lifted up, looking steadfast upon the Divell, still saying the words thrice over, till the picture was made. The picture had all the parts and marks of a child, such as head, eyes, nose, hands, feet, mouth and little lips; and the hands of it were folded down by its side. They laid the face of it to the fire till shrunk, and put a clear fire about it till it was red like a coal. After that they would roast it now and then; each other day there would be a part of it well roasted. The Laird of Park's male children were to suffer by it.

Issobell made in all four confessions containing the above, and instances in the enormity of lust and ill-willing, penitently spoken furth of her own mouth, saying *Alace I deserv not to be sitting heir, for I hav done so manie evill deidis, especially killing of men. I deserv to be reivin upon iron harrowes, and worse, if it culd be devysit.*

There is a small difference between the Aberdeen dittays and the Auldearn confessions. The Aberdeen witches were pathetic and petty—a sort of quack doctors who pretended a knowledge of simples and sympathetic magic; at the best, nature curers who fell into the hands of a more terrible medical council. The figure of Johnnet Wischert is not unfamiliar—the rough and ruthless woman who has a power of ill-will in herself and attracts ill-will from others. These were handy victims for a popular hunt with the king himself as master of the hounds. They may also have been the scapegoats of the hunters. Perhaps the provost and bailies of Aberdeen believed in spite of themselves in the old practices, may themselves have engaged in Halloween dances in the Mealmarket and had a sense of guilt which they purged by committing the scapegoats to the flames. These things need to be seen in their place in history. The devilish dances, often referred to in burgh records of that earlier time, may have been tolerated a little before; and, before that, encouraged. The Roman Church, always careful not to make the burden of conduct too heavy, allowed the saturnalia of the Abbot of Misrule as a natural exercise for animal spirits. The Kirk of Scotland kept or tried to keep the beast on a tighter rein. But the beast remembered and occasionally or often broke out; and had a sense of sin thereby. How convenient to purge that sin on the bodies of the less worthy citizens at the cost of some cartloads of peats and small coal. In witch trials such as the Aberdeen ones I suspect it is more rewarding to speculate about the conscience of the judges than the arts of the unfortunate panel.

The cases of Andro Man and Issobell Gowdie are different. There is something more than the observance of the Halloween dances and the knitting together of gossip into a fiery shroud. What is there in all the organisation of the coven, that secret commonwealth that terrorised the countryside? What is the imagery about the Divell and the Queen of Elphen? Andro Man is at least a figure crazed with the ballads of Fairyland. He may have been a little more than that. Something comes through in the dittay against him, a force of something that once was valid; and, whenever something comes through, there must have been power of life and imagination at the root of it. There cannot be any doubt about Mistress Gowdie. She is a tragic figure. She stands up from her confession as a woman of character and intelligence, a woman of sensibility and imagination, a creature of no ordinary sort. The living voice and the ardent mind ring and flash through her words. There are no frenetical flummeries; every sentence is a deed and every deed shown immediate, horrible. Of course, Pitcairn has given only the depositions as recorded by the clerk of the court, but anyone who has been a reporter in courts or other places knows well enough just when the person interviewed was giving, and when the reporter was making the best of a blatter of words. Issobell rises out of Pitcairn's pages, out of the magnificent and factual Scottish words taken down at the tip of the tongue, a woman real and ardent and damned. Beyond all doubt she believed in the Devil and believed that she had taken part in his evil works. I wonder if she were not a character of a very high order, living in a soceity that could give her no sufficient good scope and by that frustrated and driven to moral destruction. Or what was John Gilbert, her husband, like? There is no mention of children. Could the good Professor Freud have helped her? Was she only in need of that superior witchcraft? I wouldn't know, but I am fairly sure that Issobell was a woman caught in a tragic situation. What did happen around Aulderne? Did Issobell truly ride on a windlestrae and spang elf arrows off her thumbnail at the ploughman in the field? Who was the meikle blak roch man who could have taught de Sade something? What were the intolerable tensions between society and the individual which found release at the Old Wardis of Inshoch? These questions remain for infinite speculation.

All these things happened long ago and almost, as you might think, in a different country. But I have no longer the clear ideas about time and geography I used to have. Time as measured by the clock and the vigour of the heart seeps inexorably away, but change, as apart from decay, does not keep any such equal pace. Time, as measured by the conditions of the human race, is a slower and more uncertain thing. There are advances: there are retreats: some things in a lifetime are gloriously amended while others no less valuable insensibly decline. We need a sense of time as long as eternity to be sure that the human race makes progress. Which doesn't, however, set us free of looking for a way ahead or justify us in scratching hopefully all the time at the places where our tails used to be. As we move on we carry the bad as well as the good along with us. The forms of good and evil may change, but the spirit behind them often survives. That is why I have spent so much time at the dark side of the moon. I had a female relation not so long ago who was reputed to be a witch, and she may have been, for she went about raising hell among her family and acquaintances.

She is dead now and gone, poor woman, where the wicked have no chance to trouble anybody—not even themselves. Only the question remains—was she really a witch? I think the answer is yes.

One or two qualities of a witch emerge from our examination of the subject. The witch inspires fear among the people with whom she lives. People fear her because she has the power to do them powerful harm; or they think she has it. She has also terribly superior knowledge; not perhaps superior but infernal, since it must come directly from the Devil. It must come from the Devil because the witch has the power to find out things about you that you alone know and the Devil must have whispered it in her lug. Well, of course, I am inclined to discount the Devil—even the Kirk that used to have a strong vested interest in him has refined him down to a philosophic notion and now seems inclined to replace him entirely by the governors of Russia. Let us count the Devil out entirely with his hooves and his horns—and the witches show up all the better, or worse. They are the Devil in themselves. They are women (and men) with a power of malice far above the average. They can see through the attitudes we erect to screen our secret thoughts and actions. They are the psychologists who can smell out the trauma behind the nervous tic. Their seemingly infernal knowledge comes through acutely perceptive eyes and ears tuned to catch the note which betrays a man about some devious ploy, overcome by irresistible seductions. They always smell it out. They always know. Then they have very strong emotions—dominant, dominating emotions. They are masterful people. In that combining of strong intelligence and strong feeling there should be a rather wonderful person—the sort that are kings and queens in the story books, the sort that when we meet them resolve all troubles by the power of the mind and the power of the spirit. The true witch has everything —nearly everything; all except one thing and that is love, and without love she carries all Hell in her heart. She is evil incarnate. Now when I write love, please don't mistake me. I don't mean the commodity that is written about in the books for disappointed housewives. Between ourselves I am not very sure what I do mean. Or I know quite well but can hardly define it. I know it includes the impulse to help and unwillingness to interfere; to impose nothing on others; to make pleasure; to cultivate kindness; to get rid of fear. With it one can get along. Without it one dies an early death, though the body may live to a dry old age. And when there is a strong mind and strong emotions but no love, there is hell in the heart and another witch walks abroad. The pubs of Bloomsbury and Charlotte Street have been full of them in my time.

That was the case with my female relative. She always knew what everyone was up to before they knew it themselves; and she always knew how to make a scandal out of someone's secret intentions. She was a master-player on all the small jealousies and dislikes that people try to overcome in order to live decently together; she could work up a few discords into a danse macabre of nervous fury. She was the wrecker and we feared her because we felt in her a power that was evil. If she wasn't a witch who was? But how far away from the auld widow woman and the three barren wives.

It is a curious thing that the spirit of the witch should remain while the old beneficent rituals and beliefs are forgotten. Or is it curious? Perhaps there cannot be active evil until good has been denied. But what has all this got to do with the north as it is today? And with people such as we are, so very, very rational? Or are we so very rational? Or do we make ourselves conform to a pattern of rational well-doing? I wouldn't like to say, but I can't help asking.

CHAPTER VII

DIVERSIONS AND PASTIMES

THE diversions of the northerners are very various. Forty thousand people may go to Pittodrie on a Saturday to watch the Aberdeen team, but there are more who find a lasting and cheaper excitement in watching the misfortunes of their neighbours. There are still a few who get their evening's fun by going down to the village to see the bus come in. Some pursue the drama and some the tennis, some women and some the drink. We are not different from other people; but just more thorough.

It is a curious thing that we have no great passion for the horse. We have been great breeders of the Clydesdale, and some farmers still have for that noble draught horse the same unreasoning loyalty their ancestors had for the exiled Stewarts. But for sporting horses— hunters and racers and such lovely, useless cattle—we have no great fancy. There are no race-meetings north of Perth, and no popular desire for them. I can remember at least one attempt to hold races in Aberdeen but it had little success. We do have an interest in racing, however, and many backers who have an extensive knowledge of form and are ready to wager on it, though they may never have seen a horse. There was a shepherd I once knew from the Braes of Moray who played the horses regularly and became a grocer's vanman in Glasgow where there were better facilities for study and investment. I said to him, "What'll happen to the van when you're away at the races?" He replied, in some surprise and even resentment. "Me at the races! Never! It's a sinfu waste to keep aa thae useless horses so that thousands o idle folk can stand and stare at them when they should be at their work. If I was the Government, and had aa the brains they think they have, I'd find a way tae put down the racin, but still let the bets go on." We have no foxhunting, except with guns to exterminate the vermin, for it would be unthinkable to encourage foxes in a countryside so populated with chickens. Any hunt with horses and dogs would itself be hunted and the members broken up by packs of infuriated henbreeders. So the few riding clubs are restricted to following a prepared scent over a carefully defined trail —the free hallooing hunter reduced to the ambit of a tramcar. That is perhaps not very exciting but may be more civilised than the full sport.

It is often said that in Scotland golf is everybody's game, played by the rich and the poor alike. Such statements are nearly always false, but this one is true, except that the poorest seldom have the heart for play. Golf began as a common pastime played on the links along the shore, and it has remained that. Of course there are clubs to which you cannot be admitted unless you are of a good social position, but very few people who wish to play the game are prevented because of the expense. It is easy to get the necessary tools—or at least it used to be. From the time I was twelve I lived in a small village beside a sea-side course, a private course on which the best people played. Sitting on a sand dune and out of reach of sliced shots, I used to watch the players who came in glossy motor cars and played in clothes that had never been mended, and paid boys to carry round their clubs in leather bags that would have held four stone of potatoes. They seemed so noble and elegant in everything—even in missing the ball—that I thought golf must be a game for gods, and that people would have to be as rich as gods to play it. I soon discovered that all the boys in the village had at least one club apiece, with which they used to play on the edges of the course, and even on the greens when the greenkeeper decided not to be looking. They had, they explained, bought their clubs with the money they had earned as caddies. I thought I should do the same. But there I got a sudden setback. It was explained to me very clearly by the older boys that there were too many children hanging about the caddie-master's for all the jobs there were, and that any newcomer would get his head punched, his ears screwed and likely be deprived of various members. However, I discovered there was another way. The course had many hazards made by dense old clumps of whin that trapped a loosely played ball. Very rich gentlemen who played into such hazards sent their caddies among the whins as retrievers, but caddies who were very vulnerable about the knees seldom looked long, and so balls were abandoned. That was a chance for the likes of me. From a convenient dune I watched where exactly each ball had disappeared, and when it had been abandoned I nipped across and looked about till I found it. On a good Saturday, and if I had chosen the right whins to watch, I have got three good, unmarked balls. The next thing was to find a market. Nobody need think the Black Market was invented in 1940. It probably began when the first golfer lost a ball and somebody found and sold it. There were people who would buy those balls for twopence and threepence apiece, and I found my way by some immoral instinct to those people. So I was able to save up enough to buy a putter and an old-fashioned cleek, one of the loveliest and most difficult instruments in golf. With those I played golf when the gentlemen had gone home, or before they arose.

There is something incredible about being young. I that never see six in the morning, unless I am on my way to bed, can hardly believe there were once summer mornings when I rose at five and walked down to the river mouth with a slice of brown bread in one hand and the cleek in the other. The sun was only stirring under a blanket of pearly cotton clouds. The wind blew off the land with the smells I had always known, of the dark green leaf and the farm middens; thyme wet with dew gave up a sharp savour, mingled with the green bitterness of the bent crushed underfoot. The lark ascending rose straight into dawn and the sea beat lightly on the shore beyond the sandhills, with a long swish, as if God were sweeping his carpets.

Having put off my clothes in a hollow of the sand hills I ran down and threw myself splash into the water, with a cautious abandon, as one returning to the bosom of mother nature, though uncertain of the welcome he would get. Some caution was needed, for the old lady ran hot and cold. There were on the sea bed table lands and deep abysmal valleys. On the table lands there was water still warm from yesterday's sun, lagoons that the tide had missed, but the valleys ran currents from the cold deep sea that were as much as flesh could bear. Hot or cold, there was a virtue in that ocean, the sewer of a continent and the solvent of dead men's flesh and bones, such an enlivening and cleansing thing that I laughed and shouted and heard, or imagined I heard, Triton blow on a horn wreathed with seaweed. Afterwards, as the sun came out, I played golf on the dewy fairways, hitting the ball prodigious heights among the skylarks. It was not often I managed to hit the ball in the desired direction, but that was of small importance: I hit it hard and high and out of sight and stood with my breath held and my mouth open at the magnificence of my own power as the ball, hooked most splendidly, darted like a tern out to sea. So I will always be a golfer, though it is a long time since I have had the seriousness to play at any game.

I progressed to the status of a *bona fide* golfer. When I got a permanent engagement at one and sixpence a week to look after an old lady's garden, I could pay my sixpence and play on the town's course on the cheap side of the river. It was not really as good a course as the one I learned on. When the wind came from the south-west you got a smell off the gasworks—not a bad smell, yet not a fine smell like farm middens; and when the wind blew from the west you got the smell from the dead horse factory which was sick with corruption. There were other disadvantages, small family parties—father, mother, grannie and four children under seven—were likely to dawdle across the line of play and you couldn't ask them to hurry, for one or all of them would have replied, "This is the toun's links and tounsfolk can go where they like on them." It was a difficult remark for a democrat to answer. It was even more difficult when your ball got into a bunker and you found that the bunker was occupied by a courting couple as well. If you asked them to move over, the gentleman of the party said, "Get tae hell out o here." There was nothing for it but to break the rules of golf and keep the peace. But there were compensations. Even on the town's course there were rough places where a ball could go out of sight and small boys lurked there perhaps with the ambition to acquire the capital to buy a cleek. How good it was to be able to tell them off, and how well I did it, knowing exactly what was in their minds.

Among golfers golf is such a companionable game. It so happened that I seldom went to the course with a companion, but when I got to the paybox there was usually someone waiting for a game. Waiting, I think not for someone to beat, but for someone to walk round with. I walked round with a lot of them in six or seven years. Sometimes I won because my muscles were free and my nerves regardless: more often I lost because an older man has a discipline that can eventually beat the exuberance of youth. I had some fine times with those chance acquaintances. There was a reporter (poor man, he is dead now, and has at last got the big story he can't turn in) who said if he didn't have a round of fresh air in the morning, he couldn't have stood the office for the rest of the day. I always beat him, because it was so easy to ease my ball into a better position while he was talking about the press, in a way which puzzled me then and which I recognise now as a mixture of pride and shame.

There was an old shepherd, a man from the country who had retired to the town and taken up golf when he was well over fifty. He played a canny game, never in the rough, always straight for the green: a cunning, intellectual, cattle-market sort of game. When I was going to putt, with a stroke in hand, he would hold the flag for me, and look at the shot I had to play, and say portentously, "A missable putt. Aye, a missable putt." And sure enough I missed it. Another was a labourer in the slaughterhouse, a short, broad man with bandy legs, who never wore a collar, and smoked a short clay pipe. He had only three clubs, a driver, a cleek and a mashie that had a home-made look. His style was extraordinary, comical, for he stood far away from the ball and suddenly swung at it, as if he were felling an ox. The ball did not go a great distance, for it was stunned rather than driven, but it went straight, and my correct style and natural exuberance never got me within a stroke of that strange, square man, who smelt of thick black and offal.

After such an apprenticeship it is natural that golf is never quite right when it is played away from the sight and smell of the sea. I know there are some fine inland courses, but even the ragged prospect of the Grampians from Gleneagles does not make up for the loss of the salt wind, and the springy seaside turf, and the wash and rumble of the waves. We have some splendid seaside courses in the north—at Aberdeen, Cruden Bay, Peterhead, Fraserburgh, Cullen, Lossiemouth, Nairn and Dornoch—where the best golfers play, but I prefer the village courses, often of nine holes, that belong entirely to the village. All sorts of people play there—fishermen, roadmen, shopkeepers, schoolmasters, boys and girls. There may be only nine holes, but you can play round and round for hours, because there is no queue at the starter's box—nor a box, nor a starter. Even one round of nine holes may take some hours because of the retentive rough, with the whins like prickly forests, for on those courses a lost ball must be found, and to give up after a short search would be a sign of ostentation or infirmity of purpose. You need never fear that you are holding up the game, or that you will lose your place, or that anyone will pay you any attention except of a friendly sort. Family courses.

I used to play on one such with a gentleman who boasted that he never lost a match or a ball on his own course. I believed him. Though he was often in the rough, he was relentless in searching, and left no blade of grass unturned, no whinbush unbeaten. Especially if the game was going against him and his opponent was all tensed up for the kill, the old gentleman exercised fine gamesmanship in the rough. He would find a yellowhammer's nest, which led to an argument about birds; or some miserable plant that, he said, rightly belonged to Lapland or Coromandel. Or he would search and search till his opponent sat down on the warm side of a bush where, lulled by the chirp of the grasshoppers and mazed by the steam of light on the ocean, he fell into a deep dreamless sleep. Then the old gentleman wakened him with a shout of incredulous joy, having found his ball nicely cocked up on a tussock of grass. The sleep and that stroke of fortune always undid me and I lost the game. It was there I was cured of golf, as I was cured of bridge and poker about the same time, because I could not keep awake enough to watch my opponents. Still it was something to have known those little courses. The grand places are just a little too grand, too efficient machines for playing golf on. Those beautifully mown fairways, the fringes of carefully cultivated rough, the bunkers sited to catch the professional's drive and my second; the greens innocent of worms and guile, they offer no alibis for the incompetent. But the small seaside courses offer every possible excuse. You venture out on them like an explorer into virgin country, and to get back alive is in itself success.

We are great ones for the football nowadays, and the number of clubs that have been started in the last five years is one of the happier things in the countryside. Every village of any size in my part of the north has now got its team that plays in the summer leagues. Football might seem out of place as a summer game in some countries, but not in the north. It is for us a social occasion and social occasions are hardly possible out of doors in winter. Besides games in winter seem against nature. Games should spring from a merry heart, else they are just a mortifying of the flesh. How right then that our football season should begin when the days lengthen and the corn is green.

Between six and seven in the evening you can see the young men of the district cycling to the village, along the narrow country roads, each with a pair of football boots slung round his neck. Besides the Team there are the hopefuls who turn up for the preliminary kick-about in which they may take the eye of a selector: all the male children over five years of age. While the team gather in whatever does duty as a pavilion, the hopefuls and the children slam the ball about the goals. When it is ten or twenty minutes after the advertised time for the start of play, the village people begin to come from their houses, not in any obvious excitement but as if they were only stepping out for a breath of the evening air. It would not do if anyone thought they were intending to go to the game. Besides, the opposing team might fail to turn up and any spectators who had gathered by the pitch would have been made to seem ludicrous—which is something none can afford who lives in a village. So there is a casual gathering on the road towards the playing field of people who say they are not going to the game but may drop in for a minute or two. Their caution begins to look wise enough, for the opposing team has not yet arrived. The children, and even a few who should be wiser, begin to say, "They've cried off. They canna raise a team. They've cauld feet." But the committee of the home team are glad enough that the opponents are late: their own centre-forward has not yet turned up.

You see, it is not easy for everyone to get there on time. Our football teams are made up of the young village tradesmen and the farm boys. A plumber or a joiner may be working on a job ten miles away. The cow may be calving. And even the best laid plans may go wrong. The centre-forward arrives at last. Then the opponents drive up in a bus accompanied by a crowd of their supporters. But there is a new crisis. When the centre-forward left home in the morning he told his mother to send his football boots down to the field by his little brother. Either the mother did not understand or the little brother did not listen—but there are no football boots and the centre-forward lives in a cottar house three miles away. Somebody tears off on a motor-cycle to get them, as on some desperate errand, which makes the hearts of the little boys beat faster.

Meanwhile the opposing team have run on to the field, where they practise kicking goals, cheered on by their supporters. Those supporters demand to know why the home side are still in the pavilion, and insinuate that they are deliberately wasting time in the hope that night may fall before the game can be finished. When told about the missing boots, they cry back "Fine day" and other things that express total disbelief in the rudest terms, which greatly infuriate the children, who reply even more rudely. The adult supporters of the home team are now even less evident, having retreated into the shelter of gable ends, or even into the public house if no one is looking. At last there is a roaring of the motorcycle up the loans; the missing boots arrive. Two minutes later the home team come on to the field; the hopefuls and the little boys retire behind the touchlines; and the game begins. The home supporters now drift down towards the pitch—all except those who always watch from the roadway, where, of course, one is not committed to anything.

Some playing fields of the north are windswept and bare even at midsummer, but our own one is a pretty place. It is a level haugh between the road and the river, overlooked by the Kirk, the Bank and the Pub. About half-past seven in the evening the sun shines full and fair down the valley in a great stream of light which puts a bloom on the world. In that brief and golden hour there is colour everywhere: on the bare heads and faces of the players; colour and shadow on the steep sides of the valley where the young cattle stand in groups at the corners of the fields; a colour of green and gold on the corn where the young rabbits bob out from the edges of the wood; a flash of blue and gold down the river which turns the heron for a moment into a bird of paradise; lakes and islands and wandering continents of blue and gold in the territories of the sky. Our brittle, brilliant air takes on softness, depth and mystery all the way up to highest heaven. The air is cool and fresh and you can feel the irresistible growing and unfolding towards ripeness. It is the proper time for a game, because in the hour when the dew falls there is a recreation of energy, when one is young. However the day has been eaten up in the tiresome things that weary the muscles and the spirit, the cool of the evening makes you new again for the things you glory in doing. You have a second chance. It is one of the sad things about growing old: there is no second chance.

Place, then, for those to whom evening has brought the chance of glory. The twenty-two go at it, expressing the vigour of their youth, such skill and intelligence as they may have, impeded a little by the pitch, and greatly by each other and the referee. There are not many signs of the scheming brain that saves the feet. There are many movements that begin and few that endanger anything but life and limb. That does not worry the spectators. We do not greatly value what are called the finer points of the game, because a man who indulges in them gets everybody confused, especially himself. What we want is goals. Bash on, barge through and charge the goalie down:

that is our idea of a good play. Win by ten goals—that is what we will our team to do. We identify ourselves with the team and demand they win for our own glory. It is all rather primitive, our tribe against the tribe from over the hill, and gives play to some strong emotions. If Aristotle the rationaliser had seen the summer leagues he might have defined football as a public spectacle that arouses in the spectators and players alike the feelings of self-assertion and violence and by allowing those expresssions within the limit of certain rules purges them so that men are more willing to live at peace within the rules of society. About the time when the shadows grow out from the woods and the river mist creeps up and the kirk bell sounds ten, a long shrill of the whistle ends the game. We drift away in little companies, feeling for the moment each one part with another because we have felt a common emotion, regardless of ourselves.

As the children go home along the country roads, they play over again in high voices the moves of their heroes, or damn the referee for partiality with oaths that ring far and clear and die sweetly into the gathering night. I am a little past being excited by the football, but it makes me happy for the children and the young men. Especially for the children. They must always be giving their hearts to something and it is well they can give their hearts to a game that is innocent, uncompromised. Their lives need to be full of intense feelings and satisfactions if they are ever to grow into men. It is a fine thing too they should feel themselves part of a community: and not only as spectators. Every child on the touchline has the ambition to play in the team and when he cheers he is cheering for his inheritance. I must think those children fortunate and the young men too: they have one more thing that can bind their hearts to their own place so that, however far they may travel into the deserts of the unhappy world, they will always have a point of return. Those who have ever enjoyed a good life, even for a short time, are thereby armoured against fate.

The so-called highland games are a popular spectacle of the north in summer. They may be of great antiquity but I doubt if they are peculiarly highland, although they are sometimes very tartan affairs. The highland part of them can be seen most highly coloured at Braemar, Aboyne, Lonach and the Northern Meeting at Inverness. At Lonach in Strathdon the members of the Lonach Society meet on the morning of the games, dressed in the kilt and carrying pikes. Headed by pipers and their chieftain, they march through the glen to the games field, where the rest of the day is spent on athletics, piping and dancing. Most of the events are confined to young men of the district. At Braemar, Aboyne and Inverness the meetings have become grand public spectacles at which the gentry are as much on show as the athletes, the bagpipers and the dancers. The dozens of smaller meetings at small towns and villages are expressions of local enterprise. All of them encourage the locals to take part, but for drawing the crowd they depend on a small number of champions.

Those champions go the round of the games, competing against each other two or three times a week all through the summer. They are of several kinds—heavyweights who putt the shot, toss the caber and throw the hammer; sprinters, vaulters, bicyclists, bagpipers and highland dancers. There are not so many of them, because only the best can get a big enough share of the prize money to make it worthwhile. But those few do pretty well: and the heavyweights become popular heroes. This is a little different from the summer leagues. This is part of the entertainment business.

The scene is always the same, though it may vary in small details. A green field—perhaps a pleasure ground, or just a field from which the cows, but not their traces, were removed last night. A marquee for teas. Another for bottled refreshments. A tent for the judges. A tent for the competitors. A few sideshows put up by travelling showmen. The vans of sixteen ice-cream hawkers, and a fried potato man. Hundreds of motor-cars, from the large and glossy to the kind that rattle in the wind. Some thousands of people sitting or standing round the wide ring in the middle of the field. Over all the windy summer sky, with the threat of a shower blowing up from the west.

Affairs proceed briskly inside the ring, for there are usually two or three things happening at one time. Sprinters sprint; slow-bicyclists totter on the active side of inertia; girl dancers, hideously dressed in kilts and velvet and hung with little silver medals, posture and pirouette to a monotonous highland noise from the bagpipes. And all the time the heavyweights go about their ponderous business, like mountains at labour. They are of course very big men, with great knees and calves displayed by the kilt, and great biceps and abdominal muscles that bulge out their woollen sweaters. Not the sort of fellows to move in an athletic way: nor do they. Throwing the hammer as they do it must be about the slowest sport on earth. Each competitor is allowed three attempts. The first man comes forward, making the ground tremble as he walks. He takes off his sweater, eases his muscles, takes up the hammer, examines it, polishes the shaft, tests the balance in his hands, looks over the ring, the crowd and the distant hills, as if doubting the occasion worthy of him; then just as you fear he will decide to go home in disgust, he suddenly whirls round and round, winding himself up faster and faster, while the hammer rises to shoulder height, until the man, having spun himself into a blur of kilts and thighs and muscles, lets go and the hammer flies a great distance through the air. Small boys cry "ooooooh" and sound critics say "Ayyyyeeee". Stewards run forward and stick a peg in the dent made by the hammer head as it landed. It was a great moment but it is past and time slows down to a crawl again. The champion resumes his sweater and withdraws, either to inspect the place where the hammer landed or to join the other champions, while the second comes ponderously forward.

There is plenty of time to enjoy the other excitements in the ring; to look at the dancers or listen to the bagpipers as they compete in the exercises of their intolerable noise. Only the initiated can enjoy the esoteric beauties of piping, but even musical persons can get some fun out of watching the judges. You see, any laird who has served in a highland regiment is thereby a judge of highland music (and rightly so, for in his term of service with a regular battalion he has had to contribute to the upkeep of the pipe band). Therefore at a games it is likely that two of the judges of piping and dancing are lairds and the third in his day has been a pipe major. As each piper steps up to do his piece the two lairds listen very hard, while the pipe major stops listening after the third bar. At the end of the piece the judges huddle together. The pipe major says, "Well, gentlemen, what do you think?" The senior officer present says, "I don't know—er——", and the junior officer says, "D'you think his grace notes were—er——". The senior officer says, "Pipe major, what do you think?" The pipe major says, "Well, gentlemen, I agree with you. There was a something." The gentlemen now gratefully leave it to their pipe major, as during their service they always did leave it to the pipe major. The next bagpiper is already screwing overtures of agony from his pipes.

When you return your interest to the heavyweights the same figures are still moving slowly about the business of heaving blocks of iron through the air. Perhaps you have missed something: perhaps not. Prizes have, of course, been won, but you need not be very curious about the winners. It is likely that each has got a share. I would be the last to hint at any collusion among competitors, but people who meet each other so often may sometimes show Christian charity towards each other. That is as it should be. There cannot be any great virtue in throwing a hammer seven inches further than the other man. The whole thing is a spectacle of human beings going beyond nature, like pigs that count and elephants that dance. And the farm people love it. Having been unfaithful to the Clydesdale horse for the sake of money, they feel a double loyalty to the next best thing for the sake of art.

I am not sure that the hammer throwers and the girl dancers are quite the draw they used to be. At any rate most games organisers now provide faster excitements in displays of motorcycling and in five-a-side football. The whole thing ends with a dance in the big marquee which may go on till the small hours of the morning. The dancing itself might once have been classed with the athletic events, especially that part of the lancers where all linked arms in circles and moved round at a great speed until the girls were swept clean off their feet and swung out like gondolas in a merry-go-round. It was great fun; and, if the set collapsed, all the funnier. But not now, for the popular dances are all of the ballroom sort. Even those are sometimes complicated by the antics of the drunks, but those lads are not as numerous or as drunk as they used to be. People do not fight or fall about as their grandfathers did, and a nice girl leaving a dance need not step carefully among blood, bottles and bodies.

The old set dances that everybody knew fell sadly out of favour in the 'twenties. Dancing masters no longer went about the country each with his fiddle, giving lessons in barns and smithies. It seemed as if all might be forgotten, with so much else, in those days when rural life became so attenuated. But there has been a revival of what are called country dances. The name, I suppose, has been taken over from the English country dance people, but I doubt if it is a good one. The English dances go clipperty-clop to a very pedestrian country beat, whereas the Scottish ones move quickly and with spirit. They are complicated, they allow elegance—they demand it: they are essentially of the court as against the village green. In view of the long and close relations between France and Scotland one may reasonably think to find a French influence in those dances, an influence tempered with the energy proper in a cold climate. The old measures are coming in again and new ones have been invented in their style. They are good to perform and they are incomparable for giving poise and confidence and lightsomeness. Of course they do not offer the same proximity that the ballroom dances do, but our people have always been able to find proximity in circumstances where it can be most effective, and that is seldom in a ballroom.

The games have become almost wholly professional, but the drama is more and more the sport of the amateur in the countryside and in the small towns. I should think there is no village between John o Groats and the North Water Brig that has not a dramatic club, while women's rural institutes, church guilds, youth clubs, and every social group except the bowlers, the curlers and the small-bores, sooner or later decide to do a play in aid of. That is delightful: it is a sign of health and spirit in a community when people get together to amuse themselves. They do not stop there, but in an excess of goodwill they insist on amusing the public. They succeed, now and then, but not always in the way they intend. Amateur dramatics can be good: at least, there is no overpowering reason why they should not be good. But they seldom are; and at their worst—when a producer who knows nothing about production and a cast who know nothing about acting

perform a play by someone who has no knowledge of the theatre—
the result can hardly be believed even when it is seen. There is nothing
like amateur drama anywhere in the world. Amateur musicians are
often very bad, but they can sing or play reasonably near the note, and
they have at least tried to learn, however unsuccessfully. Amateur
actors are the only people who perform in public without having
made any effort to learn the trade: and, what is worse, they charge
very good money for it. Of course, their performances are always
in aid of. They drag out their friends, relations and neighbours in the
name of charity, and bore or infuriate or dumbfound them for three
long hours. There are times when one suspects that charity was invented by amateur dramatic societies as the only hope of getting audi-
ences to watch them. Charity and the amateur drama go hand in
hand, making one pray for professionalism and a great extension of the
welfare state. The amateurs do not even confine themselves to boring
their near neighbours. The demands of charity being insatiable, there
is an infinity of clubs in need of funds, and any dramatic society that
has got up a play is sure of invitations to perform far and wide. The
drama often is not an entertainment but an excuse for taking
money off the public: a sort of confidence trick by which you are
relieved of half a crown under a promise of amusement that is seldom
fulfilled. Attendance at amateur drama is accepted as one of the duties
of country and village and small town life. One expects little and is
not disappointed, or annoyed or anything. One endures. At one performance the producer, acknowledging the polite applause of the
audience, said the cast had then performed the play in eight different
village halls—and nobody was impolite enough to suggest it was then
time the players knew their lines. Sweet charity: what things are done
in its name.

The drama is a competitive sport, the winter equivalent of the
summer leagues. Comparing the two sports one may say that football
is played with regard to certain standards of art as laid down at
Pittodrie, Hampden Park and Ibrox. The amateur drama has no
discoverable standards, not in our countryside. There are, I understand, competitions at which teams perform plays and are awarded
marks by a referee brought from a distant place to which he returns
as soon as possible. A knock-out competition of that sort does give a
wonderful illusion of quality to the least bad; and amateur actors
are very susceptible to that illusion, which is perhaps the one thing
they have in common with the professionals. I cannot help thinking
that the football is superior. However well our heroes play, we know
they are not in the class of George Hamilton or Tommy Pearson;
and when we praise them we do so with implicit reference to those
most skilful players. They are in no great danger of conceit, for they
perform in a critical atmosphere and the spectators are always recalling

them to first principles. But in the amateur acting there is no reference to Olivier or Rachel in the acting; nor in the plays to Shakespeare or Shaw or even Coward. I have sometimes wondered in those hours of desperate endurance why the audience did not behave as football spectators do, and if it would not be a most salutary thing for the players if we did. They never get hard criticism, and they will never amount to anything until they get it. But we must not be hard, because they are doing it for charity. And well they might, considering the charity shown them by their audience.

It is interesting that we do better in music, but it is no surprise, for there are some recognised standards, and professionals who know, even if they cannot always apply, them. The conductor of a choral society has had a professional training and thus can drill and discipline his choir. Then, of course, singing has been in good repute longer than the drama. The presbyterians tore away the frills from public worship, but even they allowed the psalms and paraphrases. The choir of men and boys, turned out at the Reformation, came back long after as the choir of men and women; and from singing hymns in church it was an easy step to oratorio in public halls. From *Messiah* it was only another step to *The Mikado* and *The Merry Widow*. Most towns in the north have a choral or operatic society that performs some popular work, in whole or in part, at least once a year. The standard of performance may not always be the highest—people that work all day for their living can seldom be great singers in their spare time—but it is on a standard and one can hear that the conductor had an idea of the work in his mind. They do perform some of the greater works. When a choral society sings *Eliah* it is as if a dramatic society were to present *Julius Cæsar*, but while the town's dramatic club would never risk Shakespeare, nothing will keep the choirs away from oratorio.

Just what can be done to make pleasure of the highest sort even in a country district, when professional standards are steadily, even ruthlessly applied, can be seen in the productions of the Haddo House Choral Society. Haddo House, as I have put down earlier in this book, is one of the stateliest homes. That Earl of Aberdeen who was Prime Minister during the Crimean War lived in it. During late Victorian and Edwardian days it was one of the great Liberal houses—Mr Gladstone planted a tree. Its master then was a great figure—Viceroy of Ireland and Governor-General of Canada. Its mistress was a leader in Liberal society. As they say hereabouts, she was a spender. Profusion flowered around her, not only of money but a profusion of the spirit. She is on the way to become a legend. For instance: Haddo House had most things—drives, cottages, lakes, vistas, whatever the heart could desire; but people kept on asking where the ruins of the older house might be. Tired of explaining there were no ruins, she had some built, and the walls of the Old House of Kelly stand above the Kelly Lake today. There was a ball once at Haddo House in wintertime and all the roads from Haddo to the nearest station, Udny, some miles away, were lit by lanterns. I have talked to old men and women who saw those lanterns, or think now they saw them. I suspect it is a lie, but a beautiful lie that has a heart of truth in it, like a fairy-tale. If she did not do it, it was the sort of thing she might have done. There was a profusion in her charity. Orphanages and hospitals sprang up around her, out of the fruitful mould made by dung in the fields of central Aberdeenshire. She was profuse of her time for things that were civilised. When she was very old I remember her appearing on a vile winter night at a lecture in King's College on the rare books in the Library. She apologised for being late by saying she had travelled by train that day from London and the train had been delayed; but, late though it was, she could not resist seeing once again the rare old books. I thought then the books though older were not more rare than she. It is wonderful to have seen her. Though she was in many ways a very modern woman she was at the same time one of the last flowers of the old Whig aristocracy. The economics of these times make it certain we will not see her kind again.

The present mistress of Haddo House is a musician trained to a professional standard. In the last few years she has gathered and trained a large and very various band of singers and those have formed themselves into a choral society. They are the people of the district—a wide district. They are tradesmen, teachers, farm boys and girls, shopkeepers, farmers—no different from the members of any other choral society. They began with the easier things—carols and the like—and then went on to Gilbert and Sullivan. Cautious people would have been content to stop there, but caution has no good place in the arts. Going on the principle that we needs must love the highest when we see it, or at least should be given the chance, the conductor persuaded the society to attempt Bach's *St Matthew Passion*. She also persuaded them that a great work must be done in a fitting style. The solo singers must be the best of their kind; so too the orchestra. It became the speak of the countryside as the details were made known. Elsie Suddaby was coming, Mary Jarred, Eric Greene—famous singers of oratorio, archangels of music in perpetual attendance on the *Messiah*. A whole orchestra from the south. An organ coming all the way from Glasgow by road. If all the tickets were sold the money would just about pay for the fiddlers. Interest quickened and even a little sympathy. The affair was bound to be a disaster, but it would be a disaster on a grand scale. It is worth while quoting from the programme:

ST MATTHEW PASSION
John Sebastian Bach

Sunday, May 21st, 1950, at 2.30 p.m.

SOLOISTS

Elsie Suddaby   Mary Jarred
Eric Greene   William Parsons
Gordon Clinton

A String Section of the Scottish Orchestra

Leader: Jean Rennie

1st Orchestra   2nd Orchestra
Violin: Jean Rennie   *Violin:* Daniel Hall
Oboe: Leon Goossens   *Oboe:*   Michael Dobson
Flute: John Francis

Pianoforte continuo: Jean Murray
Organ: David Murray

CONDUCTOR: JUNE GORDON

Hammond Organ supplied by Messrs. Boosey & Hawkes

The choruses were sung by the Haddo House Choral Society and the Turriff Choral Society; ripieno by the Haddo House Junior Choir and the senior pupils of St Margaret's School in Aberdeen—in all, about two hundred voices.

There had been nothing seen like it in the countryside before—the great house in the classical style set high above the ornamental lakes among hundreds of acres of wood and parkland; the wooden pavilion built in ampler times for five or six hundred; the choir banked high against the eastern gable; the strings on the floor below; the solo singers, the priestly ones, set high on the dais before the people; and the people drawn out of all the corners of the countryside and from the towns beyond—so many so different elements all together in the one place at the one time. In the middle of those discrete elements stood the conductor whose will had brought them together and whose will must then command and fuse them so that the music would call out responses from the people and that power released enforce the music; until, by giving and receiving, players and audience might rise together into the high places where art is eternally born again. At the beginning of a performance there is a second of breathless silence, as there might have been before the first word was spoken that made the world, for the conductor must raise the baton over a chaos of emotions and none can tell what the result may be—worlds of divine harmony unfolding or chaos worse confounded. There were some anxious ones that afternoon; and perhaps old Bach may have turned away for a minute from tempering the claviers of heaven to say God speed you.

All went well from the start. There was authority in the first bars of the music which asserted that matters were to be conducted on a high standard and no charitable listening asked for. As the choir stood up for the first chorale and we saw the rows of very familiar and often not very expressive faces, irrelevant and unkindly thoughts came into our minds, Could voices accustomed to calling the cattle home really rise to *Come, ye daughters, share my mourning?* But as they sang those doubts fell away. The sounds they made were music whoever they were that made it. They were at least competent. Now competence is a very wonderful thing, for out of it so many more exciting things may grow. That afternoon was securely based on competence —of choirs that had been trained until they knew their words and their music, and of professional singers and players who could have performed their parts in their sleep but did not sleep in them. Then slowly the magic began to grow in the air. Everything was in its favour—the hall filled with a modest, willing country crowd ready and patient to make the best of the day; the day itself so mild and warm that you could almost smell the damp ground under the young corn; the pavilion full of a greeny golden light cast by the sun shining through the trees; the lowing of distant cows and the scoldings of the contentious rooks that fell in so nicely with the lyrical passages between the flutes and oboes; these and the conductor so slender and handsome and commanding—each in their own way were so disposing to pleasure that even the professionals may have been quickened by them. Professionals can always be relied on to give a competent performance and that is sometimes all they give, but when magic begins to work they respond and rise. That was how it was. I know nothing about music and cannot say when and precisely how it happened. The spirit of the place may have had something to do with it by starting that process on which all public performances depend. You know: some felicity in a phrase played or sung above the level of competence calls out another. The level of performance rises; and when one rises, all rise; and all together rise further than any one of them could rise alone. So it was that afternoon. The orchestra, the solo singers and the choir became one, and possessed magnificently the courts that Bach had erected out of sound. They carried us with them, as far as we could go. I would not say I understood what Bach was meaning, but some of the grander passages, when the choir sang all together like a great wind, made my nerves shiver as if I had been touched by some unimaginable splendour; tears sprang out of my eyes, and at the end I felt I had travelled far among exaltations, that I had been carried up beyond myself to the higher levels of experience. I was so exhausted, so riven and borne above myself, that I could have lain down and slept, for ever. I could not endure any more: I doubted if there could be anything further worth enduring.

As we came away, out into the sunlight and the green woods, we thought what a wonderful thing to have happened on a Sunday afternoon in the middle of Aberdeenshire. Nothing of all the elegant and important things that had ever happened in that place was likely half as wonderful. It must have been in some degree an experience for all the singers and most of the audience, since you cannot so intromit with the greater works of art and remain exactly as you were before. On the morning after, the society began to make plans for raising the money to pay the bill. It was a privilege to help them: and no charity. There was not any money that could pay for the value received.

A word about fishing. Salmon run in all the rivers from the North Esk to Thurso and sea trout can be taken in the estuaries. These are preserved, as, unfortunately, they must be, else there would soon be none, but a day's fishing can usually be had somewhere for a few shillings and some of the burghs have free fishing for a limited number of rods. The brown trout of the burns are free, as they might well be, for they are hard to land. Those are the only fresh-water fish I have ever taken, and it is a thing about which I should be ashamed to write, for I took them with the help of an intelligent worm. To fish with bait is of course a vile thing compared to the use of the fly, but I doubt if any fly needs more skill and patience than the taking of burn trout on a clear day with a worm floated under the hang of the bank. It is not a way to be used when hungry.

The sea also has some fishes in it. There are brave men in Aberdeen who fish off the rocks to the south of the town. With a bamboo rod and a hook baited with a piece of herring or even a scrap of red flannel they have great battles with coarse fish, battles that end with the fish on the rocks or the man in the water. I in my time was devoted to fishing for flounders at the mouth of the Don. Those flat fish, that could be passed off as Dover soles in the best restaurants of London, came in at the mouth of the river with the tide. Any afternoon in summer there were a dozen or twenty of us (as there still are) along the mouth, each having two or three lines baited with fresh herring. Now and then the flukes came up in families and we worked furiously for half an hour, pulling in a dozen apiece, and hurrying off home to the frying pan. At other times, with a threepenny line and a hapenny hook, I have fished for podlies off the pier at Fraserburgh. Once and once only I dared to go out with two elderly men in a small motor boat after haddocks and it is only a deep distrust of the sea which has kept me from going again. There is no experience quite like it— to float on the nine-beat bar of the waves till the divine moment when all the fish of the sea leap on to your hooks in a miraculous draught of fishes. And so to home and a fry and strong black tea.

Fishing, like golf, is still the sport of the common people; and where the common people cannot afford it, they do a little poaching. The illegal taking of salmon is considered the king of sports by some people whose opinion I value, in other things. There is not only the battle of wits and strength against a cunning, powerful fish, but also the chance on being taken in the flank by a water bailiff at the crisis of the battle. There is, too, the excitement of breaking a law without feeling really a criminal, for no one can really feel that a landowner has any property in a fish that happens to be swimming along the borders of his land. The true sporting poacher feels himself a Robin Hood. I have noticed that many people take a little pride in breaking the rules made by governments in recent years, especially the sort of people who own salmon fishings. It may be no worse to poach a salmon than to break what seems an unjust regulation of government. It may in fact be much less a crime. A government, representing the people of the country, has some right to say what shall be done with the goods that are in the country: but has a landowner any more property over a salmon that passes up the stream through his estate than I have over the landowner who drives up the road through my farm?

Unfortunately poaching has fallen into disrepute these last few years because it has been done for the black market and in a really criminal way. The salmon often lie in the pools — when they are on the move a single pool may hold a hundred or more. Now if you lightly toss in a stick of gelignite, the shock will stun every fish in the pool so that they float belly upwards on the water and can be whipped away to market—all except the most of them that will have been blown to pieces. There are even worse dodges. Some substances thrown into the water will poison every fish in a few minutes. That is the best commercial way of poaching, because the fish are not marked in any way and all can be sent off to market—though I would not care to eat a poisoned fish, perhaps I could name a few expensive restaurants where I have probably eaten worse. No decent person could approve of such poaching, which is private enterprise at its deadliest work of killing the goose by the ruthless extraction of golden eggs.

But I myself am not entirely innocent. My own and only experience of the sport of salmon fishing was enjoyed at the twilight of a summer day on a northern river. My companion and I walked casually up to the bank of the river in the gloaming, across the empty desolation of the moors, when the air was crystal clear and the mountain peaks seemed to crowd in around us looking over our shoulders as if privy to our intention. It was a lonely place; we were the only human living creatures on land: and a quiet place, not even the sound of a muirfowl, only the wash and rumble of the stream leaping between great boulders into a series of dark pools. We selected the middle pool, lit the fuse, held it as long as we dared and threw it into the water. It sank: there was a thud which shook the ground, and a sudden turbulence on the pool. A big salmon floated up on its back with its belly showing white in death.

Simultaneously a loud and startled voice cried, "What the devil's going on here?"

From behind a rock came a tall and saintly figure with white hair and a holy face that we recognised as a distinguished minister of the Kirk.

"You've been using geli," he said in sadness and reproach.

We all looked at the dead fish being washed out of the pool.

"Criminal: criminal," he said. "But now that you've done it, don't waste the fish. Here, man, I'll bring it in for you." He went to the side of the water with a stick that he had in his hand and very neatly brought in the fish. "A fifteen-pounder, but you shouldn't have done it."

I said "No" and I was black-affronted. But my companion, more experienced than I, looked at the stick in the reverend gentleman's hand. "A gaff?" he said.

The minister said, "A gaff? Surely not." He had every right to be shocked by the accusation, for a gaff, which is a stick with a hook at the end of it, is a most illegal weapon for taking salmon.

My companion said "Oh" and went to the rock from which the minister had come. He looked and cried back to us, "Come and see what I see." We went—the minister slowly—and saw a fish of seventeen or eighteen pounds lying on the stones, neatly taken with the gaff. We looked at the minister. The minister looked at the salmon. "And you a minister of the gospel," my companion said.

The old gentleman hung his head and said, "Mea culpa, mea culpa," very gently, very sadly. Then he looked up with a glint of triumph and said, "But the fact remains—my fish is a bigger fish that yours and I didn't use explosives."

He had a cutter of excellent malt whisky on him, for he said the evening air was dangerous on the moors but the same God that sent pain to us pointed the way to solace. We parted unwillingly and I never saw the saintly old man again, but I will always remember him as he plodded away into the dusk, bowed down with years and the big salmon under his raincoat, and disappeared into the shadows of the mountains.

Traditionally the second most popular of indoor sports in the north was drinking, and here we must notice a great decline. Most people cannot afford to drink in the old heroic style. A glass of whisky used to be threepence when a man's wage was fifteen shillings a week; with a glass at four shillings and sixpence a man would need £13 10s.* a week to keep up with his grandfather. But even the people who employ good accountants and still have the money cannot hold the old measure. The modern constitution is debilitated with white bread and reduced with patent medicines and cannot stand up to the assault of liquor. The heroic drunkards were men who lived on brose and porridge and boiled kale, varied with braxy mutton, salt herrings and foul salmon, with the leg of an old hen on Sunday. Illicit whisky was halesome fairin compared with those.

The evenings they held. There was a greatly respected farmer in these parts who had several farms, at each of which he kept a manager and a two-gallon greybeard of whisky. Whenever the news got round that his gig had been seen going up the road to a farm, the neighbours yoked their horses in their gigs and went to call on him. By evening a fair company had gathered in the dining-room for cards and conversation. There was a sort of ritual on these occasions. The host sat in the armchair by the side of the fire, handy for the bell. Whenever the need arose he rang and the manager brought another kettle of boiling water with which he made another bowl of toddy. That went on for a long time, while the gentlemen grew happier and louder and the host, smoking and sipping, watched and encouraged them with a rather mischievous delight. After midnight there were new orders to the manager. "William, just step out and bring Eastie's gig to the door." Having brought the gig the manager helped Eastie into it, steadied him as well as possible with the whip and the reins and set the pony off in the direction of home. By two or three o'clock in the morning all the gentlemen would have gone or been quietly helped away and wise ponies were homing to their stable doors. Then the host and the manager had a quiet and a modest drink and the master set off on the long drive to the farm where he lived. At eight o'clock next morning he was ready to catch the train for Aberdeen market,

---

* Besides, present-day whisky is 70° of proof, whereas our ancestors drank it around proof and would have no water in it, from fear of microbes. A famous minister in Aberdeen said, "If God had intended you to drink weak whisky He'd have made it impossible to distil it strong. Only Evangelicals water down God's mercy."

his white beard shining and his bright eyes clear. It may be that people did feel a slight hangover in those days, but it was not a thing you mentioned as if it were an athletic distinction: you sweated it out by mid-morning and were ready for a dram or two at dinnertime.

Markets were tremendous affairs, because most of the business was done in the bars and every bit of business needed at least two drams. After the business there were hours of social intercourse and more drams, and when the farmers raced each other home in their high gigs, women and children ran and hid themselves, for it was like the riders of the Apocalypse thundering by. Weddings—they were even worse. There was a northern crofter married the daughter of a neighbour and the wedding was held in the hotel three miles away. Doing the thing in style the principal parties hired a horse brake, one of those open carriages where the passengers sat facing each other along each side with straw down the middle to keep the feet warm. It was a capital wedding: it must have been, for, on the return journey, the bridegroom lay dead drunk among the straw under the feet of the guests while the bride was on the box alternately weeping for shame and kissing the best man out of pure friendship.

But I must not multiply such instances which can only raise disgust or nostalgia. We don't do that sort of thing nowadays. We have not the chance: perhaps we have not the equipment. Those people kept their tonsils, their appendices, their gall bladders and most of their teeth. Their blood had not been corrupted by vaccines. They could take their drink neat and survive it. Of course, there were then, as there are now, the defeated souls who could not face the light of day until they had had their mornin. The pathologicals are always with us. But there has been a decline. There was something orgiastic about those booze-ups in the country, which are less common now. People now drink in the hope of feeling good: our ancestors drank because they knew they would feel better. That is a distinction in which there may be a difference.

It is time to make an end of this business of sports and pastimes. There is a great amount of social activity, whatever its value. The dancing class on Monday; the pictures on Tuesday; the dramatic on Wednesday; the small-bores on Thursday; the concert in aid of on Friday; the dance in the hall on Saturday; and besides these, the junior agricultural club, the woman's guilds, the W.R.I., the British Legion, the Scouts, Guides, Cubs and little Brown Owls; the Curlers' Ball, the Farmers' Ball, the ploughing matches, hoeing matches, the Burns Supper, the choir, the youth club; and all the private occasions and the bridge. Once you are established in a district you need not spend an evening at home from October to April as long as you have the price of admission. It is easy to be superior about many of those activities, for they are not very exciting and they might be far better than they are. But they may give some real satisfactions and bind the heart to some piece of earth so that the spirit is refreshed. After so much denial of our social instincts in the long horror of the industrial ages, anything seems good that brings people together to work for a common purpose and to make pleasure together. It is a satisfaction to feel a part of some society and be not lost between the deserts of eternity.

CHAPTER VIII

THE LAD O PAIRTS

THE people of the north have prospered by making the most of what lay to their hands. That includes their heads, for education has been one of the most valuable resources and we have tilled the human brain as ardently as any crofter ever tilled the stonier fields of Britain. Scottish education has been greatly praised for a long time and with some reason. Long before the Reformation, learning was held in respect; and since the Reformation, it has been remarkably accessible to those who could profit by it, perhaps more accessible than in any other country. John Knox, the Reformer, laid down the rule that there should be a school in every parish. At the time when England, a rich country, had two universities, Scotland, a poor country, had five—however poor they may have been. To have a clever boy in the family was a great honour, a great responsibility, entailing a duty to send him to the university whatever the sacrifice. No humble birds ever worked harder for a young cuckoo than a Scots family of crofters or tradesmen for the bird of paradise in their nest. They realised the boy had talents that must be put out to advantage as the New Testament directed.

It is not easy now, and soon it may be impossible, to understand the sacrifices made to get education. There is a legend in the Scottish universities about the students who went to college at the beginning of each ten-weeks term with a bag of oatmeal and a parcel of salt herrings and lived on those, with little else, in some miserable unheated lodging. Unlike so many legends, that one has truth in it. Young men often got their learning the hardest way; and George Macdonald's *Robert Falconer* has a very good account of it.

A long time ago an old man told me how he got his master's degree. After three terms at the parish school he, the second of eight children, had to fee with a farmer at £2 in the half-year with a shilling of arles for a working day that was usually twelve hours long and often longer. His old schoolmaster had faith in him and encouraged him to go on with the Latin and Greek by coaching him in the evenings when he could get away from his work. At other times he studied in the chaumer above the cartshed when he could steal the doup of a candle to read by. In that way he continued, saving every penny he could. It meant the denial of every extravagant impulse, but nothing mattered beside the chance of a master's degree. In his middle twenties he had saved enough to pay for a year at a grammar school, where he sat and construed with the growing boys. He then won a small, a very small, bursary which took him to college. With the bursary and what he could make at farm work during the long vacations, he just managed to live through the university terms. He got a room for 1s. 6d. a week and lived on oatmeal, with an occasional egg or herring. He could not always afford a light, but there was a street lamp outside his window by which he studied. In these conditions he underwent the discipline of classical reading and philosophic method and so got his master's degree. The old woman with whom he lodged was as poor as he; there was never a blink of fire in the house after porridge time: "I'd hae been glad enough to jump intae bed aside her for the warmth o't, and Homer wi me and aa the Argive host, beside Joseph Hume and Bishop Berkeley, and we'd hae been naething but a warmth in her bed."

The days of which he spoke are far away and he was a tough old relic of a hard time. Not all got through as well as he did; and some did not get through at all. There were always those who drove themselves to the college by the light of a penny candle but could not last the course. The strain broke them and they returned to the plough and the conjugation of an endless furrow. They may have been fortunate in returning to the life for which they were fitted. Others broke down completely and died. It is all very nice and noble to praise plain living and high thinking, but high thinking is a fire with a forced draught and must be well fed, otherwise it may burn out the body. A few years ago an old gentleman, a Fellow of the Royal Society, retired from his chair in the University of Aberdeen. Asked what had been the greatest change in the university since he had gone there as a student sixty years before, he said, "Fewer students die before they get their degree." While we praise the older state of Scottish education it is well to remember those who died of it.

The ordinary unacademic child did badly, or not so badly, according to your point of view as to the value of suffering in education. Before the Act of 1872 which made education universal and compulsory, children attended school when their parents could spare them and pay the fees. My grandfather, who would be a hundred and ten if he were alive today, had only a few terms at the parish school though he was the oldest son of a fairly prosperous farmer. He went to school unwillingly when he was nine and left it gladly when he was eleven, but in that time he learned enough to be able afterwards to read and write and count as fluently as most people do now after nine or ten years of strenuous instruction. I would not like to say that schools were better a hundred years ago than they are today. An old gentleman, describing his parish schoolmaster, said, "Aa that he taught me in two years was the weight o the taws." But however bad some of the schools and brutal the schoolmasters, there was one saving grace—school life was short and there was less danger of being bored beyond all further taste for knowledge.

It may seem that children then got a very small equipment of learning; and yet they may have got the important part. When you have put people in the way of reading, writing and counting perhaps there is not a great deal more you can do for them. Anything they learn after that, if it is real and useful knowledge, they must learn for themselves, and the teacher can help only by making opportunities for discovery and providing information when it is required. Cramming neither feeds thought nor sharpens wit. I have sometimes wondered why there used to be more rich individual characters and why there are fewer of them today. Could it be that children eighty years ago got just enough education to sharpen their wits and not enough to bore them? I wouldn't know: but it is worth thinking about. However, I am not suggesting, nor will suggest, that formal education need be bad.

That so many children got only a few terms at the parish school did not mean that they were denied any further intellectual adventures. Those parish schools turned out a remarkable number of literate people who were willing to continue learning on their own, for the pleasure of knowing. It was pleasure with passion in it, and hunger satisfied. Some of those same people who delivered such a mighty assault on the waste land had a hunger for more than agricultural knowledge. That is no matter for surprise. When people have been stirred up and have discovered their powers in one direction, it may give them ideas and aspirations in other things. When they broke out of the bounds of the old farming they discovered new and for them unbroken fields of knowledge. After agricultural improvement came mutual improvement. At the beginning of last century the men of Rhynie in Aberdeenshire formed a society for mutual improvement through the discussion of scientific ideas and philosophic notions. The society was copied in many other places, a proof that it arose out of and satisfied some real need. The story of the Rhynie society has been told in a monograph, now very rare, called *A Village Propaganda*, an ingenuous work, but also a record of the expanding mind and spirit. The members got a lot of fun out of their society— real fun: not crying hee-haw at the road-ends or listening passively to entertainers, but adventures among words and ideas while they composed papers with their legs writhed round the kitchen table. As agriculture and so many other things were developing at a great rate, there was a vast new knowledge to be overtaken. Those village and farm people with their little schooling made some effort to overtake that knowledge and made some part of it theirs and handed it on as the general heritage a country child breathes in with the air and never bothers about. Hugh Miller, the Cromarty mason who became a

distinguished geologist, was one of them, as he told so beautifully in
My Schools and Schoolmasters. That they were able to do so much says
a lot for the old dominie. He had given them the tools and had not
discouraged them, or had not had time to do so. Perhaps that is the best
a teacher can do—to not discourage: unless he can add the supreme
gift of inspiration. And there is also the moral so obvious but often
overlooked, that the essential condition of learning is the desire to
learn. It is all a matter of the climate of the mind. Given the right
climate learning will flower in the stoniest fields. Without the right
climate pedagogues scourge in vain.

Perhaps we make too much fuss about the amount we teach or try
to teach and pay too little attention to the climate of the mind. It is
incredible the mass of facts taught, or at least presented, to children
in schools. By the time I was nine or ten I could tell you about Omsk,
Tomsk and Tobolsk, the Obi, the Yenesi and Lena; I could draw
you Kamchatka and tell you within fifty miles where were Guadaveri,
Krisna and Cauveri; I knew there were storms in the Straits of Magellan. It was all right for me; I had the imagination to enjoy maps;
I like maps better than the countries they represent. But I am not
ordinary in preferring the shadow to the substance. I wonder now what
my companions got from all those to them so weary hours. Perhaps
the Obi and the Yenesi have flowed clean into oblivion: and no
great loss, since the Russians probably call them by other names.
Why not be happy to forget them? Our parish is more productive
and therefore of more value to the human race than Cape Horn and
all the storms in the Straits of Magellan. If our children studied it
they would get geography they could see with their own eyes; more,
they would inevitably pick up some of its geology and ethnology too
—and these are things without which geography has no significance
beyond a list of names. But in schools children must be given some
remote contact with Cape Cod though they do not understand a
tenth part of what is happening at their own doors. It would be comic
if it were not such a waste of intelligence: if it did not make an arid
climate of the mind.

There is little future in giving children a large number of discrete
facts about the universe. No mind is ever likely to contain as many
facts as the *Encyclopædia Britannica*, so why try to force it? And what
would a mind be like that was as disconnected as the *Encyclopædia
Britannica*? Besides, facts have very little meaning unless they are
intimately related to experience. Perhaps school education can only
show children the significance of facts within their own experience
and encourage the imagination to apply that knowledge to new experiences and to things outside immediate experience. Anything beyond
that is a piling up of facts, most of them dead and many of them
wearing out of date. So many "facts" at any one time are only

half-knowledge, or a distant glimpse of the truth. Anyone who has lived even half a life must have seen how "facts" change. The things I learned about farming as a boy are, it seems, no longer true; some of the principles by which I farm I doubt profoundly, although at the moment they pay. Knowledge is not constant. Facts are often fashion. But one thing constant is the ability to understand an experience, to relate it to other experiences and to reason therefrom. To encourage and develop that ability may be the greatest service we can do any child.

It is quite true that we can acquire a degree of skill in certain things although we do not understand them. We can scrape through examinations in algebra and Latin grammar, just as the performing elephants and the educated pigs do their simple tricks, with the same patience on the part of our teachers and the same amount of understanding on ours. So many come to the end of their education in that state; by ten or fifteen years of perseverance they have learned a number of tricks, enough to get them an undistinguished living so long as they stick to performing those tricks in the accustomed way. But when they are suddenly faced with a new set of facts they are helpless, just as the pig educated to distinguish letters would be helpless if suddenly confronted with numerals.

I sometimes fear that our schools are concerned with many sorts of ability, except this one of understanding experience, without which all the others lose most of their value. Perhaps there is no time for understanding; children must get on with so many facts, especially if they are proceeding to academic or professional careers. The universities and professional bodies demand certain standards of fitness, and the common standard is the certificate of the Scottish Education Department for which the student sits examination about the age of seventeen. From the time the child is eleven or twelve, the schools make a powerful drive towards the target five years away, a drive that takes on terrific momentum in the last year. There might be a little more to education than getting up facts out of books—adolescents have bodies and emotions as well as minds and are sometimes very disturbed in both at that age; but the drive towards the examination is so intense that every effort must be concentrated on bookwork. There are secondary schools where no games are played in school hours, where no communal activities are encouraged and where social life is almost impossible after school hours because of the prescribed homework. After seven hours in school a boy or girl is supposed to do three hours' preparation at home—a longer working day than is expected of any other worker, except a housewife. It seems a little too much to put on a creature at a difficult period of growth. School is now the only place where a child is supposed to work harder than an adult. To a farmer concerned with living things, that seems very bad husbandry indeed; we never expect the colt to carry a heavier load than the draught horse.

Many people know it is wrong. The more enlightened parents complain that their children are overtaxed and blame the teachers who give out too much homework. The teachers complain that too much work is prescribed and blame the inspectors. The inspectors say, rightly, they are only the servants of the Scottish Education Department. The officials of the S.E.D. have humane ideas and will agree that the curriculum is sometimes weighted too heavily on the theoretical side; but, if it were not so, parents would complain. The S.E.D. may be right, for some parents begin pushing towards the certificate the day a child goes to school at five. There is thus a circle composed of people of goodwill but often vicious in effect; which is usually true of goodwill that does not get to the pitch of action. Outside the circle the universities remain aloof and intransigeant, erecting always stiffer barriers to prevent themselves from being overwhelmed by students, many of whom, exhausted by learning the elementary tricks of the trade, could not hope to finish the courses they might begin.

Something must have gone wrong somewhere. One is tempted to say that genuine respect for and love of learning have been replaced by the idea of learning as a means to social advancement. It is the entry to a white-collar job. But then education has been regarded as that for a very long time. It is true that many unfortunate children have been pushed into higher education because their parents wished them to have a "respectable" way of life. That, however, can hardly explain the sense of strain in the secondary schools and the sense of futility that overcomes so many primary teachers.

If the academically minded children are too often overstrained, the others are too often wasted. Now I notice in myself that it is very easy to learn anything from Canasta to the criminal code, if the mind is interested; and quite a few grown people agree they have the same experience; equally, we agree it is rather fruitless trying to learn if we are not interested—and being adults we are fortunate in that we seldom have to try. If that is true of grown people, it is likely to be even more true of children; and in my experience it is very true.

Most very young children are vitally engaged with the world around them: they are the great explorers voyaging on the Amazons of human experience. In all their play they are learning—the shape of things, the smell of things, the weight and taste of things; how to walk, how to run, how to sing and how to dance—learning by doing, by experience. The climate of their minds, then, is expansive like a late spring day. Then at five they go to school. The first two years are often very fruitful, for the infants (as they are perhaps no longer called) are often allowed a good deal of handwork and some freedom of movement in the classroom. They can go on learning by experience, by doing; and often learn more than they did at home, for the school has the proper materials and apparatus, and kindly, intelligent women who have the time as well as the impulse to attend to small children. But at the age of seven the formal instruction cannot be longer delayed.

That may be right enough. But the method is often wholly wrong. The instruction is so often not at all related to anything the children know or are interested in. It becomes entirely mental. It is a sudden and tremendous specialisation. For, look you, up till that point the learning has been a thing of several senses—of touch, of taste, of smell, of hearing, all of them feeding the mind or the brain or whatever you call that co-ordinating sense. But, at that critical point, the child must change its way of life and put away childish things, and sit still at a desk and deal with data that cannot be tasted, smelt or handled. The child is presented with facts that exist in a purely mental world and are not directly related to experience. They are taught that eight pints make a gallon, but they are not given the measure called a pint and the measure called a gallon and set to fill the second by the first, and so discover it takes eight of them. They must think of an abstract thing called a pint which is the eighth part of an abstract thing called a gallon. They are presented with those abstract facts and drilled to memorise them although they have no meaning in experience: no wonder the children grow weary under such task work and then bored and cease to learn. Their time and abilities are wasted and so too the time and skill of their teachers.

Not all are wasted. Some children can make the change without any great distress; they have the sort of mind that can relate the abstract pint to the abstract gallon of milk; they can go on with understanding, although, as we have senses as well as minds, they might go on more fruitfully and more quickly if the methods were not so exclusively mental. All true knowledge comes through passion (in the older, wider and nobler sense of the word), and a passion from which the senses are excluded is more than I can imagine. Still, the children that have a very active mind do well enough. The others are too often sadly wasted.

Scottish education is a very efficient machine for administering a standard education to a standard child. If a boy or a girl is at the right stage of development, the machine serves quite well; though, as I think, not well enough. But so few are ever at the right stage and no machine can deal with a wide variety of material. The system has not been made to fit the children, having regard to their varying natures and rates of growth—physically, emotionally and intellectually. The children must fit into the system, and since they cannot do that themselves, their teachers must compel them, more or less gently. So the years at school, which should be the time of development in every direction, are often used to force children into a pattern. The more sensitive conform, at some expense of misery and wasted ability; the tougher ones go dormant, to awaken long afterwards when they find some practical matters that interest them, or to sleep for ever. It is a sad affair and all against the rules of good husbandry that say you must work with nature, not against it.

Let me make it quite clear I am not arguing that children should do no work at school. I am not suggesting that children should do just what they like and have complete freedom. I have heard there are schools run on such lines, and there may be, but I have not seen them, though I have seen a few schools that are called progressive. However, as far as schools are concerned I am not progressive. If I am anything, I am reactionary. As I have noticed, it is in the nature of children to work hard when they are interested and also they are happiest when they are thus engaged, enlarging their experience.

My idea of a good school is that is should be a place where children's interests are fully engaged and then subtly directed—at the right time for each child—towards those essential tools, reading, writing and arithmetic, without which interests cannot develop fully. Then the school must have order, method and discipline; for man is a social animal and order, method and discipline are the bases of society. But those six essential things are not ends in themselves: they are only means to a civilised life and a good society, and if they are treated as ends, which they often are, the effect is to defeat understanding and kill interest and not only put an end to real work in the school but start a prejudice against all work thereafter. I do not think that the drudgery can be taken out of learning, but I am sure the drudgery is vain unless the drudge knows and feels there is some purpose in it. In the late war, as I remember, the Army Council always emphasised that the ordinary soldier must be put in the picture and know the purpose of every tactic. There are too many schools in which the purpose is never put across: where the climate of the mind is cold and stormy.

There are times when one begins to think there is no progress— only change. The old Scots way of education was often too hard for those who were short of money. But it had some advantages — few got much of the academic sort unless they really wished it; the interest and the desire had to be there first. Today every child must go through the motions without any regard to interest or desire. That has a certain likeness to mass production or mass reduction—the method of industry for dealing with inanimate matter, but applied to human beings. No wonder it sometimes works rather badly, that the amount of knowledge and the ability to use it which remain in a child at the end of a school course are small in proportion to the time and energy spent by teachers in imparting the knowledge and the children in resisting it.

Education is a chief industry of the north. The child who can take it, and some who can only just, must proceed to higher education and thence to the Civil Service or the professions. The stock is hardy and can stand the pace and survive it and do well enough. There is, however, always the thought that if education were less of a machine process such a good stock might do even better. We are a remarkable people with many useful qualities. We are conservative (in the wider and the political sense of the word), conscientious, practical and full of commonsense. Our patience and perseverance have taken on something from the granite and the tortoise. If only we had the little something more. If only we had a sense of wonder and the vitality that bursts all bounds of custom in the search for new worlds of experience; that unpredictable quality, imagination, and, at its highest, genius, that is the breath of life to nations. Now I do think we have made quite a lot of our talents. We have produced hundreds of doctors of divinity; thousands of doctors of medicine; colonial and Indian administrators—whom the English offended they pacified, and saved the Empire for a modest pension. So much good work well done. Lots of talent put to advantage; lots of talent but little inspiration. Many have gone from the north with academic honours bright upon their brows, with all the world and time at their mercy, but how few lived up to that bright promise. That applies in some degree to all universities; but, considering the vitality of the North-east, one might expect that a few more would have passed into the legendary state where the inspired ones live on after death.

Let us look at Alexander Cruden and Thomas Davidson, so different men and both so truly of the North-east.

Alexander Cruden was born in Aberdeen in the last year of the seventeenth century, son to Bailie Cruden, a person of some consequence. When he was thirteen he went to Marischal College, took his degree, had an unfortunate love affair followed by what would now be called a nervous breakdown, and then went tutoring in England. By 1726 he was in London correcting proofs of classical and learned books for the press. He was by far the best corrector in the country. Through that employment he was engaged as French reader to the Lord Derby at Halnaker, and must have felt that his fortune was made. Alas, one reading was enough. Cruden could read French perfectly, but in his own way, which was to spell out every word; he had no idea of pronunciation, in which many graduates since then have resembled him. It was too much, or too little, for Lord Derby, who terminated the engagement amidst screams of wrath from the corrector. Cruden then returned to London and set up as a bookseller, in which he was very successful, and received a Royal Warrant from Queen Caroline, the wife and better part of George II. It was then he compiled his great work, the complete concordance to the Bible. The seed of this work was the Sunday sport of word-chasing through Holy Writ. A word was selected—say, myrrh—and it was sought right through from Genesis to the Revelation, its occurrences noted down and the score totalled up. It was a simple extension to note the loci of each work on strips of paper and to preserve them; and, when every word had been accounted for, there was the material for the complete concordance. It was a remarkable book; it remains so; a reference book two hundred years old that cannot be improved on, except for the addition of two words that Cruden overlooked; an invaluable work, but as a book unreadable, a monument of patience, perseverance, accuracy raised to the height of passion. There have been other concordances but only one complete concordance. Am I going too far in suggesting that only an Aberdonian could have done it, and done it so well? It brought him nearly a thousand pounds, which was a lot of money in the middle of the eighteenth century.

Thomas Davidson was very different, as the phœnix from the ant. His father died when he was very young, but his ability was so marked that he could not be denied an education. He served as a pupil teacher at the parish school in Old Deer and entered King's College at sixteen, where he graduated four years later, in 1860. After various teaching appointments in Aberdeen and in England, he went to London, Ontario, and then settled in St Louis as a classical teacher. There he met and was influenced by W. T. Harris, founder of the *Journal of Speculative Philosophy*, who encouraged him to develop and write down his ideas on the philosophy of education. Four years later he went to Boston, where his house became the meeting place for a small group that included William James. At that time he was described by James as "a contagious example of how lightly and humanely a burden of learning might be borne upon a pair of shoulders." In the summertime Davidson used to take his private pupils to Europe, where on the high roads between London, Paris, Berlin and Rome, he sought out and disseminated ideas. He was always the teacher, but in the style of Aristotle, leading small groups in discussion and inspiring them to seek truth in the world and knowledge in themselves. A group of his English disciples founded the Fellowship of the New Life, aiming at "the cultivation of a perfect character in each and all". That may sound a little precious; but the Fellowship was a seminal group. Havelock Ellis was a member; and Hubert Bland, H. S. Salt, Edward Carpenter; Ramsay MacDonald was its secretary. Those young men of the 'eighties were to influence, some of them profoundly, the social ideas of the twentieth century. Frank Podmore led a schism from the Fellowship that developed into the Fabian Society, which was to provide the intellectual leaders of socialism and its strategy for action. Davidson himself was no leader; he sowed the seed, he inspired, and moved on. Back in U.S.A. he held courses of lectures at Farmington, New England, where one of his assistants was John Dewey, whose ideas have had such a creative influence in education. Then for ten years he conducted a summer school in the cultural sciences on his farm called Glenmore which spread his ideas among some of the liveliest minds of his time.

But it is perhaps wrong to write of his ideas; he had one idea: that there was no substitute for culture. This culture is "Man's spiritual nature, his intelligence, his affections, his will, and the modes in which they express themselves. This culture includes a history, a theory and a practice, a certain familiarity with which must be acquired by every person who seriously desires to know his relations with the world and to perform his part worthily in these relations." He was looking for "a philosophy of actual experience . . . based upon the results of carefully digested science". In that philosophy "you must avoid all one-sidedness, all over-devotion either to the past or the present. You must correct Karl Marx by Isaiah and vice versa. If you do this loyally and persistently, the meaning of life will gradually break in upon you, and you will find yourself filled with a hope, and animated with a courageous purpose which will make earth a heaven for you. If we cannot make heaven here, I see no guarantee that we will be able to make it anywhere." He brought all the weight of his learning and the power of his constantly revised and refined experience to the consideration of the individual's place in and duty to an always more complicated society. That, as we are increasingly aware, is our greatest concern. He was the opposite of all specialists, all scientific and intellectual barbarians, who see no greater good in the world than their own speciality, whether it is the anatomy of atoms or the obesity of Hamlet or the weather at the backside of the moon. Since I am indebted to Mr W. H. G. Armytage of the University of Sheffield for these facts about Davidson's life (taken from Mr Armytage's essay in *Aberdeen University Review* of Autumn, 1950) may I quote the final words of that essay: "Not only was he one of the twelve most learned men of his time, but also one of the most humane, whose stature gains significance as we ride the crest of the twentieth century."

If the parents of a twelve-year-old child in the north today were allowed to choose the future for their son and had to decide whether he would be the Queen's Bookseller and get a thousand pounds for writing a useful, unreadable book, or be a creative spirit influencing men and times unborn, they would have little hesitation. The bookselling would be safer. I mean, they would prefer that the child should take a good degree and settle down to steady advancement in a profession in which he might be insulated from the greater emotional and moral experiences. We don't think there is any future in experience, unless it is the sort that gets you better wages. Any other experiences are useless, for the purpose of life is to lay by for your old age, and those experiences are death to saving and endanger your pension.

Perhaps we have become the prisoners of our more ordinary qualities. We are cautious, conscientious, practical and well ballasted with commonsense. Our patience and perseverance have the nature of the granite. The only things uncultivated are a sense of wonder, and vitality in the search for possible worlds of experience. We like to think that is how we should be, reliable machines rather than various human beings. We are quite right to be proud of ourselves, for we are very useful citizens. But just a little dull? I think so; I bore myself at times with my own social virtues. The sense of wonder has been denied and the vitality has been withered.

I use those words with a purpose, because I think we have those qualities when we are children, though everything possible is done to kill them. Our ancestors too were often a little more than sensible, industrious and plodding. They made songs, dances, ballads; carried out elaborate rites at seed time and harvest; had a very active emotional life from which they probably got deep satisfactions. Their great evils were poverty, and starvation when the harvest failed. They were very much at the mercy of their environment.

The Industrial Revolution and the improvement of the farmlands showed what could be done by taking thought and getting some control over that environment. Opportunity dawned on people's minds in a sunrise of wonder at what could be done with the things that lay to their hands, and that sense of wonder called up great primitive energies in the service of the new ideas in trade and husbandry. The passion to make farmland in the unlikeliest places cannot be explained by anything less than a surge of vitality in one of those times when the mind, the emotions and the muscles are all tuned to attain some greatly desirable end. The same thing can be seen in the expansion of Aberdeen. The laying out of Union Street was as much an act of faith and an assertion of mastery as the labours of a crofter to scrape up a little soil between the stones on Belnagoak. How quickly the Aberdeen shipwrights learned how to build clippers, the loveliest things that ever flew the seas. We are too accustomed to judge those times by their bad effects—the slums and the degradation of labouring people; and we overlook the tremendous sense of liberation and opportunity, the sense of power in a man's head and his hands. There can be no doubt about the liberation in the north. Those were the days of endless discussion round the fire at nights on philosophy and science and the principles of agriculture. Those were the days of heroic labour in the fields. Anything was possible through knowledge, and with knowledge hard work was a pleasure for the sake of the work well done and the good life that would follow. There was at that time, I think, a sense of wonder, of glory, in the north which made any discipline tolerable, however hard.

The sense of glory has gone, or withdrawn through neglect, blasted in a cold climate of the mind; but the discipline remains. We have adapted ourselves to maintaining what our ancestors made and we do it with admirable commonsense and perseverance. We have cultivated just those qualities that would help us to keep our farms and our businesses together and repressed the dangerous things, such as imagination. We have felt we could not afford a sense of wonder, of glory, except when drunk. And we have kept those out of our schools. They are not examinable.

It is possible that we have been right. In a machine world it may be necessary to behave like machines until we have got the machines into their proper place again. But the pity is that we try to convince ourselves that we are machines, cautious, unemotional, unimaginative, full of commonsense and calculation. There, I think, we do ourselves a violence. Our forefathers were not like that two hundred years ago. I doubt if children are born like that now. I remember a few men and women of two or three generations ago who had great vitality and imagination imperfectly contained inside the bounds of conventional behaviour, because there was no real scope for expression in creative work. I know some of that sort still. The vitality and imagination are wasted because they are not encouraged, are considered dangerous, even immoral. Those people never do the work their talents are fit for. There is something in them that does not get through.

Perhaps we have gone in for specialisation in the intensest way; we have specialised in producing an Aberdonian, a good hard-wearing wage-earner, whether in divinity, medicine, Eng. Lit., accountancy, paperhanging, plumbing or orra work. Even worse, we have been successful. Aberdeen has produced more nearly-distinguished people than any town of similar size, or five times as large. That is a pity. If they had been less thoroughly drilled in the duller virtues and been a little more developed on the side of imagination they might have been the incomparable commanders instead of the deadly efficient seconds-in-command.

It is in the schools that we perform this curious indoctrination of dullness; or, if not begun, it is mightily enforced there. The clever children are reduced to absorbers of facts—all their various human abilities denied so that memory and reason can have all the precious hours—hours which will never come again though the children live to a thousand years old. During those most formative years they have to specialise on facts; is it any wonder that when they go to earn their living they are so often incapable of understanding or handling human beings? And the children who are not clever: they are bored because there is nothing in the diet of facts that can feed their hunger; they suffer from malnutrition and lose vitality and lose the taste for and joy in work and think of nothing but the football and the great day when they can leave the prison, even though it is now the enlightened sort of prison with much talk about ideals and only a little corporal punishment. Poor little brutes, clever or otherwise: they are the victims of an idea that schools can take in an infinite variety of human beings and turn out a standard article, inspected, guaranteed and true to type. Another thing: I have noticed among my contemporaries that some of them came from homes that had a fine, rich character (the beautiful use of the dialect with its wonderful power of imagery, especially when used against friends and neighbours), but as they progressed in learning they began to lose that native richness. One might have expected that thoughts enlarged would have gone far and wide, bringing back honey to the nest, where it would be stored up with a subtle and distinctive flavour. Or take it another way. There are distilleries where each pot still produces a different, a subtly different, flavour. The same malt goes in, but a different spirit comes out. Now in one or two of my contemporaries I have seen that character at work. The routine ideas were poured in, but the spirit had a flavour of the north. I remember one night, when I was a student, we were discussing Plato's theory of ideas, which was expounded to us by one of our company as that everything which is in the universe also exists in the mind of God. There was a fellow from Strichen or New Pitsligo or maybe Drumlithie—these things slip my memory now, for they are of no importance, but he had the figure of a land worker and the feet of a horse—and he had some difficulty with that idea.

He said, "Ye mean for all the tables in the world there's one table in God's mind?"

The expounder said, "Yes—a prototype, friend."

The fellow said, "And for aa the chairs, there's one chair in God's mind?"

The expounder said, "Yes."

The fellow said, "And for pots and kettles and plates and saucers, and railway engines?"

"All of them."

"Even lavatory seats?"

"Them too."

The man with feet like a horse said, "Well, then, the mind o God must be like a country roup, for there's one of everything there, and everything well worn."

That was, I think now, a happy distillation of Plato in a pot still from New Pitsligo, or wherever it was. But how seldom it happens. The result of education is so often that the native character of wit is lost for a very remote grasp of a very different culture. So few can make the wider learning their own, because, in order to get that wider learning, they must first deny that which they grew up with.

Our peculiar sort of civilisation has progressed so far, is so much the work of the human mind and spirit, that we need even greater powers of mind and spirit to preserve, let along extend, it. I am often misunderstood. I think with difficulty, and write with the left hand in a confused style, and my words often do not convey what I intended. Let me for once be clear. I am saying nothing against the lad or lass o pairts. They are born with powers of the mind and spirit by which they should be the interpreters of experience to, and the leaders of, the rest of us. Civilisation depends on their powers. I hope I have expressed myself well enough so that it is plain I am saying only that I think those powers are not encouraged enough in our schools, though sometimes they are so strong in a few individuals they can survive the schooling.

One question remains—what about the university?

Well, I could say something about universities, in unfavourable criticism of them; but nothing of that sort about King's College. For a university is unlike a school. A school is as it is, or its headmaster intends it to be; the pupil either gets under or gets out, or in some cases fights a long-drawn battle. A university is different: it is protean; it is what each senior member thinks it is and what each junior member gets from it. Now what the authorities thought I should get may have been quite different from what I did get; and what I did get was plenty.

The secondary school I attended was not a bad school: at least, I did find a few teachers who inspired me and whom I will always love, yet in my six years in that school I always knew a sense of strain. Whenever I neglected a lesson that I knew was ridiculous, I always had a sense of moral guilt—not fear of punishment. It was, of course, all the drive towards the certificate examination and the bursary competition set up by the university. Every class there was a football team training for the Cup Final. I have forgotten so many things that have happened in these last thirty years, but I still remember the last day of my last term there when I walked out under the arch into School-hill and knew I need never go back. I was so glad to leave: and yet I felt I should not feel that way. I had no hatred against anyone. I just felt glad that it was over.

I spent four years at King's College in the school of English Literature. And now, if you will put up with me for just a few pages more, I would set down what I remember of that time. My memory is not what it was: I have forgotten so much—it terrifies me sometimes—but I have noticed that I forget things only as they cease to have any value, and that surely is a great God's blessing.

I remember the library, the high, long, narrow room, lined with books and vaulted with oak, where all human knowledge was there hanging like fruit on a bough, and you had only to reach out your hand and take your fancy. It was a vast collection numbered by the hundred thousand. Besides those in the main hall there were others in the stack room. And in the stack room one might have long conversations with some person, charming, earnest, or both, but wholly feminine, between Hansard and the *Encyclopædia Britannica*. And—and this was the wonder of it all—there was time for everything. No master hounded us on to the certificate or the bursary competition. There was, of course, an examination to come, and if we failed, it would be a nuisance, or worse. But the decision was left to ourselves. No one there set a term to human knowledge. It had taken many hundreds of years to write those books in the library and the writers of those books had had assignations in their time. It made us rich in days and hours and centuries. We could use them or waste them as we pleased. Not irresponsibly, however. We knew that what we were using up was our own time which no one could ever make good to us. Some of us, as I think now, used it splendidly, scattering it about, like great kings in an older time did jewels and provinces. But perhaps more wisely than kings, for we spent the time that should have been devoted to winning prizes in class to filling up the vast and empty spaces of our minds. Conquistadors never hunted the silver of Peru with a greater lust than we among the jungles of the written word. We spent time splendidly but we knew it was our own time. Earlier on in this chapter I wrote something about the fertile climate of the mind. Now that was the climate of the library. The first time I went into it I knew I had come home: as soon as I had snuffed up that sub-tropical heat and mustiness I knew it was the climate I had been dreaming about in the muddy closes and the frosty roads of Aberdeenshire. Why that should be I wouldn't know: perhaps we are less barbarous than our teachers think, or make us. But there it was, and there it remains. I went to the university too soon: or I studied English Literature before I had the experience to know what Shakespeare and Shelley were making all the song about. I have thought I might have done better to have gone there when I was thirty-five. But, of course, I couldn't. There is a time for instruction and afterwards one learns alone. Teachers can do little more than help us to get on our feet. The great libraries remain when the teachers have dropped behind. The great library of King's does still remain for me the high arched gate out of childhood to the living world. But I am a little sad to notice that a new generation cannot make assignations in the stack room there. One may enter only by permission. There is, as I fear, no progress, only change. But the great library remains. I have used it many times in writing this book: and even now I enter it, as I did so many years ago, the first time, a boy come from the raw yards of Aberdeenshire. The noblest of God's men live there though dead, and the climate of that place to me is the Kingdom of Heaven—the only heaven I know of for sure.

I wish I could remember the lectures I heard at King's, but there are few I do remember. Almost nothing in the English School beyond a few speeches exquisitely declaimed by Professor Jack and the endless patience and goodwill of W. D. Taylor. But then I was too young: how could I appreciate Shakespeare when I had had so little experience? and I wasn't in the mood to get up facts as a substitute. In all those four years there was only one class that did excite me. Professor John Laird was supposed to instruct us in the rudiments of moral philosophy. He was a man of the north, of the north-east, born like so many native sons without the bump of veneration, and, unlike so many native sons, had never learnt to venerate. His lecture room at the end of an hour used to be like one of those sideshows at the fairs where (long ago) you were allowed to throw balls at piles of china for the joy of seeing how many you could break. You see, he began his lecture by setting up, say, Plato in the corner, and spent the next fifty minutes in throwing cricket balls of hard logic at him. It was hard on Plato. It was even harder on the class. They went there dry sponges, all hoping to soak up enough nicely tabulated information to get through the examination; and some of the larger sponges hoping to get a prize. John Laird, however, was no substitute for a text-book. He went on the assumption (maliciously) that every student had read the prescribed text and that all he had to do was to criticise it. He set up the philosophers and he knocked them down.

It was bewildering at first, to a good little boy like myself who thought every philosopher had all the knowledge; but it gradually became exhilarating. It was exciting to see the great men turned inside out and shaken and beaten against the wall and smashed to bits and cast away, as the conditioned products of their day and age. There was an exhilaration in it, a guilty exhilaration, as a peasant might have felt at the Reformation when he saw the sacred idols thrown down and trampled underfoot. But it was not just iconoclasm; when he looked round the shambles at ten minutes to the hour, he hitched up his gown, gave a little dry cough and, in a spare, clear form of words, stated what small enduring part of truth Plato or Bishop Berkeley had ensnared in a web of words and error. But it is not the last few minutes of truth restated that I remember. I could not tell you now what Plato thought, or Bishop Berkeley, nor what high matters were treated so eloquently in the *Prolegomena to Ethics*. Those weren't the pasture this little sheep was looking for. I remember, I will never forget, how he displayed the great in their human fallibility. A negative service, perhaps; but I think not. Anyone who comes through an official Scottish education, as I did, has far too great a veneration for the great: a sort of intellectual fascism is induced

by scholastic and professional gauleiters. The growing mind is put
in chains to the past. Not by John Laird. He was the one that knocked
the chains off. It is my regret that I did not value him enough at the
time. I value him plenty now. He has saved me from an intolerable
deal of dead philosophy. It is only a great teacher who can set you free
from his own subject.

Above all I remember the summer terms. Perhaps I was fortunate,
perhaps I do not remember very well, but it seems to me now that all
our summers were warm and all our nights were long and clear. We
played tennis, or went for long walks by the sea and the Don, and day
was infinitely prolonged in the long northern midsummer. There was
time enough for examinations and living too. There was such a
feeling of ease in those days and amplitude. We had been taken up
into a high place and shown the kingdoms of the mind and told,
They're yours for the taking. And for a little while we could take and
take and not worry about the long years ahead and the so desirable
pension at the end of them. How very fortunate we were that we had
those few years in which to grow, between the narrow anxieties of
school and adult life. So you may forgive me if I seem a little maudlin
about that time.

Of course I was not a good student. I was not a bad one of the sort
that needed disciplinary action, but equally I was not likely to be a
credit to the place. When I said I wished to be a journalist, my teachers
were relieved at such modesty: it meant one less student who must be
discouraged from ideas of going to Oxford or Cambridge. I was a
little disappointed at their willing agreement, but also a little relieved.
It showed I would be left alone for the rest of my life: and to be left
alone to myself seemed then and still seems the greatest good. I really
don't want to be what anybody thinks I should be. I just want to be
what I am. That, however, is a very, very difficult thing to be.

I could wish that the university would give more people a chance
to find out what they are, because it is their last chance before the
business of making a career overtakes them. I cannot see that the university does so for enough of the students who attend it. The whole
trend of university education is towards more and more intense
specialisation, a narrowing down to smaller and smaller fields of knowledge. The scientists and that sort of people have been allowed to run
away with the business. There are more and more people investigating
the atom and few and fewer who have any idea of how to apply the
knowledge for the good and glory of mankind. Please make no mistake: I haven't any barbarian distrust of knowledge; but of specialists
I have a great distrust. For specialised knowledge is not necessarily
wisdom. I have seen it in agriculture. Some fellow, breeding grasses,
manages to make four leaves grow where one grew before and all the
problems of British agriculture are solved. And some other fellow,

timing a cow as she feeds, with a stop watch, says the fewer yards she must walk to fill her belly the happier a cow she is. So you put the cow on to the lush pasture and she fills her belly quickly and gets diarrhœa and mastitis and suffers from sterility, while other cows, kept on a poor pasture where they have to work for their living, suffer from nothing but tired feet.

I would not undervalue the work of specialists, some of whom are my friends and many more of whom I admire, and whose work I know is valuable—but specialisation, alone, is not enough, though we tend to it in the north. There is hardly conclusive proof that the narrow sort of specialisation does pay the highest dividends or that wide humane interests dissipate a person's talent. The truth may be quite opposite. Knowledge may be indivisible: and, while it is always essential to discover the facts, those facts have only a limited value until they can be seen in relation to each other. For that reason the widest ranging minds may also have the deepest insight by a power of imagination working on the facts and discovering their significance or divining their implications. The power of imagination may be the highest human quality. No one has been able to demonstrate it by dissection, but I guess it lives and grows in the free air and the warm climate of the mind. It is perhaps a temper and a tone, as in a body that is well cared for and exercised. Whatever it may be it is alive; and not only alive but breaking out of the bounds of ignorance to a fuller sort of life.

It is a pity about our education. We really deserve something a little better. The stock is excellent. Being a little remote from the rest of the country and having escaped the worst of the Industrial Revolution, we have a certain native vigour and independence. If only those could be encouraged to range more freely and widely through human experience. There is little need to worry about any normal child of the north being able to make a living: we are the kind that can always get along. If only the climate of the mind were more favourable there is no saying how far we might get. When we breed lads o pairts, we breed them with more pairts than we allow them to develop.

CHAPTER IX

THE CATTLE SHOW

IT is not easy to finish a book like this about a story which does not have an end. My mind keeps turning back upon things; as, for instance, upon the cattle show.

What an excitement there was about the show when I was a boy, say thirty years ago. I used to live part of the summer with a farmer who always entered horses, cattle and sheep at his local show; and we must have spent the evenings of a week, and some of the days, in preparing the animals. It was an extensive beauty treatment. We brushed and combed the horses until we were afraid to touch them, in case electricity came out of their hair. We washed their feet and dried them with clean sawdust, then brushed and combed the fetlocks until they shone, long and silky, like a girl's tresses. Finally we took new halters and whitened them with blanco so that nothing common should detract from the bloom of the animals. Cows, being inferior creatures, got less attention: as I remember, their tails were washed and brushed out and their hooves dressed, but that was all.

The sheep, however, got the most lavish treatment. To begin with, we washed them in a deep pool in the burn. Being Border Leicesters, they were big, heavy and obstinate. It took a strong man to throw them into the pool and an agile one to avoid going in with them. When they were thoroughly soaked they were allowed to come out and shake themselves, which they did in a way that threw cold water in all directions. Then we caught them and washed their fleeces with soap and water, even the little tracks of dust and tears that ran down from the neuk of each eye, which took time, patience and cunning, for they were always ready to jump away from, or over, us. Then we threw them in the pool again, and kept ducking them there with a long pole until the soap was rinsed from their fleeces. Next day we began again, to dye them. After they had been soaked in the pool we worked yellow dip very thoroughly into the fleeces until they looked like melting butter, and then let them run in the sun to dry themselves.

So far it had been apprentice work: now the artist took them in hand with the shears. Slowly and with many pauses to observe them from all angles, he clipped them into an ideal shape for a Border Leicester, hoping thus to hide small defects from the eyes of the judge and also to bring out the good points, if any. When we had done with them, the beasts were curious rectangular objects of a remarkable yellow colour, still sheep, but sheep stylised, the products of *haute couture*. Schiaparelli could not have improved on them and only Dali could have gone on where we left off.

There was a rising excitement about the morning of the show. The ploughmen appeared in their second-best—the tight trousers; the shapeless jackets of thick cloth like a pelt; the white shirt but no collar, each neckband being confined by a bright brass stud; and the new cap askew on the closely cropped hair. Even the cattleman, who lived in such close community with his beasts that the dung had dried on him, that one morning had used the scrubber and the dandy brush. At intervals, the slowest animals first, we set off to the show in the market town. Along the road we began to see our rivals, all the way being spaced by little flocks and herds and teams, with now and then a man riding a single mare or a crofter driving his only cow. People came out from houses and steadings to see us go by, sometimes with off-taking comments on our animals, sometimes with the long silent stare of those who live alone upon an island of distrust. So it went on till we came into the little town, where we had no time to think of anything but confusion and disaster. Every street converged its flocks and herds into the narrow lane leading to the showyard. By that time the animals had been excited. Chased by all the town dogs, harried by all the town children, shouted and sworn at by their drovers, they made sudden sallies into shops and gardens. At the head of the lane a few stewards tried to regulate the traffic, but they might as well have tried to regulate a herd of buffalo. All the beasts that had not been lost crowded past them, bellowing, baaing and slavering; dogs barked and sticks slapped over fat black quarters; the dung flew free and everybody shouted "Hell". When we got inside the showyard the confusion spread out as each drover tried to find his own and did find them and stalled or penned them in the appointed places.

The ground was suited by nature to the occasion. It was at the foot of a steep slope from the town to the river, so there was a high bank on the north side that made a natural grandstand. On the south, trains ran slowly behind a screen of young beeches and, beyond, the river glinted through the leaves while it swished and rumbled among the silvery stones. To the east there were old beechwoods that clattered with contending rooks. The ground was thus a small, enclosed and shady place, warm when the sun shone, but frequented by the river breezes, cool with a touch of spray. The animals were held in temporary pens all round it while the attendants worked hard with brushes and sawdust and mysterious small bottles of oil to give the touch that might win the last deciding point. The middle of the field was roped off into several rings for judging the various sorts of animal, by far the largest being for the horses. Along the railway side there were two big marquees, one for the dairy and baking and the other for the refreshments. Two small tents, one labelled *Secretary* and the other *Judges*, stood side by side under a wide elm tree and looked somehow both official and conniving. In the far corner, out of the way, there were a few ploughs, rakes and carts, maybe a dozen in all, put there by local merchants in the hope of trade, but little regarded in the festival of living things. At five to eleven in the morning the spectators were disposed around the stalls and pens, giving advice to their friends, depreciating with silent contempt the property of their enemies, and taking up postures of immobile obstruction while they discussed the weakness of a hock or the uncertainty of the weather.

When the clock struck eleven from the parish kirk, all the attendants doubled their efforts, making the sawdust fly like snow round the horses' feet. Spectators looked at their watches, then at the two tents, official and conniving under the elm tree. They saw a man with a very large badge in his lapel passing from the one to the other several times with bottles and glasses. It was a sign that the judges were being loaded and the battle would soon begin. Stewards, wearing badges of silver cardboard, ran about waving catalogues, calling on competitors to get ready, and urging the spectators towards the rings so that the animals might have room to move. After a monstrous deal of shouting, attention was fixed in the middle of the field. The judges came from beneath the elm tree in pairs. Sometimes there might be only one judge, but it was considered better there should be two, on the principle that two heads were better than one and each judge could keep an eye on the other. As they stepped into the ring I used to think they had awful majesty. They came from a distance. They were so famous you could sometimes read their names in the paper. And on that day, when the best of the countryside had been gathered together, they were the arbiters of judgment. They were, I thought, in a wonderful position and maybe they thought so too; for, although they were quite ordinary bodies, they took on a remote, impartial air for the occasion. During the next two hours their word was law, beyond all question.

Whatever the animals, the judging was a time of almost intolerable suspense; as a spectacle, the judging of the horses was supreme. Perhaps a dozen, or even twenty, mares would be led round the ring, first at a walk, and then at a trot. They frisked, they bounded, had moments of pretended fright and real panic in the walk while the attendants tried to make them hold up and show their points. But when the walk became a trot, the more rapid movement filled them with pride and joy. The great beasts, shining with health and care, pounded over the hollow turf, throwing back their hairy hooves till their bright shoes caught the sunlight. Strong and irresistible, necks arched, manes flowing, neighing, blowing out great cannonballs of breath, they carried their attendants along at the halter's end, as if it had been some old story of gods in animals' shape at sport with the sons of men. When the judges had seen enough of it they signalled that the animals be ranged before them, and somehow that was done, with the obviously good at one end and the obviously bad at the other. The judges proceeded with their priestly office. They ran their hands over the beasts, stood back with half-shut eyes, walked round, drew attention, shook their heads, agreed, moved one beast up a place and moved another down three. Meanwhile the spectators hung over the ropes, or leaned on their sticks if they were fat, important men, and all criticised the animals and the judges, at first with caution, but afterwards with feeling and force as the spirit kindled in them. Sometimes the judges took a long time to agree, and you could see emotion trying to win through on faces long schooled to express nothing but wary incomprehension. And when the decision was made, there was a surge of triumph and protest round the ring and one mannie would cry, "Dammit, the grey mare's got it." And his neighbour in disgust, "Eh, dammit, aye."

By one o'clock all was decided and done with for another year. Some had gotten red tickets and silver tickets to nail up in the stable or byre. Some had gotten nothing but a deepened sense of injustice. Most had just the feeling that it was dinnertime, that the refreshment tent was open, and they had all afternoon before them.

The members of the Society dined in the hotel, where they all sat down together along with the judges. The menu was simple, traditional—cold salmon followed by cold roast beef; and, for those who drank noxious liquors, a cup of coffee. Before the dinner, and during it, the gentlemen had fortified themselves against the speeches. So they returned to the field about a quarter to three in an excellent good humour. The crowd was now greatly increased, for the farmers' wives had come in, and the young men and girls, and hundreds of the town people. It was now a purely social gathering where old friends met and old sweethearts were reviewed. Through it all, those unfortunate creatures who always get drunk at dinnertime on public occasions weaved their uncertain courses round the fixed centre of the refreshment tent, causing laughter, embarrassment and shame, while their wives put a brave face on it, saying pleasantly, "Oh, come now, John", and other wives thanked God their husbands were not like that and never would be, at least until much later in the day.

There was also a band, a good old-fashioned brass band in a uniform, honest tradesmen of the cornet and bombardon. With a lorry as a platform they took up their positions for offensive action and began with one of those arrangements that were always familiar but always somehow different. It was fine, virile stuff. The big drummer made the drum go boom, cymbals clashed, the bombardons grunted in a subterranean chorus, a man wrestled in the coils of a flashing serpent from which he drew blasts of pain, the trumpets affirmed the theme over and over again in brazen clangour and the cornet, O sweet and heavenly horn, warbled above all a song of happy glee. How beautifully they sounded in the field, now borne towards us on the wind with a more than martial din, now carried away into the beechwood, thin and faint and far, like the horns of elfland calling among the rooks. Horses neighed, cows mooed, sheep and pigs called after their fashion —the music assumed all noises to itself. Even a shunting engine did no more than reinforce the man in the coils of the serpent. I'll never hear that sort of band again, good country tradesmen with their simple rhythm like the feet of horses on the road at night, for I'll never be the age again to enjoy an hour so much when all the senses are eager and the response immediate. It was all good—the heat of the day when the breezes failed, the smell of the trodden grass sharpened by herbs, the smell of dung and urine in the sun, the smell of the animals, the smell of food and beer from the refreshment tent, of whisky on men's breath and scent on women's sweat; everything —the attendants sitting beside their animals with sandwiches and beer, the old men that stood in twos and threes talking and listening absently as if the words did not much concern them; the drunks in all the stages through urgent friendship to collapse—everything, everything; and everything was wonderful. Not good. Not bad. There was no place for judgment. It was enough that so much existed. Wonderful there could be so much in the world and I in the middle of it.

Sports were always held from three till five. Some of the events were for professionals—running, jumping and cycling. The others were restricted to the people of the district. Pillow fights, pony races and tossing a sheaf of broom over a high bar—those brought shy young men out into the merciless criticism of the ring, where they were approved, condemned, even applauded—as often for their parents' qualities, or money, as for their own. While the entertainment took its appointed course, the spectators circulated and performed the social act with more or less grace according to their nature: seeing and being seen, impressing and not being impressed, attacking and defending and now and then even making an exchange of real friendship. In the country no act, however lightly done, is ever finished and forgotten; and those involved have its restraints between them as long as they live. Even on a fine summer day at the cattle show, resentment at ancient acts, imagined insults, winked ready in the corner of the eye above the social smile. But the social act was performed till even the spirits of pride and enmity grew tired; or, gorged on the shame of enemies put down, rested for a little while in peace. Then it was time for wives to collect their husbands and go home; and soon it was time to go home without them.

Such a day could not be abandoned at half-past five with the band getting into their stroke, so the dancing board became the centre of the show. The band now played dance tunes, mostly eightsome reels and old-fashioned waltzes. The younger people crowded the board and danced as well as they could. The hot night and the dancing made the round country faces drip with sweat. Spirits grew hot too in such close company. The cries rose louder during the reels, arms gripped closer in the waltzes, desire grew bolder, suggestions were made and refused, to be granted on the long road home. All round, spectators leaned on the rail, drunk and sober, making insinuations, hotching with excitement, hating, hungry or despising; their emotions, raised by the drink, the music and the dancing above the bounds of custom, made plain upon their faces, for all to see. So much. And all so wonderful. And never to be seen again like that, the world unfolding. How delightful it was as the sun went down and the level rays gilded the rooks on the tree-tops. From the high grassy bank, where couples withdrew to sit, the band sounded a little thin, a little remote; the dancers, jigging on the boards that rose and fell with them, seemed strangely small and innocent. When the sun went down under the hills, men lit flares round the board and it was as if we looked down from a high gallery on a stage; and not on a living play but on a marionette show where the dancers jumped on hidden strings, and the band went through their gestures to the music of one old man on some ingenious instrument.

Soon, too soon, it was over. The band packed up their instruments. The flares were put out. The rooks shook out their wings with a last angry slap and went to sleep. The dancers went home along the by-paths through the woods. It was over and it will never be the same again. Not for me, anyway. I have not gone back there for twenty-five years. I shall not go again. If I did go and felt those old emotions I would be a customer for psychiatry. There is a time for wonder; and I have had it.

The shows go on and they may be as much or more to others as that one was to me. Some things have changed. There are few horses now and a great deal of machinery; and the ingenious tools by which a tractor can be used to take the heavier burdens out of farm life may fill a country boy's mind with wonder, at the opportunity which lies to his hand.

Perhaps that is what this book is all about. It was, of course, written in the hope of fame and fortune. Now that it is so nearly finished I realise it will bring little enough of either. But the want of them may have little importance because I begin to suspect they were not the real purpose of the book.

For I undertook the writing with the confident feeling that it would be easy. I knew the countryside so well and the curious or

amusing types who live in it. Besides, I had written all or most of it
often, for the newspapers. It would be, I thought, an enjoyable
exercise for a winter season, between lifting the potatoes and sowing
the corn. But it has not happened that way. I found myself taken up
with my subject. It is, I think, a good story in itself, however I have
told it—the growing up of the industrial town and the winning of so
much farmland from the waste, the making of so many material
things by the power of the human will. And not only material things:
there has been intellectual and spiritual creation in the north-east,
of an architectural solidity, a little utilitarian and earthbound perhaps,
but things of the mind and the spirit all the same. I became absorbed
in the immediate past; at first, I thought, for its own sake; but now, I
suspect, for my own. I was looking for the things that made me, in
the hope of finding myself.

It is not always easy to grow up in a community like the north,
where there is a strong sense of social conduct. A pattern is constantly
being imposed on you, however strange to that pattern you may be.
You submit to the imposition, or you rebel against it, or you do both
at the same time; then tensions are set up in you, and distortions. You
leave and seek a different society, a more congenial one, but it too
has its patterns. So you are thrown about a bit more until you don't
know what you are. At least, that is how it was with me. I have tried
to be many things in my time—been a client of fashionable cultures,
worshipped strange gods (though not religious ones), and all the time
been conscious of a residual disappointment. And I think this book
has been an attempt to discover what I am. In writing this book I
seem to have been admitting myself sprung from the north-east and
admitting a stream cannot rise higher than its source. But at the same
time, if I may vary my metaphor, I am not willing to accept my
mother just as she is. I can't help suggesting ways in which she could
be more worthy of me. I have lost much, but not my conceit in myself.
I am indeed a child of the north-east.

There is something else. The condition of the world is confused
and dangerous. We incline to fall in doubt and be lost among the
immensities of human cleverness and unreason. In such times one
has an instinct to return to one's own place and one's own people.
Not so much physically as emotionally, spiritually—call it what you
will. It is something to know the men that lived before us, and to
know that they too may have looked into the face of fear. I would not
say I am sure there is any continuing purpose, beyond survival: but
again it is something to realise that we have continued in business for
quite a while and may continue for quite a while yet. I had my
moments when I was young and lived in the north. The cattle show
was wonderful, and it will never be like that again. Not to me. But
there was a misty evening two summers ago when Methlic beat New

Pitsligo at the football and won the Brucklay Cup, in the second replay. I had taken a car load of small boys to see the game, and we came back glorious with victory. If ever an old Austin 10 sounded like a celestial omnibus, ours did so then. The boys may live a long time before anything to which they have given their hearts will repay them with such magnificence. The summer leagues may be all very foolish and so may the cattle shows have been, but such things can give their ecstasies and it is by the ecstasies that we are lifted high enough to live through long ill times. Perhaps it is only those who have given their hearts to something that have the heart to endure misfortune.

I wouldn't know. I know less and less for sure as I grow older. I have found myself very willing to give my heart to some of the people I have discovered, or found again, in writing this book—to John Shanks, the poor glover, who took Elgin Cathedral into his care; Isobell Gowdie, the Auldearn witch; Archibald Simpson, that honest architectural tradesmen in a good style; Thomas Davidson, the wandering scholar; Cruden, the mad corrector; Auld Johnny More and young Johnny More and Jock o Noth, aa three; William Thom, the poor weaver, with his flute and his wheepling pœsie: though dead they are more alive to me than some I could name who gant in the balcony seats today. Of all those old ones, our ancestors, there are two that wholly possess my imagination. One is Old Ronald, my friend, and in so much wisdom my beloved master. I will never get very far away from that barley field and the fairies in the hills of Dyce. Sir Philip Sidney knew one such—an old blind crowder that kept the young men from play. Ronald was one of the poor that are rich in spirit, and I loved him then and always will do. As for the second— well, I have been accustomed to disapprove of capitalists, and still do, though I am one of them, but the heart, as I begin to discover, is various—the second is Alexander Anderson. That I should be so taken up with one who operated what at times looked mighty like a bucket shop—five years ago I would not have believed it. But, although my political beliefs have not changed, I do not feel obliged any longer to hate the capitalist for the sake of principle, not when he is rich in spirit, as it now seems to me Alexander Anderson must have been. No man that was rich merely in money could have so treated any town council of Aberdeen. And no man that was merely a financier could have become Provost of Aberdeen after so endangering so much of the citizens' capital. Old Ronald and Alexander Anderson would probably have got on very well. They were both raised on the same side of the hill—the hill Parnassus. They were both imaginative men, though their imaginations worked on different materials.

I would stop here, with Old Ronald and Alexander Anderson. I couldn't get any pair that better expressed the character of the north between them, not even Cruden and Thomas Davidson. If I thought

they were in any sort of heaven where they could be conscious of human affairs, I would dedicate this book to them. Since I doubt that, I would dedicate it in the hope of giving a little pleasure to those who have given me so much of so many things, and I make an end by offering this book

To the Town
and the University
of Aberdeen

From an often ungracious
But never ungrateful Son

NORTH-EAST LOWLANDS OF SCOTLAND

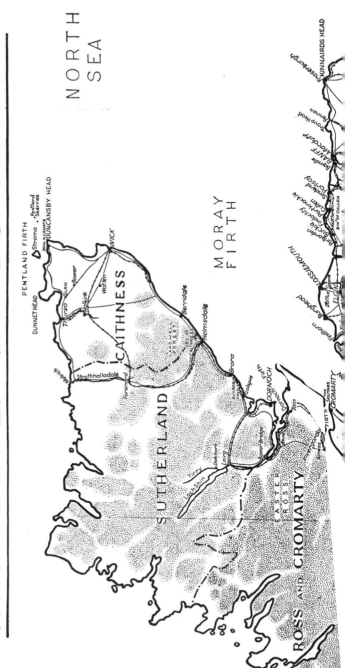

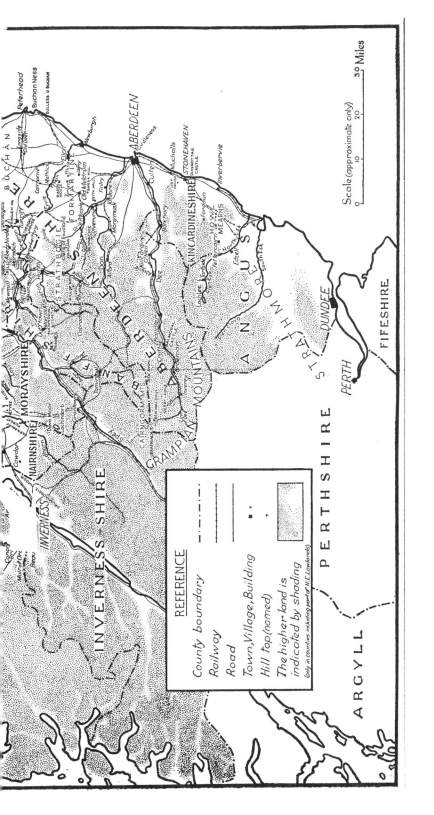

INDEX